CREATING A SCHOOL MEDIA PROGRAM

CREATING
A SCHOOL MEDIA
PROGRAM

John T. Gillespie
Diana L. Spirt

R. R. BOWKER COMPANY
New York & London 1973
A Xerox Education Company

XEROX

Library of Congress Cataloging in Publication Data
Gillespie, John Thomas, 1928–
    Creating a school media program.

    Bibliography: p.
    1.   School libraries—Administration.   2.   Instruc-
tional materials centers—Administration.   I.   Spirt,
Diana L., joint author.   II.   Title.
Z675.S3G53   027.8   77-164032
ISBN 0-8352-0484-7

Published by R. R. Bowker Company (A Xerox Education Company)
1180 Avenue of the Americas, New York, N.Y. 10036
Copyright © 1973 by Xerox Corporation.
Printed and bound in the United States of America.

CONTENTS

Appendix IV

Audio Equipment / Microform Equipment / Motion
Picture Projectors / Still Picture Projectors / Television
Receivers

PREFACE

In recent years a number of books have been published that deal with the philosophy and educational possibilities inherent in the school library media center concept. Other books have concentrated on selecting and organizing particular elements of a media center collection. Few, if any, of these books, however, can be considered a basic or overall text on both the principles and practices of creating, organizing, and administering a school media center. The authors hope that *Creating a School Media Program* will fill this gap. Although background material on the history of school libraries and recent developments in education pertinent to media centers have been included, the focus of the book is on practical considerations for establishing and operating the media center within in a single school. The authors have tried to emphasize the elements that distinguish a media center from the conventional school library and in so doing have attempted to anticipate difficulties that media personnel might encounter in trying to convert from one type of center to another.

There has been a deliberate de-emphasizing of certain elements that are sometimes found in conventional manuals of this sort. For example, only brief mention is made of such technical services techniques as cataloging because the authors believe these routines are best performed through the use of commercial processing sources or district-wide preparation centers. As another example, while the authors have discussed the principles and criteria for choosing selection aids, they have omitted a detailed listing of bibliographies and review sources because so many of these lists already exist. There is, however, extensive coverage, particularly in the appendixes, of the characteristics, strengths and weaknesses, and evaluative criteria connected with the selection and use of various educational materials and equipment.

In this manual the authors have concentrated on topics that reflect recent developments in organizing and administering the school media center. In so doing, they hope it not only will find an audience with media personnel and students, but will also be of value to librarians who want guidance in redesigning their programs as well as to other educators interested in providing good media services in our schools.

In the course of the research for this book, the authors traveled across the country from Maine to California, Michigan to Texas, and Washington to Florida visiting school media centers and talking to librarians about their programs. Some of these programs have been highlighted in chapter 4, but all that we observed appears in one way or another within this book.

To the state supervisors who helped us identify centers to visit, to the media specialists who graciously spent time explaining their media programs to us, and particularly to our patient editor, Madeline Miele, we are grateful.

We are also pleased to thank the Research Committee of C. W. Post Center, Long Island University. Over the past two years the committee has continued to support our work as have our research assistants, Christine (Evans) Weil and Dale (Dalton) Hodges, who worked diligently and cheerfully with us on the detailed and voluminous business of preparing a manuscript and still found time to get married.

Finally, we wish to mark the completion of this piece of "fifth business" by saying Thank You to each other and to our friends in the field to whom we dedicate it.

JOHN T. GILLESPIE, *Dean*
DIANA L. SPIRT, *Professor*
Palmer Graduate Library School
C. W. Post Center, Long Island
   University

PART 1

INTRODUCTION

1

SCHOOL LIBRARY
TO MEDIA CENTER

THE ERA OF THE SCHOOL DISTRICT LIBRARY

As early as 1740 Benjamin Franklin included a library in plans for his academy. However, the real beginning of the school library movement in the United States did not occur until almost a century later. New York State, under the leadership of Governor DeWitt Clinton, began the pioneer work. In 1835 the State Legislature passed a law allowing school districts to use limited amounts of their tax monies to establish and maintain school libraries. When only a few districts decided to use their funds for this purpose, to spur further action a second act was passed in 1839 setting aside a sum of $55,000 annually to be given on a matching-fund basis for the establishment of school district libraries. The effects were dramatic. During the school year 1841–1842, for example, more than 200,000 books were added to these collections. Several other states followed New York's leadership and passed similar legislation. In 1837, chiefly through the efforts of Horace Mann, Massachusetts enacted its first school district library law to enable school districts to raise funds for libraries. This law was liberalized in 1842 to give $15 per year from state funds to each school district that could supply a similar amount for library purposes. The Michigan law, also passed in 1837, stipulated that school districts that raised $10 maximum in taxes per year for libraries would be returned a proportion of the fines collected for breaches of the "disturbing the peace" laws! Connecticut followed with legislation in 1839; Rhode Island in 1840. By 1876, 19 states had passed some sort of law designed to promote public school libraries.

Yet the movement to build school district libraries during this period is generally considered a failure. The collections were usually unattractive to children. They contained mainly textbooks or adult materials suitable

3

only for a teacher's use. To capture this new book market, many unscrupulous publishers glutted the market with cheap, poorly written and produced texts, and without competently trained personnel to select library materials many of these shoddy products found their way into collections. Facilities for housing these collections or the requisite abilities within each school district for organizing and administering them effectively were also insufficient. Consequently, the collections often became scattered; books disappeared and frequently were incorporated into the teacher's personal library. In time disillusionment set in concerning the value of this type of library service, and in many districts the money was diverted into other channels—supplies, equipment, and even teachers' salaries. One evidence of the decline of this movement is that New York State school district libraries in 1853 contained twice as many books as they did in 1890.

Perhaps a more important reason for the demise of the school district library is the growth of public libraries. Legislators as well as many educators began to support the development of a more broadly based agency that would be able to supply library service to more than a small segment of the community. In Massachusetts, for example, the 1837/1842 school library law was repealed in 1850 and replaced the following year by a law providing that tax monies be used to establish and develop public libraries. In time the public library superseded the school district library.

Although the school district library movement was perhaps premature —a phenomenon far in advance of existing social conditions—it is important historically for two reasons: the principle was established that a library facility in a school could have some educational value and a precedent was created for the use of public funds to support these libraries.

THE GENESIS OF THE SCHOOL LIBRARY

The year 1876 is considered the birth date of the modern American library movement. In that year the American Library Association (ALA) was created by librarians (led by Melvil Dewey) who were attending a series of meetings on national library development during the Centennial Exhibition in Philadelphia. The first issue of *Library Journal* also appeared that year, as well as an extensive report, *Public Libraries in the United States of America: Their History, Condition and Management*, issued by the United States Bureau of Education. The report's title is somewhat misleading because the publication also includes information on other types of libraries. According to the report only 826 secondary school libraries were in existence in the United States (no elementary or grammar school libraries were reported) and their collections totaled only a million volumes.

Dismayed at the condition of school libraries in New York State and the seeming inability of local school districts to improve these conditions, Melvil Dewey, then Secretary of the Board of Regents and Director of the State Library, and Andrew S. Draper, Superintendent of Public Instruction, drafted a bill that the Legislature passed in 1892. This law, a pioneering effort, allowed for the growth of school libraries in New York State and also served as a model for library legislation in other states. As in the earlier, 1839 school district library law, the new legislation provided that a single school district could receive monies on a matching-fund basis (no more than $500 per year) for the purchase of library books. In time other schemes were used to appropriate this money, and eventually a formula based on the size of the pupil population in the district became the yardstick. Only books approved by the Department of Public Instruction could be purchased with state funds. Lists of recommended titles were issued periodically, and they consisted of reference books, supplementary reading books, books related to the curriculum, and pedagogical books for use by teachers.

To prevent a reoccurrence of the disastrous ending of the school district library, these collections were intended to remain in the school at all times, but teachers, administrators, and pupils were allowed, on occasion, to borrow a single volume at a time for a period not to exceed two weeks.

A classroom teacher was to serve as school librarian, and by annual reports to the State Superintendent of Public Instruction, these "librarians" were made responsible for the care and upkeep of the collection. Given these rigid regulations, it is easy to see that many schools were discouraged from applying for state funds. That modifications were necessary soon became apparent, and in time they came. Gradually other states passed similar legislation.

In 1892 New York State also formed a School Libraries Division within the Department of Public Instruction. Annual reports from the department show an increased concern with the development of school libraries, and for the first time, in the report of 1900, a tentative standard was issued for libraries in elementary schools:

> A small library is becoming indispensable to the teacher and pupils of the grammar school. In order to give definiteness to this idea of a small library, suppose it to consist of five hundred to one thousand books, containing the best classic stories, poems, biographies, histories, travels, novels, and books of science suitable for the use of children below high school. . . . It is evident that a carefully selected library of the best books of this character should be found in every grammar school.

Other developments indicated an increasing interest in school library development. In 1896, the National Education Association created a Library Section partly because of a petition requesting action circulated by

John Cotton Dana, then President of American Library Association, and partly because of the impassioned speech on the importance of libraries in education delivered by Melvil Dewey at an NEA national convention in Buffalo. ALA created a committee to cooperate with NEA's Library Section. (In December 1914 ALA founded its own School Library Section.) In 1900 the first graduate of a library school in the United States to serve as a school librarian was employed at the Erasmus Hall High School in New York City. Several state teachers' associations began developing sections for school librarians. In 1910 New York State once more led the way, this time by creating a High School Library Section within the New York State Teachers Association. That no mention is made of elementary school librarians reflects the absence of any significant development in this area.

At this time the role of the librarian was considered primarily a clerical one, and in schools that hired professional librarians there developed a struggle for recognition of equal status in position and salary for librarians with teachers. New York was one of the first cities to recognize that librarians were essentially teachers rather than clerks. In 1914 its Board of Education adopted regulations that made salaries of qualified high school librarians comparable to those of teachers and also recommended that prospective librarians should be graduates of a one-year course in an approved library school.

Although library schools were often requested to add courses for school librarianship to their curricula, progress in this area was slow. What little professional training was available was supplied usually through courses taught in teacher training institutions and normal schools or by brief summer workshops and institutes usually sponsored by a state education department or a teachers' association.

The statistics for this period show a gradual and encouraging growth in size of school library collections. The actual sorry state of school libraries was revealed, however, in a *Library Journal* article of April 1913 entitled "Development of Secondary School Libraries," in which the author, E. D. Greenman, comments on the status of these collections:

> Most of them are small collections of reference and textbooks, poorly quartered, unclassified and neither cataloged nor readily accessible for constant use. Of the 10,000 public high school librarians in the country at the present time, not more than 250 possess collections containing 3000 volumes or over.

A further indication of how school libraries lagged behind development in other library areas is the national statistic, revealed by M. E. Hall in the *Library Journal* of September 1915, that only 50 trained librarians had been appointed to schools (all secondary) between 1905 and 1915. The sad conclusion is that, although some foundation had been laid during this period for the development of school libraries, most schools had either no libraries or ones that were inadequate in size, staff, and organization.

In addition to the school library operated as an integral part of the school organization, various other structural patterns for supplying library service to children emerged during this period. These often involved attempts to combine public and school library service. The four most important methods were: (1) In rural and remote areas without even public libraries, the state library agency provided traveling or "package" libraries to schools. (2) In urban areas, students used the public library resources exclusively, and liaison between the school and public library was maintained by such devices as visits to the school by professional librarians and placing loan collections in the schools. (3) A branch of the public library was created in the school to supply library service for both the children and adults in the community. In 1895, for example, a public library branch was established in Cleveland's Central High School, and four years later another was set up in a high school in Newark, New Jersey. Unfortunately these book collections usually were more suited to adults, and often this division of interests resulted in neither population being served adequately. (4) A system of joint control was established by which a public library branch to be used exclusively by students and teachers was placed in the school, but organized and administered by the staff of the public library. Once more problems arose involving the divided loyalties of the librarians and the inability of the library to respond immediately to changing curricular needs. More important, under this system of joint control the library was never an integral part of the school program, but was looked upon as an outside agency.

Although some of these variant patterns of organization persisted into the middle of this century (and, indeed, in some areas are still in existence), they were gradually found unsuitable, and the prevailing pattern that emerged was an independent library in individual schools under the control of a Board of Education. Following this development several larger school districts formed central library agencies for supervision and guidance. In the interests of efficiency these agencies later expanded to provide such services as centralized processing, selection centers, and district-wide circulation of special collections.

THE AGE OF DEVELOPMENT

The rapid growth of school libraries following World War I parallels the similar general growth in public education. School population increased tremendously. In the 30-year span between 1900 and 1930 the elementary school population alone rose by 50 percent, and at the secondary level the growth was even more phenomenal.

A general population increase coupled with sustained faith in the importance of a general education were primary factors in producing this situation: less child labor was employed and there was a more stringent enforcement of school-attendance regulations. Centralization of schools helped promote the development of larger units that now could afford what was sometimes regarded as the luxury of a library and the services of a qualified librarian.

Teaching systems also changed. The use of a single textbook and rote memorization were often supplanted by other teaching methods that stressed individualized instruction and a recognition of the differences among children. New curriculum structures, such as the Winnetka Plan (1920), the Dalton (Massachusetts) Plan (1920), and the many others that grew from the influence of John Dewey and his progressive education movement, underscored the need in schools for quantities of various kinds of educational materials. The logical source for this material was a well-stocked, well-administered school library.

The beginning of this period also saw the publication of the first national school library standards. In 1915, a nationwide survey on the teaching of English was conducted by the National Council of Teachers of English. Through this report the totally inadequate condition of school libraries in the United States came to light. This prompted the NEA to appoint a committee of both librarians and educators under the chairmanship of Charles C. Certain to study secondary school libraries. The committee's final report was submitted to the NEA in 1918 and was approved. ALA's Committee on Education also approved the report, and it was published by ALA in 1920. The report's official title is *Standard Library Organization and Equipment for Secondary Schools*, but it is commonly known as the "Certain report."

The Certain report begins by painting a gloomy but truthful picture of the status of the post-World War I school library: "There are few well-planned high school libraries in the U.S. Sometimes there is a large study hall for the library—generally just one room with no workroom or conveniences of any kind for the staff." Specific quantitative standards are given for secondary school libraries in schools of various sizes and grade levels. Included are liberal recommendations for physical facilities (the library should accommodate 5 percent to 10 percent of the school population), qualifications of librarians (an undergraduate degree, one year of library science, and a minimum of one year of library work with young adults), size of book collections (between six and eight books per student), as well as details on equipment, supplies, and budget.

The report is adamant on standards for the professional role of the librarian: "Clerical work of the high school of the nature of office work should not be demanded of the librarian." The standards are forward-looking and even prophetic in their espousal of the media-center concept long before the term came into existence:

> The Library should serve as the center and coordinating agency for all material used in the school for visual instruction, such as stereopticons, portable motion picture machines, stereopticon slides, moving picture films, pictures, maps, globes, bulletin board material, museum loans, etc. Such material should be regularly accessioned and cataloged, and its movements recorded, and directed from the library.

The Certain high school standards (and their supplement of 1932) had a beneficial effect on school library growth. They provided the first yardstick to evaluate local libraries and also created a framework from which other accrediting agencies, library departments—regional, state, and local—could develop other sets of standards.

A second Certain report, *Elementary School Library Standards*, appeared in 1925 and received once more the endorsement of both NEA and ALA. In these standards the integrated media approach was restated:

> There is need, therefore, of a new department in the school whose function it shall be to assemble and distribute the materials of instruction. . . . In its first purpose, that of school library service, it may be thought of as the one agency in the school that makes possible a definite systematic manipulation and control of the materials of instruction. . . . [The collection should include] moving picture films, pictures for illustrative purposes, post cards, stereopticon slides, sterography, victrola records. This material shall be recorded by the librarian and distributed from the library.

Once more these standards were exhaustive in the amount of specific detail given. For example, included in the extensive supply lists are the length of the ruler needed in the library office (18 inches), the brand of paper clips to buy (Gem), the color of bookends to be purchased (olive green). There is also appended a list of 212 basic books for the elementary school library. The twelve fiction titles include *Peter Pan, Heidi,* and *Water Babies.* Because most elementary schools had no libraries and the need for them was still generally unrecognized, the impact of these standards was not as great as that of the 1920 standards.

In 1924 the North Central Association developed the "Score Card for School Libraries," a set of standards that began concentrating attention on programs or qualitative standards rather than on quantities of materials. In 1927 this association required each member high school to score its library.

That the Certain standards overemphasized the quantitative aspects of school library programs was criticized in other areas as well, and when the Cooperative Study of Secondary School Standards was formed in 1933, a new study was begun. This resulted in the publication of a numerical scoring technique to evaluate the secondary school (including the school library). Through numerous revisions, this publication has evolved into the *Evaluative Criteria,* an instrument still widely used by many accreditation associations and by schools for self-evaluation.

Other documents of the period focused attention on school libraries. In 1932, a national secondary school library survey was conducted by B. Lamar Johnson as part of the National Survey of Secondary Education sponsored by the U.S. Office of Education. The resultant publication, *The Secondary School Library,* supplied data on 390 libraries as well as special information on exemplary programs. Although no specific recommendations are given, indirect guidance for library program development is suggested. The Department of Elementary School Principals of NEA devoted their 12th Annual Yearbook to *The Elementary School Library* (1933) and in 1943 the second part of the 42nd Yearbook of the National Society for the Study of Education was called *The Library in General Education.* Many monographs also appeared that supplied, for the first time, guidance on how to establish and maintain a school library. Lucille F. Fargo wrote an ALA publication, *The Library in the School,* which had a publishing history of several editions and became the standard textbook on administering school library services. A detailed and sophisticated evaluation device for gathering data and measuring a school library's development appeared in 1951. The authors were Frances Henne, Ruth Ersted and Alice Lohrer; the title, *A Planning Guide for the High School Library* (ALA). Other important administrative texts for various types of libraries and levels of professional competencies were written by Hannah Logasa, Azile Wofford, Mary Peacock Douglas and Jewel Gardiner.

The second set of national school library standards, *School Libraries for Today and Tomorrow,* appeared in 1943. This was one of a series of documents on standards that were developed under the leadership of the ALA Committee on Post-War Planning. This publication represents the cooperative efforts of school library specialists then prominent in their field. The work is primarily descriptive. It contains separate chapters on the purposes of school libraries and the various services that can be offered through the school library. Quantitative standards are presented throughout the text and summarized in chart form in appendixes. The standards reflect a progressive and forward-looking view concerning the role of the school library in relation to the school's objectives and the equal importance of both elementary and secondary libraries. They are, however, less definite about the place of nonbook materials in the library than the Certain standards. For example:

> The wide use of many books, periodicals, prints, maps, recordings, films and other audio-visual aids has made it imperative that information regarding all materials in the school be available from some central source.

The school library appears to be the logical place for this information even when some of the materials are housed outside the library.

Requirements for certification of school librarians improved and became more rigidly codified during this period. A U.S. Office of Education study conducted in 1940 showed that some provision for certifying school librarians existed in every state. Eight states provided this by specific state laws, 24 states allowed their education departments to provide their own certification requirements, and 16 states allowed local school boards to certify their librarians. The requirements varied considerably. For example, while one state required only two years of college and eight hours of library science, another required a Bachelor's Degree. New York State had the highest certification requirements, followed closely by California. By regulation effected in 1930, New York State required for permanent certification as a school librarian an undergraduate degree, 36 hours of library science (the maximum and minimum number of semester hours in each area of course work was specified), and 18 hours in education, including student teaching. In 1925, New York State mandated the appointment of a secondary school librarian (or, when necessary, a classroom teacher to serve in this capacity) for all but very small secondary schools in the state.

Although these certification requirements were written down, in many states, school districts often ignored them simply by not creating positions for school librarians. In most schools the library was still administered on a part-time basis by volunteer help or by classroom teachers who were given released time for this function.

The amount of statewide supervision of school librarians increased markedly during this period. In 1939 only 13 states employed full-time supervisors, but by 1960 more than half the states had developed these positions. Primarily because of increased Federal spending for school libraries, virtually every state had some form of statewide supervision under qualified personnel by the end of the 1960s, and many had increased the number of the supervisors to four and five times more than there had been before World War II.

The question whether education for school librarianship should be based in library schools or in teaching training institutions continued to receive a great deal of attention. Many arguments favored the latter: teacher training institutions were more numerous and better situated geographically; library schools were primarily public- and academic-library oriented and unwilling to give courses in time slots (summers, for example) that were convenient to school personnel who wanted to be school librarians; certification requirements were generally so minimal that teacher training institutions could easily offer these basic courses; school administrators frequently wanted to hire only part-time librarians who were also qualified as subject specialists for classroom teaching.

During the 1950s a decided shift was noticeable from schools of education to library schools for courses in school librarianship. No single reason for this change can be given, but certain factors are apparent. Increased state standards for certification were adopted that often could only be met by attending a library school offering a complete program in library science. The proliferation of library schools during the period also helped. Some of them, ironically, developed from teacher training institutions. This tended to break the pattern of most library schools being oriented mainly to adult services. As library schools and library school degrees became common, curricular programs and the number and variety of courses offered in library schools were expanded and became more specialized. Pressure was also placed on library schools to extend into the school library area from within the library profession. For example, the 1951 standards for accrediting library schools and the interpretive document that accompanied them stressed the importance of developing multipurpose curricula that would not be confined solely to a single area of library service. The standards permitted only five-year programs to be eligible for accreditation—which weakened the drawing power of undergraduate programs offered within teachers' colleges.

In spite of these encouraging developments, national statistics continued to show the sorry state of school libraries in the United States. The Office of Education report on *Public School Library Statistics for 1958–59* noted that about one-half of the nation's schools had no library and well over one-half did not have the services of a qualified librarian. Even in schools with libraries, collections averaged fewer than five books per student. The most seriously deprived area continued to be elementary schools of which two-thirds were without a school library.

The decade of the 1960s is considered one of the greatest periods of school library growth. The period began with the publication, in 1960, of a new set of national standards developed by the American Association of School Librarians (AASL) of ALA with the cooperation of 19 other professional associations. In addition to their national impact, these standards influenced development and expansion of state and local standards. Although they deal primarily with various services offered by a functioning school library and make quantitative recommendations, these standards stress the responsibility of school boards, administrators, and various kinds of supervisory personnel in developing successful school library programs. The statement concerning school libraries as instructional materials centers, adopted by AASL in 1956, is reprinted in the standards, but there is no strong recommendation that the library and audiovisual collections must be combined physically. Increased cooperation is suggested, however, where these collections are administered separately. Specific quantitative standards are included for audiovisual materials and equipment.

In the early 1960s while school librarians were trying to implement their new standards, the NEA's Department of Audiovisual Instruction (DAVI) had two committees working simultaneously on developing standards for audiovisual programs. The Committee on Professional Standards was working on quantitative standards and the Consultant Service Committee on the qualitative aspects. In June 1965 the quantitative standards were approved as the official guidelines for the organization.

In 1967, the Canadian School Library Association (CSLA) published the first set of standards geared to meet the needs of Canadian school libraries. *The Standards of Library Service for Canadian Schools* (Ryerson Press) includes recommendations for types of media and also supplies detailed recommendations for services, personnel, and collections in various types of schools differentiated by size and location.

The greatest impetus for school library development in the 1960s came from increased financial aid from Federal sources. The forerunner of this aid was the National Defense Education Act of 1958 that had as its aim the strengthening of teaching in the areas of science, foreign language, and mathematics through expenditures that could include purchases of equipment, library books, and other educational materials. Even more important was the passage of the Elementary and Secondary Education Act in 1965. Through Title II of this act, provision was made for millions of dollars to be spent on developing school libraries. Other sections of the act supplied additional funds for providing library materials for disadvantaged students and for setting up model projects and demonstration libraries.

There was also an increased flow of money and support from private resources. Most notable was the Knapp School Libraries Project that funded the establishment of several "ideal" school libraries across the country from 1963 through 1968. Thousands of educators visited these demonstration centers and thousands of others learned of them through written reports and other materials that were prepared to publicize the project. The Knapp Foundation later financed an intensive project to determine manpower needs in the area of school librarianship.

The effect of these new sources of support was phenomenal—hundreds of new libraries were founded, others were able to expand considerably their collections and services, and the demand for qualified librarians far exceeded the supply. Although Federal support has subsequently varied considerably, the momentum for developing school libraries has continued.

THE EMERGENCE OF THE MEDIA CENTER

The aims of American education are usually expressed in terms of a dual responsibility to society and to the individual. The societal aims involve not only the preservation of those important values accumulated through time but also provisions to insure growth and change in society. Education also attempts to equip the individual with knowledge to fit into the existing society and to contribute to that society's betterment.

When translating these aims into theories of learning, educators and psychologists become involved with the conditions of learning: How, where, why does learning take place? What outcomes can be expected after the learning experience? The examination of these questions has led to a number of schools of thought on the subject—of which many are in partial conflict and others seem to be based on irreconcilable dualisms. For example, the behaviorists and associationists, among them E. L. Thorndike and B. F. Skinner, believe learning is essentially a mechanistic response to external stimuli, or in short, a conditioning procedure. The Gestaltists and field theorists maintain that learning is a cognitive process involving personal perception in problem-solving situations. Practical applications of these theories—programmed texts and simulation games, for example—are increasingly present in today's schools.

Regardless of differences in theories, basic principles involving learning remain unchanged: (1) children learn as individuals; (2) children learn at various rates; (3) children learn according to different styles and patterns; and (4) education is a continuous process.

Their attempt to translate these principles into practice has led educators to pursue many new teaching strategies and organizational patterns that break with traditional modes. Among these have been the widespread adoption of unified media programs administered through a school library media center. Once more, professional associations helped lead the way. In 1969, the first joint standards cooperatively produced by the DAVI and AASL were issued, *Standards for School Media Programs.** The development of these also involved 28 advisers from other professional associations. In addition to emphasizing the positive results that unified media programs can bring and supplying detailed quantitative guidelines, the media program standards also stress the necessity of fusing facilities and services if media personnel hope to meet the challenge of today's education. Since the issuance of this publication, many state and local audiovisual and

* In late 1973 joint committees of AASL and AECT (Association for Educational Communications and Technology, the new name for the former DAVI) were planning to issue revised standards for school media programs.

school library organizations have merged and others have instituted cooperative projects. Increased support for the media center concept from other agencies, organizations, and professional personnel shows that many persons who are involved in education now realize that a sound media program is a prerequisite for high-quality education.

PART 2

SCHOOL MEDIA PROGRAMS

2

THE NATURE OF
MEDIA PROGRAMS

The emphasis on the individual nature of learning has led educators to question methodologies that promote only teaching facts and rote learning, curricula that departmentalize knowledge into unrelated units, and organizational structures that promote artificial grade levels and perpetuate unrealistic expectations and rigid standards. Recently many schools have been developing new, freer approaches to teaching. Numerous organizational patterns have been developed: individualized instruction, team teaching, flexible and modular scheduling, large-group/small-group instruction, independent study programs, interdisciplinary studies, nongraded or multigraded classrooms, contract teaching, extra school internships, and tutorial or directed study programs.

The role of the media specialist has become that of an organizer and guide, one of whose chief responsibilities is to provide a learning environment appropriate to the needs of the school community. Among the elements essential to creating this environment are a variety of media at many levels of comprehension and interest that have been organized for easy accessibility and a range of services and activities that involve the learner. The need for a unification of both media and services to promote learning through programs has led to the creation of a new agency within the school, the school library media center.

The concept of a unified media program developed as education responded to the changes in society. Ideas in any medium—print, pictorial, sound—together with the mechanical, electrical, and electronic means to use them are the basis of knowledge. To present them in any situation requires a program that has a unity of purpose; any arbitrary division or fragmentation of resources and services for use in an instructional setting can weaken the educational potential of a school. It is the responsibility of the media center to provide leadership in developing new methods of

19

instruction, designing curriculum, organizing materials and equipment collections, administering programs, and improving communication between the school and the community. The media center is an arena composed of many programs in which all types of collections and services exist in arrangements to facilitate rather than restrict use and that encourage progress toward present and future educational goals. It is a center of purposeful activity, the vortex of action in a school where individuals learn.

The threefold intent of this chapter is (1) to define briefly the nature of media programs at all levels, emphasizing the program in the individual school; (2) to describe the resources, services, and activities that together comprise the overall media center program in a single school; and (3) to outline a plan for inaugurating or strengthening a media program in the individual school.

The media center program in its largest sense is the sum of all the activities in which students, teachers, administrators, and others in an educational setting use materials and equipment to facilitate communication and promote learning.

LEVELS OF SUPPORT FOR MEDIA PROGRAMS

Media programs exist on the national, state, regional, school district, and individual school building levels. By purpose and design those of the first four types are meant to be of assistance to the media program in the individual school. The programs on the national and state levels offer the least amount of direct help to the individual programs. Although there is only one national education program—in the U.S. Office of Education— that heads the hierarchical structure of education, there are fifty state education departments and thousands of school districts, many of which have unified media programs. The media programs both of the state education departments and the school systems exhibit a range of differences, from traditionally separate divisions for audiovisual and library resources and services to totally unified media programs. Over the last two decades, a pattern of change has been visible in state education departments. While some states—New York, for example—with a long history of compartmentalization of audiovisual and library services have found it difficult to make appropriate changes, others—Maryland, Michigan, North Carolina, etc.—have adopted a forward looking, unified state media program by combining formerly separate divisions.

FEDERAL PROGRAMS

On the Federal level, the Bureau of Libraries and Learning Resources (BLLR), headed by an Associate Commissioner of the U.S. Office of Education, traditionally administers library programs in the public and college fields. The BLLR also includes three programs directly related to public education: the School Library Resources Program, the Equipment and Minor Remodeling Program, and the Undergraduate Instructional Equipment Program. All three place the responsibility for the unified media program management within the school media center.

One of the main purposes of the BLLR is to help the U.S. Office of Education develop ways of delivering all kinds of instructional services to the American educational community. The intent is to provide leadership for continuous improvement in the nation's educational system by maintaining an informational clearinghouse at the Federal level. The program is directed toward conducting research, encouraging training programs, developing resources and services, and exploring technological developments and facilities. It also serves in a liaison role with the state departments of education and, when requested, in an advisory capacity to the U.S. Congress.

STATE PROGRAMS

Within each state department of education, it is increasingly common to find that the responsibility for the development of media programs, with the exception of such highly specialized elements as instructional television, rests in a library bureau under a division devoted to instructional services. Each bureau generally includes a staff professionally trained in educational technology and library science that can serve as liaison with the U.S. Office of Education, Bureau of Libraries and Learning Resources, with other divisions within the state education department, and with the schools in the state.

The state bureaus are also increasingly acting as agents in linking media centers with already existing large public libraries and regional resource centers in order to form statewide media networks. The ultimate goal is to provide access to any material needed in the schools. In newer efforts, some state bureaus are initiating research projects to identify specific staff and student needs as expressed by the patrons. They are also establishing criteria for evaluating programs that will be suitable for use with newer budgeting systems, an increasingly important area for development, in the light of the new emphasis on accountability for program results.

REGIONAL PROGRAMS

An emerging level of media services similar in many ways to that available under large school district operation is the regional networks that attempt to unite public libraries and school media centers in an effort to broaden and enrich the programs of individual centers. In many instances public libraries, through regional and state systems, have been the trend setters in this type of organization. In the past, Federal funding has often provided the seed money. Although school media centers have not been able to initiate comparable school network systems because of the restrictions in their local government type of funding, they have in some instances joined these cooperative regional networks. This type of plan assumes that efficiency, economy, and better service will result from shared resources and services. The regional plan has been noteworthy when the contract services have supplied educational items too costly for small school districts, such as instructional television supplied to midwest states by Midwest Program for Airborne Television Instruction; media workshops for educators in New York provided by the Board of Cooperative Educational Services (BOCES); films, diaramas, and other expensive or infrequently used materials loaned to schools in San Diego County, California, by the Resource Center. Regional networks are operating successfully in smaller school districts for special groups, e.g., the academically talented, the handicapped, the culturally disadvantaged. They are also providing such special services as automation capabilities and inservice courses.

Regional cooperation for media services and resources can be beneficial among schools in districts that are not large enough to support a centralized district resource center as well as employ a director of media. However, it is desirable for a district with a minimum of six school buildings to use the centralized method in addition to regional cooperation. The larger school systems, suburban Montgomery County, Maryland, and urban St. Louis, Missouri, for example, generally find that centralized district media services for the larger operations, such as film and professional libraries or centralized media acquisitions and preparation, etc., have been important first steps toward excellence in school media program operation.

SCHOOL DISTRICT PROGRAMS

A media center program at the school district level functions both as a centralized resource for the district and as support for the program in individual schools. The resources and services that form a base of operations at the district level can provide the services needed by many of the schools. Each school can retain its own individuality by its own selection and use of resources, as well as by its own unique use of the district services. Maryland and other states with a small number of school systems are exploring school system state networks based on the practical knowledge that no system with fewer than 40,000 students can sustain all centralized media center needs.

The district media program includes several internal district responsibilities: (1) preparation of annual budgets; (2) interpretation of the total media program (central and individual schools) to the public, to the Board of Education, and to the staff; (3) application for funds from Federal, state, and foundation sources; (4) administration of the funds for special projects; and (5) formulation of reports for the district Board of Education, the state department of education, and the U.S. Office of Education.

Two of the major tasks of the school system media program are planning and evaluating. These tasks are the foundation for media services on the system and individual school building levels. Planning is generally based on knowledge of: (1) the educational philosophy of the school system and the objectives of the instructional program, (2) staffing patterns, (3) curricula, (4) various methods of instruction, (5) availability and utilization of technology, (6) awareness of newer technology. Evaluation is a continuous process of measuring the quality and effectiveness of the programs available to the users, i.e., the administration, teachers, students and community, in order to make decisions about program modification and changes. The results of this regular evaluation are essential for use in the Planning, Programming, Budgeting Evaluating System (PPBS; see chapter 5, Budget).

On a district level, media services under the direction of a coordinator who is knowledgeable both in the library field and in the field of educational technology and who exhibits leadership capabilities will insure greater development of media programs at the individual school building level. To provide these services on a system level requires appropriate staffing, funding, and facilities. The district professional staff also should have general competence in the library and audiovisual fields and some degree of specialization in both media and subject areas.

Seven percent of the instructional budget is recommended to support a district program. Any distribution of media that is appropriate to the district's educational plan is permissible. One that is commonly suggested for schools with a beginning district media program is: (1) 25 percent textbooks; (2) 25 percent traditional media (books, films, recordings); (3) 50 percent newer media and equipment (video tape and audiovisual equipment).

Although enthusiastic administrative support and financial backing by the Board of Education are of prime importance, staff and facilities for the center are also vital. The district media center is best located in or close to the district's administrative center. In many instances, the district center is located equidistant from the majority of the schools, an important factor for bringing teachers and media specialists to the center and for sending resources and services to the individual schools. Ideally, the media center should have space for its many components: (1) professional collection,

(2) examination center, (3) processing, (4) media production, (5) film and tape libraries, (6) equipment services, (7) inservice activities, (8) printing services, (9) television services. The facilities should also include areas for administrative offices and professional reading, viewing, and listening. An outside entrance and first-floor delivery access are also important.

INDIVIDUAL SCHOOL PROGRAMS

A media center in an individual school building is actually a multiplicity of activities and services that together are sometimes called the program. The operation of the center provides the base for the other activities or programs. The media center operation may itself be considered a fundamental program. Often, because of limitations in monetary support, staff, and facilities, it has been the only program. These factors have slowly changed with the increasing recognition that the use of media in schools is important in the teaching-learning process, and as a result the media center has developed other programs for its school audiences, such as local production of film and tape and dial-access media presentations. These programs expand the educational potential of the media center and make it an exciting and vital part of education.

RESOURCES, SERVICES, AND ACTIVITIES IN AN INDIVIDUAL SCHOOL

RESOURCES

The school provides in each building a collection of materials and the equipment needed to use them that fits in variety and scope both the curricula of the school and the interests and abilities of the users. The range can be broad: from books and jigsaw puzzles or videocassette tapes to community resource files and games or microfiche. The collections should include some material in every available medium. The national standards and standards suggested by some states—Illinois and Maryland, for example, can serve as guidelines for collection size. The following suggestions are based on Maryland's recommendations. Basic initial collections should be available in every school. Each school, regardless of enrollment, should have a fully cataloged and processed print and nonprint collection. The quantity of material in a basic collection will depend on enrollment, range of grades, variety of subjects taught, and special needs of the school population. The funds needed for initial collections should be included in capital outlay budgets. The acquisition of a new collection is time-consuming because selection, acquisition, and technical processing must be done before the collection is ready and the media program can be initiated. The building of a collection should ideally therefore begin when a new school building or remodeled media center is first planned. Some duplication should be anticipated if decentralized resource centers by subject area or grade levels are to be in the same building.

The size of the collection in a media center can be established by recommending media based on enrollment for different levels of schools. This approach to collection building reinforces the unified concept of a media center. The following are guidelines for quantities of items that are necessary to carry on a basic media program:

Elementary schools (K–6)	Twenty items for each pupil (8,000 pieces of materials for 400 students).
Junior high or middle schools (6–9)	Twenty items for each pupil (10,000 pieces of materials for 500 students).
Junior or senior high schools (9–12)	Thirty items for each pupil (36,000 pieces of materials for 1,200 students).

No one way of assigning print and nonprint materials according to a predetermined percentage scale is necessarily the best for each school. Instead, a primary consideration should be that the subject matter—instructional or recreational—be represented in as many formats and to the same degree that it is needed by the faculty and students of the school.

Recommendations for quantities of equipment follow the same pattern because the equipment is so closely tied to the materials with which it is used. There is no maximum or minimum quantity; the amount depends upon the school's program. However, care must be given to equipment purchasing because obsolescence is an integral part of technology. This fact should not, however, prevent the media specialist from incorporating into the program new developments in equipment. It should, however, caution the media specialist that information about each type of equipment should be fully gathered.

Ideally a unified program will provide a plan for using the equipment throughout the school as well as in the media center itself. The lists of equipment shown in Table 1 suggest quantities for both of these service areas.

The quality of the program cannot be measured solely by the size of the collection; however, when only minimal media are provided, educational opportunities for students are limited. Although it is difficult to prove that a given quantity of materials and equipment will ensure that a child will learn, the knowledge gathered from experience and research is that children are more likely to show educational gains within an environment that includes a variety of media.

TABLE 1   EQUIPMENT COLLECTION FOR A BASIC MEDIA PROGRAM [a]

Equipment	Number in center	Number per teaching station (per grade level)	
Record player with earphones	5	1	(K–6)
		1/5	(6–12)
Tape recorders, reel-to-reel	5	1/5	— [b]
Cassette player-recorders			
Classroom size	10	1/3	(K–6)
		1/5	(6–12)
Portable	6	1/3	(K–6)
		1	(6–12)
Listening stations with 6–10 headsets	2	1	(K–6)
		1/10	(6–12)
Basic stereo sound system with quadraphonic capability, amplifier, turntable, reel-to-reel and cassette recorders, speakers, cart	1 [c]	—	— [b]
Projectors			
16mm sound	3	1/4	
8mm silent	5	1/10	
8mm sound	6	1/4	
2x2 slide	3	1/5	
filmstrip			
sound	2	1/4	
overhead	2	1	
opaque	1	1 [c]	
microprojector	1	—	
Previewers			
filmstrip	5	1/2	
2x2 slide	5	1/2	
Microreaders	1	1/10	(6–12)
Microreader-printer	2	—	(6–12)
Microfiche reader	2	1/2	(6–12)
Microfiche printer	2	—	(6–12)
Accessories			
projection carts	— [d]	— [d]	
screens			
wall or ceiling	1	1	
portable	1	1/5	
rear	1	1/2	
typewriters for student use	3–6	—	
lecterns			
standing	—	1	
table	1	1	
Duplicating equipment			
ditto or stencil	1	1/20	
electrostatic or thermal	1	1/20	
Local production equipment	— [e]		
Dry-mount press and tacking iron, paper cutters, Thermo and Diazo transparency			

TABLE 1 (CONT.)

Equipment	Number in center	Number per teaching station (per grade level)
production equipment, Super 8mm camera, rapid-process camera, equipment for darkroom, spirit duplicator, primary typewriter, copy camera and stand, light box, 35mm still camera, film rewind, film splicer (8 and 16mm), slide reproducer, mechanical lettering devices		
Video, TV, and radio equipment		
portable video tape recorder		
camera and monitor	1	1/5
playback unit	1	1/15
videocassette recorder	1	—
TV receivers	1	1/15
closed-circuit television	1	1/5
AM-FM radio receiver	1	1/5

a Based on 600 pupil enrollment.

b Where grade level is not indicated quantities are the same for elementary and secondary levels.

c For building use.

d One for each 16mm and overhead projector in media center and in building.

e Quantities depend on the development of the production program in the individual school. The section on Local Production of Material in chapter 9 discusses the processes, and Appendix IV contains criteria for selecting equipment.

SERVICES

The media center's program provides a spectrum of learning opportunities for both large and small groups as well as for individuals. The focus is on facilitating and improving the learning process, with emphasis on intellectual content, inquiry, and the learner. Because people do not react similarly to the same medium, the learner is encouraged to read, view, listen, construct, and create in order to learn in his or her own unique way. The media center program is a cooperative venture in which media specialists, teachers, and administrators work together to provide opportunities for the social, cultural, and educational growth of the student. The program is a coordinated effort in which activities take place in the media center, laboratory, classroom, and throughout the school.

There are several ways to describe media center programs. A traditional way is to outline the services performed by the staff. A list of 195 services (exclusive of providing materials and equipment) in secondary school libraries has been compiled by Mary V. Gaver in *Services of Secondary School Media Centers, Evaluation and Development* (ALA, 1971).

Sixty-eight typical elementary school media services have been outlined in the NEA pamphlet, *Elementary School Media Programs: An Approach to Individualized Instruction* (1970).

The Gaver list is comprehensive and has served to identify exemplary secondary school media centers as well as to indicate staff services that should be considered in developing a program on that level. Many of the services, such as posting information about TV and radio programs, also apply at the elementary school level.

Some of the staff functions basic to providing the minimal services of any media center are:

1. Budgeting balanced media programs,
2. Selecting materials and equipment,
3. Acquiring and processing (where not centrally supplied) all media and equipment,
4. Organizing collections of media and equipment for easy access,
5. Circulating media and equipment,
6. Arranging schedules that provide accessibility,
7. Handling repair procedures,
8. Preparing operational handbooks for the center,
9. Promoting the media center,
10. Instructing in the location and use of media and equipment,
11. Offering reading, viewing, and listening guidance.

Identifying only the functions, however, can be self-defeating if they are not directly related to the educational activities that they stimulate and support. Evaluation based on the educational objectives of a media program rather than on the necessary, but intermediate staff functions generally serves as a more accurate indicator of educational progress and places accountability within the framework of the entire educational community. If the emphasis is on providing only the basic operations in running a media center—as is sometimes the case where staffing is inadequate —there can be little direct and meaningful measurement of educational progress based solely on counting items that are provided and the people who are served. Thinking about media centers in relation to the multiple activities that should originate in them will highlight the programs rather than the staff services. This will lead to better evaluation and promote accountability in its constructive sense.

ACTIVITIES

Another and perhaps more valid way to describe media center programs is through the media activities that take place in the media center and the school. Activities among centers vary by type and also the combinations that they are offered in. Nevertheless, some of the same activities reappear in all dynamic centers: students or teachers, individually or in groups, listen to tapes and cassettes; make transparencies and other visuals; view films and slides; conduct a media search for a project; or prepare a multimedia presentation. Programs in existence across the country reveal numerous activities and the underlying staff functions that support them. A collection of these activities is given in the list, Staff Functions Related to User Needs. With a little imagination, the majority of these activities can be redesigned to serve in other centers.

Although the examples that are described here can apply in many instances to any of the four major audiences of a media program—students, teachers, administrators, and the community—they are grouped for convenience under the audiences with which they will be used most often. By comparing a staff function and the resulting activity it becomes obvious that any measurement of the objectives or the activity will give a truer evaluation of educational progress than will the work measures of staff functions. It should be emphasized that learning takes place only during the activity.

STAFF FUNCTIONS RELATED TO USER ACTIVITIES *

All the examples are arranged to show the relationship between staff function and the center-user's activities:

The media center staff functions so that ⎯⎯⎯⎯⟶ Students, teachers, administrators, or community members can participate in an activity resulting in a learning experience.

ACTIVITIES FOR STUDENTS

READING, VIEWING, AND LISTENING

Organize media and equipment; preview, evaluate and weed ⎯⎯⎯⎯⟶ Participate as members of a review committee to evaluate media.

Compile media bibliographies ⎯⎯⟶ Learn to use an annotated bibliography that includes books, cassettes, films, and games about a theme or topic.

Give presentations using media ⎯⎯⟶ Learn importance of using a variety of media, e.g., books, realia, globes, maps, and sound recordings, to illustrate a discussion of "courage."

Assist in developing media presentation skills ⎯⎯⎯⟶ Present programs to groups of friends or to younger students. An eleventh grade varsity ball player can highlight a talk on sports novels for eighth graders by using transparencies to illustrate game techniques; an older stu-

* Examples of several of the programs on which the lists are based are highlighted with brief descriptions in chapter 4.

dent might help a younger one select media to present to a home economics class.

Provide for local production of media ———→ Use locally produced media in a variety of ways, e.g., preparing transparencies, laminating pictures and clippings, taping and filming school reports.

REFERENCE WORK

Provide accessible reference materials ———→ Locate a variety of media by using bibliographies to establish a media reference collection for a third grade unit on nature.

Use newer media to develop study skills ———→ Recognize the need to compare and evaluate sources. A video tape unit on this part of reference work might be shown to individuals and to classes.

Correlate collections for classroom or subject area use ———→ Learn to use out-of-print books and periodicals on microfilm for an individualized American studies project.

Establish liaison with public, university, and special libraries ———→ Use interlibrary loans, e.g., a student might request a scientific monograph for an advanced placement chemistry class from a cooperating research library.

INSTRUCTION

Teach reference skills and equipment use ———→ Learn the skills for competent media and equipment use so that a third grade class can practice alphabetizing by working with the card or book catalog, or a seventh grade English class can undertake a TV production of excerpts from *Tituba of Salem Village*.

Give orientation tours and workshops ———→ Learn the organization and administration of a library, e.g., each grade level might participate in a series of workshops.

Teach use of special reference materials ———→ Learn to use essential print reference materials, e.g., fifth graders choose a suitable encyclopedia and atlas to complete an oral report on a country.

Help develop and teach a standard bibliographic form ———→ Learn the school's bibliographic rules by using a programmed learning workbook.

Develop ideas for using media ———→ Learn about other community resources by presenting a print, recording, or film project about the local pet shop's dog-care course.

CLUBS, SOCIAL AND VOCATIONAL PROGRAMS

Develop assistantship programs ———→ Learn media center work as a volunteer, as a part-time paid employee, or as part of course work in distributive education.

Assist in extra-class activities ———→ Participate in social and educational activities such as trips to local libraries, theaters, and museums; plan a media club trip to an art museum film festival.

Sponsor paperback fairs, film festivals ———→ Learn to share the experience and work of sponsoring exhibits. Examples: 4–6 grade students help to run a paperback fair; 7–9 grade students assist in planning a film festival of novels that have been made into feature films.

Plan media center publicity ———→ Help to promote center resources and services, e.g., high school journalism classes and radio clubs prepare and disseminate publicity.

Suggest media-use ideas for assemblies, PTA programs, classroom projects, and plays ———→ Assist in recording school meetings, speeches, and special programs, e.g., video tape special school programs for community use.

ACTIVITIES FOR TEACHERS AND ADMINISTRATORS

CURRICULUM DEVELOPMENT

Teach use of media through the role model of teacher-librarian ———→ Develop cooperatively a unit to be taught by a media specialist and teacher team, e.g., a unit on myths for the fifth or sixth grade.

Attend grade-level or subject-area departmental meetings ———→ Participate in designing courses incorporating new uses of media, e.g., a ninth grade survey of careers that uses resource people, films, government pamphlets, etc.

Help to design instructional systems ———→ Study existing curriculum to develop new instructional approaches; media specialist can recommend appropriate media for a second grade reading program using trade books, readers, kits, enrichment films, CAI, etc.

Learn teachers' instructional methods and media needs through individual conferences ———→ Plan to use media support for basic and enrichment programs, e.g., easy-reading materials, filmstrips, and films on anthropology for third graders.

Plan media programs for teachers' professional and recreational needs ———→ Attend exhibits of new professional materials, screenings of noteworthy films or videocassettes, and demonstrations and displays of the newest equipment.

ASSISTING IN THE USE OF MATERIALS

Help teachers become familiar with the media center ———→ Participate in video taping a media center orientation program to use throughout the school.

Teach use of a media center for research ———→ Develop with a group a local history project that can be used as a demonstration of how to use the center's research resources.

Organize routines for convenient use of materials and equipment; make self-instruction programs available ———→ Develop simple programmed instruction booklets to teach youngsters some fundamental media center skills such as classification.

Encourage local production of materials ———→ Teachers and administrators can develop their own "tailor-made" materials.

Establish departmental or auxiliary resource centers ⟶ Develop cooperatively a place for storing equipment and specialized materials within floor levels, grade levels, or departments so that they receive maximum use.

ACTIVITIES FOR THE COMMUNITY

Give talks to parents and community groups ⟶ Groups of parents of preschool children discuss reading aloud to youngsters with media staff at evening meetings; take home selective lists of read-aloud books.

Observe national media-related events ⟶ Participate in special programs to highlight the National Book Awards, the American Film Festival, the Right to Read Program, etc.

Publicize media center activities ⟶ Local radio might produce spot announcements with media staff help; newspapers run information about media center programs.

Engage community business and professional persons to speak to school and media center groups ⟶ Local persons serve as resource specialists, e.g., a florist might participate in a media center home economics program on flower arranging.

CONVERTING A SCHOOL LIBRARY INTO A MEDIA CENTER

Many things should be explored before the task of converting a traditional school library into a media center is begun. Perhaps the most important concern should be whether the person who is to run the center fully comprehends and accepts the concept of multimedia library centers as dissemination points for ideas and information regardless of the medium in which they appear. To embrace this concept also requires acceptance of the equipment that some media require for the transmission of the ideas or information. Once a wholehearted commitment to this philosophy is made, the media specialist is ready to take some immediate steps toward developing a media center and to plan for some long-range steps. The media specialist should assume leadership throughout the entire process. This leadership is vital and one of the key factors for the eventual success of a good program. A word or two of caution is necessary. Experience has shown that when introducing a new program it is best not to attempt to introduce a great number of new services and activities in the initial stages but to concentrate on developing a total media program by adding a few activities to those that have proved successful. By no means try to build a media center solely by adding new or different media; this is a denial of the basic philosophy of a media center. Instead, integrate media into the grade-level unit or course of study that is widely used in the school.

Six Immediate Steps

1. Identify a curriculum or recreational area around which to build the media concept.

2. Contact one or two teachers who are interested in working cooperatively to build a balanced media collection in the one area.

3. Encourage the students to use media in the developing collection for individual satisfaction as well as for classroom work. Simple production of transparencies and laminating pictures are two possibilities.

4. As soon as the program activity is completed, evaluate the media activities and services that have been added according to the teacher's educational objectives and the students' responses. The evaluations can serve as a basis on which to make future changes and also to urge the administration to institute the unified media concept in the school.

5. Encourage other teachers and students to participate to the extent that staff and funds are available. If necessary, postpone organizational details, such as an integrated book or card catalog, in favor of creating interest in the use of media and eventually persuading the principal to provide additional support.

6. Enlist the support of the principal and administration for instituting an increasing role for multimedia in the center.

Long-Range Steps

1. Use the educational philosophy of the district and individual school together with the specific objectives for each area in the overall curricula in order to formulate evaluative criteria for measuring the success of the media program.

2. Seek a consultant's help if possible. Visit other centers.

3. Evaluate present services, resources, facilities, etc. (See the "School Media Program Self-Evaluation Form" in chapter 4, Assessment of Media Programs.)

4. Focus on a total media center program that is uniquely suited to the school and set the priorities within multiyear phases in which the activities, services, newer resources, and remodeled facilities will be inaugurated.

5. Establish confidence and effective communication with the principal by building on the successful operation of some past program activities. Ensure a clear organizational pattern of communication as well as acceptance that only one person will head the media center operation in the school including the distribution or, more likely, decentralization of equipment for classroom use.

6. Continue to enlist the support of the teachers and students by providing activities and services they may need, but may be unaware of.

7. Revise plans as necessary, guided by the evaluation of the program against the evaluation criteria set up in the first of the long-range-conversion steps.

8. Explore the possibility of developing a unified media program on a district level.

3

ESSENTIAL ELEMENTS
OF A MEDIA PROGRAM

This chapter discusses the techniques for three activities that can help the media specialist determine the effectiveness of a school media program: (1) formulating precise statements of educational objectives; (2) defining the instructional program; and (3) utilizing public relations methods to acquaint patrons with the center's resources and services. The measurable results of these activities provide a means of assessing the success or failure of the program.

FORMULATING INSTRUCTIONAL OBJECTIVES

Program accountability is the specific evaluation of an activity in relation to its educational objectives. Each media specialist must design some way of measuring the educational results of each activity. The specialist's important first step, in consultation with teachers and administrators, is to formulate behaviorally stated objectives for each program activity. Some of the purposes for writing these objectives in behavioral terms are:

1. to develop the criteria by which materials are selected, content is outlined, instructional procedures and educational technology are developed, and tests are prepared;
2. to clarify for teachers, students, parents, and other community members exactly what students should be able to do as a result of the program;
3. to demonstrate the place of school media programs in PPBS (see chapter 5) or other systems of accountability so that the media program may receive a fair share of the school budget.

Schools have been accustomed to stating their goals in general terms, e.g., to become a better citizen, to understand the beauty of language. No matter how worthy may be these aims, they remain abstract and difficult, if not impossible, to measure. Simple, overt student behavior is most easily cast in behavioral terms, for example, a pupil will be able to locate the word "dinosaur" in a dictionary in three minutes. Since learning is based on a multitude of fundamental previous learnings (the alphabet in the illustration mentioned), starting with such a basic exercise is not undesirable. The important thing is not to confine objective writing only to the lowest level of cognitive, affective, or psychomotor learning. The following guidelines will help the media specialist write objectives more skillfully.

Since the school's responsibility is to prepare students for life in a contemporary and changing society, it is necessary to define present and prospective societal needs in order to establish curricular goals. A preliminary survey of at least five groups should be undertaken in order to determine their ideas:

1. Recent graduates—to establish the validity of objectives.
2. Prospective local employers—to identify available opportunities.
3. Community—to formulate its expectations of the school's graduates.
4. Teachers—to help pupils interpret the society.
5. The next highest school—for coordination.

The information obtained through these surveys can help define the knowledge that students should eventually possess. Moreover, to determine the emphasis of this instruction in the curricula the various objectives should be listed and ranked by these groups in a follow-up survey. The information can also provide a base for formulating many things: behavioral objectives, methodology design, instructional media programs, and a list of performance behaviors.

Essential Steps

These are the four specific points to be used in formulating instructional objectives:

1. Identify by name the behavior you expect. Specify the kind of behavior that will be accepted as evidence that the learner has achieved the objective.

Ask: What should the pupil be able to do at the end of the activity that he or she cannot do now?

2. Define the desired behavior further by describing the conditions under which the behavior will be expected to occur.

Ask: Under what limitations of time, place, etc., will the student be expected to show the desired outcome?

3. Specify the criteria of acceptable performance by describing how well the student must perform.

Ask: Exactly how well must the student perform to be acceptable?

4. Identify a suitable measure by which to judge the relative degree of success or failure of the activity.

Ask: How can the teacher measure what the student can do?

Only some general principles remain: (1) use an active verb that describes a visible activity or one that can be measured or tested in some way; (2) leave only one interpretation possible; if the behavior is inconclusive, the testing will be also; (3) as a final check to test the validity of the objectives, ask the following four questions: (a) What do I want the student to do? (b) Under what conditions do I expect the student to do it? (c) How will the student do it? (d) How will I know when the student has done it?

Putting all these elements together in a hypothetical educational objective framed in behavioral terms, the following might result: Within 20 minutes, the fifth grader will list on paper the location, author, and title of five media—including book and nonbook—about satellites or any appropriate subject, with all the above information exactly as it appears on the catalog card. The form shown in Exhibit 1 will be useful in preparing instructional objectives.

DEFINING THE INSTRUCTIONAL PROGRAM

STUDENTS

The amount of teaching of media skills that should take place in the center is a subject of current controversy. Those in favor of an extensive teaching program maintain that mastery of skills is necessary to produce independent, resourceful users of media. Opponents argue that although learning how to locate materials may be necessary, too much valuable time is spent on details like explaining the catalog card or the Dewey Decimal System when the most important aspect of reference and research work is *using* the materials. Whatever policies are adopted, the instructional program should not be conducted in a vacuum unrelated to students' actual needs. Instead, teaching should be functional and integrated with the students' other educational activities.

The instructional program is conducted at two levels: the informal and the formal.

Informal instruction. The teaching that takes place spontaneously when answering an individual student's request is an example of informal instruction. This might include supplying directions and help in locating

EXHIBIT 1   WRITING INSTRUCTIONAL OBJECTIVES

1. Behavioral task: What do you want the student to do?_____

2. Curriculum area_____   3. Estimated time_____
4. What intellectual process is involved? The student will have to:
   Learn definitions_____
   Remember principles_____
   Apply concepts_____
   Follow rules_____
   Change or paraphrase information from one form to another_____
   _____
   Look for relationships between ideas_____
   Apply principles, rules, or information to unfamiliar problems or situations _____
   _____
   Analyze something by breaking it down into its parts_____
   _____
   Produce original solutions_____
   Evaluate information, object, or solutions against specific criteria_____
   _____
5. What will you provide for the student?
   Information_____Print and nonprint materials_____
   Equipment_____Other_____
6. How will the student be observed performing the task?
   Alone_____Speaking_____In groups_____Reading_____
   Writing_____Listening_____Other_____
7. How will you judge the success of the performance?_____
   _____

material in reference books or giving a brief, impromptu book talk to answer the question: "Could you recommend a good book to read?" Informal instruction is certainly the most valuable type because it directly satisfies a student's individual needs. The obvious drawbacks of informal instruction are that it is time-consuming and repetitious for the staff and that it is dependent on a lack of reticence in students. To help match instruction to immediate needs, some media centers have produced short teaching tapes for cassette playbacks. Each tape deals concisely with a particular topic, e.g., the use of the card catalog, encyclopedia, or *Reader's Guide*; arrangement of the material on shelves; instructions for operating a particular piece of equipment. The cassette equipment is placed close to the material described on the tape. Some media centers use specially prepared or commercially produced charts and posters, and short, programmed instruction booklets to acquaint students with the library's resources. Still others have developed self-instruction laboratories where students can use tapes, filmstrips, and other materials to teach themselves media skills.

Formal instruction. This involves presenting preplanned lessons before a group of students. The presentations should adhere to established guidelines of teaching that include: a statement of goals expressed in concrete behavioral terms; an introduction that catches students' attention and explains the purpose of the lesson; an effective presentation of the material to be learned; and an opportunity for feedback and evaluation. The lessons should be scheduled in media center classrooms where materials are accessible, but disruptions to other patrons are avoided. Many commercially prepared aids for teaching media center skills are now available: packaged kits, films, filmstrips, workbooks, lesson plans, etc. Some are extremely useful and can be modified, when necessary, to fit specific needs.

The practice of scheduling groups or classes into the center on an informal, as-need-demands basis is now widely accepted. Not only does this promote cooperative planning between teachers and the center's staff; it also helps achieve the goal of making media center instruction an integrated, cohesive part of the school's curriculum. Nevertheless there are, unfortunately, many schools where rigid scheduling of classes into the media center is still practiced. Usually the reason for adhering to this traditional and outmoded procedure is more administrative than educational and often is in the interest of freeing teachers for preparation periods. Rigid scheduling can throw both content and timing of lessons off balance, causing eventual harm to the entire instructional program.

One fear sometimes expressed about a possible danger of free or open scheduling is that, depending on the teacher, some classes will not visit the center often enough or that certain skills will not be taught. In practice this fear has been proven groundless; for any such danger can be avoided in a well-run media program where there is constant communication with the faculty and where realistic, flexible instructional programs have been adopted.

Open scheduling does not mean that the teaching of media skills should be placed on a catch as catch can, unstructured basis. Every school district should adopt a sequential instructional plan that indicates the skills to be mastered at various grade levels. However, apart from a basic orientation to the media center, the teaching of these skills should be integrated with subject matter courses and student activities.

During the school year 1971–1972, the Department of Educational Media and Technology of Montgomery County Public Schools in Maryland initiated a Media Skills Project to determine a continuum of instructional objectives for media study skills in their schools. A committee of ten teachers and librarians developed the tentative schedule that is presented in Exhibit 2. Although some parts are being modified, the plan as outlined is thorough and practical. In districts where similar schedules have not been adopted, this plan can serve as a workable model.

Although formal and informal instruction are the principal ways of informing students of the resources of the media center, other approaches can also be taken. Many of these are described later in this chapter in the discussion, "Utilizing Promotion and Public Relations Methods."

Some media centers prepare and distribute a student handbook. The publications vary considerably in size and depth of coverage. The handbook should cover the following basic information: (1) a floor plan of the center; (2) general information on the size and nature of the collection; (3) a list of center personnel and the services available to students; (4) a brief description of major locating devices used in the center (card catalog, Dewey Decimal classification, periodical indexes); (5) statements on the center's policies regarding hours of service, collection, and attendance. More elaborate handbooks extend the coverage to include annotations for major reference sources, longer descriptions of locating devices, and instructions on how to use various items of equipment. To decide how extensive the student handbooks should be, the media specialist should measure its projected value and expected use against the expenditure of time and money necessary for its production.

EXHIBIT 2   INSTRUCTIONAL OBJECTIVES FOR MEDIA RESEARCH SKILLS *

The objectives described at each level are sequential. If a student is not performing at the suggested level, remedial instruction should be provided.

I. MEDIA CENTER ORIENTATION

GRADE LEVELS	OBJECTIVES
K−1	1. Name library personnel. 2. Observe library rules. 3. Handle books properly. 4. Check out materials properly. 5. Identify kinds of media (at ability level).
2−12	6. Check out material properly without assistance.

II. ORGANIZATION OF RESOURCES

GRADE LEVELS	OBJECTIVES
K−1	1. Locate "easy materials" (picture books). 2. Find materials correctly in "easy reader" section.
2	3. Locate fiction and nonfiction collection and magazines. 4. Locate card catalog, book catalogs. 5. Locate filmstrips. 6. Locate tapes and cassettes. 7. Locate film loop projector. 8. Locate records. 9. Locate encyclopedias.
3	10. Find materials correctly in the fiction collection. 11. Locate filmstrip projectors, film projectors, overhead, opaque, and slide projectors.
4	12. Find different categories of books according to the Dewey Decimal system. 13. Locate the vertical file.

* Adapted from Montgomery County (Maryland) Dept. of Educational Media and Technology Media Skills Project.

EXHIBIT 2 (cont.)

II. ORGANIZATION OF RESOURCES (cont.)

GRADE LEVELS	OBJECTIVES
5−6	14. Identify correct placement of books using Dewey Decimal system. 15. Locate indexes, atlases, almanacs, newspapers, and other reference materials. 16. Locate guide to children's magazines.
7−8	17. Locate reference materials related to specific subject areas or courses (assessment tasks for this level should be geared to locating such works as *Current Biography, Reader's Guide, World Almanac,* etc.).
9−10	*Note:* Assessment tasks for this level should be geared to locating: 1. Additional works such as *Statesman's Yearbook, Bartlett's Familiar Quotations, Dictionary of American Biography, Encyclopedia of American History,* etc. 2. Newspaper indexes. 3. Microfilm viewer, video tape recorder, video cartridge. 4. Public library *adult catalog.*
11−12	*Note:* Assessment tasks for this level should be geared to locating: 1. Additional works such as *Encyclopedia of European History,* Cambridge *History of English Literature,* Oxford *Companion to American Literature,* math dictionaries, Chemical Rubber Co. *Mathematics Handbook,* etc.

III. SELECTION OF RESOURCES

GRADE LEVELS	OBJECTIVES
K−1	1. Select materials for personal interest.
2	2. Select materials appropriate to student's reading level.
3	3. Choose a dictionary to find the meaning of a word. 4. Distinguish between the content of a fiction and nonfiction book. 5. Distinguish between the use of filmstrip, film, overhead, opaque, and slide projectors.
4	6. Distinguish between content of a dictionary and of an encyclopedia. 7. Select correct volume (using alphabetical order of encyclopedia) to find specific information.
5−6	8. Select correct materials for a specified topic. 9. Select correct index for a specified purpose.
7−8	10. Select suitable source for information on a living person. 11. Select source for quick summaries of facts. 12. Select source for short, factual articles. 13. Select source for identification of poetry and quotations.
9−12	14. Identify proper sources for information on specified subjects. 15. Select suitable books and AV materials for a specified subject. 16. Select readings that are authoritative, current, useful, etc.

IV. UTILIZATION OF RESOURCES

GRADE LEVELS	OBJECTIVES
K−1	1. Use a record and cassette player. 2. Identify a book's illustrator, title, author.
2	3. Identify a book's front, back, spine. 4. Use an 8mm film loop projector. 5. Operate a filmstrip and slide previewer.
3	6. Alphabetize to second letter of author's last name. 7. Identify a book's index. 8. Use filmstrip, overhead, opaque, and slide projectors (optional).

EXHIBIT 2 (cont.)

IV. UTILIZATION OF RESOURCES (cont.)

GRADE LEVELS	OBJECTIVES
4	9. Alphabetize to third letter of author's name, titles, etc. 10. Identify a book's title page and table of contents. 11. Identify copyright date and publisher. 12. Use card and book catalogs to find call numbers. 13. Use film projectors (optional). 14. Use vertical files to obtain pamphlets, pictures, etc.
5−6	15. Alphabetize titles to the end of words. 16. Distinguish between word-by-word and letter-by-letter alphabetizing. 17. Identify a book's appendix or glossary. 18. Use call numbers to find resources. 19. Use tape recorder. 20. Identify and state the purpose of the basic information on a catalog card.
7−8	21. Use cross references in card catalog. 22. Use general reference works. 23. Use reference works related to specific subject areas. 24. Identify the sections of a newspaper and describe each one. *Note:* Assessment tasks should be geared to student use of general works related to specific subjects such as those cited for grade level 7−8, section II.
9−10	25. Use all necessary sources available to collect information for a specified subject. 26. Use microfilm viewer, video tape recorder (optional). 27. Obtain and use materials for local public libraries.
11−12	*Note:* Assessment tasks for this level should be geared to use of general and reference works related to specific subject areas such as those cited for grade level 9−10, section II.

V. COMPREHENSION AND STUDY SKILLS

GRADE LEVELS	OBJECTIVES
K−2	1. Use picture clues to aid in understanding material. 2. Identify main idea. 3. Identify a sequence of events.
3	4. Find specific information by using pictures and filmstrips. 5. Interpret simple pictorial maps and graphs. 6. Skim to find a word, name, date, phrase, sentence, idea, or answer to a question.
4	7. Use a book's table of contents to locate information. 8. Use a specified book to locate a specific fact. 9. Summarize simple information. 10. Use a book's index to locate information. 11. Find words in a dictionary. 12. Identify key words and key phrases in a reference work. 13. Use guide words.
5−6	14. Use encyclopedias, atlases, almanacs, telephone directories. 15. Find words in *Roget's Thesaurus*. 16. Write a simple outline. 17. Compile a simple bibliography. 18. Take notes using simple procedures.
7−8	19. Paraphrase or summarize information. 20. Use bibliographies to aid in locating information. 21. Skim to get an overview of material. 22. Compile a bibliography following a specified style. 23. Organize to show sequence. 24. Take notes using prescribed procedures.

EXHIBIT 2 (cont.)

V. COMPREHENSION AND STUDY SKILLS (cont.)

GRADE LEVELS	OBJECTIVES
	25. Outline information in a topic or sentence outline.
	26. Identify topic sentence.
	27. Infer facts and ideas in a reading.
9 – 12	28. Compare figures in maps, graphs, statistical tables, to make generalizations, to infer, and to draw conclusions.
	29. Use specialized reference materials to develop and support research and select data bearing on a problem.
	30. Use preface, chapter headings, indexes, and cross references as research aids.
	31. Evaluate material for accuracy and appropriateness.
	32. Recognize digressions from the main idea of a subject.
	33. Select relevant information for a given purpose from within content of material.
	34. Skim to find material relevant to a topic.
	35. Distinguish between factual and emotional writing.
	36. Distinguish between fact and opinion.
	37. Use formal outline to organize information from reading selections and to aid in recall.
	38. Identify unsubstantiated statements.

VI. PRODUCTION (optional)

GRADE LEVELS	OBJECTIVES
K – 2	1. Construct a picture based upon ideas in a story.
3	2. Construct a picture or series of pictures to illustrate a story.
4	3. Construct a model story book with a title, author, front, back, spine, table of contents, copyright date, publisher.
	4. Construct a "handmade" transparency.
5 – 6	5. Make a tape recording.
	6. Make a "machine-made" transparency.
7 – 8	7. Make a map floor plan of the media center.
	8. Make a color-lift.
	9. Make slides.
	10. Make filmstrips.
9 – 12	11. Make a video tape.
	12. Make a film or film loop.
	13. Prepare a detailed report using audiovisual aids.

Faculty

The media center staff should also be active in developing inservice training for the faculty. This can be done on an informal basis during joint planning sessions with teachers, classroom visits, attendance at grade-level or departmental meetings. More structured presentations can be given at faculty meetings or during workshop sessions. A detailed proposal for an inservice course for teachers on the use of media in the instructional program is given at the conclusion of chapter 5, Budget.

Part of the orientation program for new teachers should be a tour of the center conducted by the staff, supplying a general introduction to the collection and the services available to the faculty. Some centers also prepare a special handbook for teachers or contribute a section to the general faculty handbook used in the school. The latter is usually a variation of the student handbook with appropriate additions or deletions. The promotion and public relations section of this chapter gives other useful techniques for working with teachers.

THE NONPROFESSIONAL STAFF

Orientation periods and close supervision during initial work sessions are two useful methods of introducing new members of the clerical staff or volunteer workers to center procedures and routines. Staff manuals are another helpful tool in training staff members.

Before the beginning of the school year, some school districts conduct special inservice courses of one or two weeks' duration for new clerical assistants. Basic topics that should be covered in these sessions are:

1. General Orientation
   (a) Recent developments in education and their relation to the media center concept.
   (b) The program of the media center in individual schools.
   (c) Media center services available outside the school (district-wide centralized services, services supplied by other libraries and informational agencies).
   (d) The administrative structure of the school district.
   (e) The role of the clerical assistant.
2. Ordering and Receiving Procedures
   (a) Forms used in the district.
   (b) Ordering procedures for books, texts, other instructional materials, bindery items, equipment, furniture, professional materials, supplies, and rentals.
   (c) Accounting and business practices.
3. Processing of Material
   (If there is a centralized processing agency, coverage of the topic will be brief.)
4. Arrangement of Material
   (a) The Dewey Decimal Classification System.
   (b) The card catalog (types of cards and their format).
   (c) The shelf list.
   (d) Arrangement of cards (filing rules and procedures).
   (e) Practice in card filing.

5. Operation and Maintenance of Equipment
   (a) Demonstration and practice with various types of audiovisual equipment.
   (b) Simple repairs required on equipment.
6. Local Production of Materials
   (a) Demonstration and practice in duplicating materials and in making transparencies.
   (b) Techniques used in mounting materials.
7. Care of Materials
   (a) Instruction and practice in performing simple repairs on printed materials.
   (b) Care and handling of nonprint materials.

Any inservice courses will have to be supplemented in two ways: (1) with district-wide sessions during the school year to update personnel on new developments or to serve as refresher courses, and (2) at the local level, with additional inservice work to acquaint new personnel with the routines and procedures peculiar to the individual school.

Hours of Service and Attendance

Media centers usually open for service at the same time as the first students and teachers arrive (about a half hour before classes begin), are open during the entire school day, and remain open for an hour or an hour and a half after the day ends, or as long as students are present in sufficient numbers to warrant keeping the center open. The number of after-school hours will depend on several factors: transportation available to students who remain after school hours; other library resources available in the district and their accessibility; the number of after-school activities that make use of the collection; and the liberality of the center's circulation policies. Some centers have experienced varying degrees of success with extending hours into the evenings and weekends, thus supplying students and other members of the community additional opportunities to use the collection. Special summer media programs are also becoming more prevalent.

The objective of policies regarding attendance is to get as many students into the center as often as they wish. Ideally, therefore, any student who wishes to use the center should have free and open access to it. In many secondary schools that have adopted flexible schedules, students in the upper grades are now given complete freedom of choice concerning where they will spend their free time. They may go home, visit the center, a study hall, or the student lounge. In more rigidly structured situations students often must obtain passes before they are allowed to come to the center from study halls. A pass system is also frequently used to admit students into the center from classrooms. In still other instances students have the option of attending a study hall or checking into the center. Restrictive policies sometimes have to be adopted to prevent overcrowding in the center, but generally they are used as methods of keeping an account of students during the school day. As each school situation contains unique elements, the merits and deficiencies of various plans should be studied to arrive at the one that best promotes good use of the center and at the same time allows students suitable access to the collection.

Whenever possible, scheduling of classes or small groups into the media center by teachers should be done at least a few days in advance of the visit. In this way center staff members have an opportunity to allocate their time and provide necessary physical space, prepare lessons, collect needed material, and check with the teacher on these preparations before the class is due. The center should maintain "sign-up sheets" that give the time and purpose of the scheduled visit. On a daily or weekly basis a master schedule should be distributed to teachers and administrators to inform them when the staff is free for conferences or last minute scheduling.

Happily, the days of the "sshing" librarian are drawing to a close and the "Silence Please" signs are no longer found in library supply house catalogs. It is natural and normal for students to talk in the media center; to try to prevent a healthy level of conversation is to fight their natural instincts. Today's students are also increasingly accustomed to background noises and seem able to block them out at will. Certain areas in the center should therefore be designated for quiet conversation. Areas around the periodical collection, lounge areas, and specified tables set aside for small group work are suitable for this purpose. On the other hand, some sections of the center, for example, areas where there are individual study carrels, should be designated for quiet study where students can be free of any distracting interruptions.

There will, of course, be discipline problems with which the staff will have to cope at times. A staff member should try to deal with the individual responsible for the disruption by a personal conference rather than before the group. Make sure that any underlying basic problems that the student might be facing are understood so that the real cause and not just a symptom may be treated. Perhaps the best advice to give in these situations is not to interpret these occurrences as personal affronts but instead to maintain a balanced view and a sense of humor.

UTILIZING PROMOTION AND
PUBLIC RELATIONS METHODS

The development of good public relations requires conscious and continuous effort; it is not something that can be turned on or off at will. Every time a patron has any contact with the media center—whether directly or indirectly—an impression is created that will either enhance or damage the center's image. Any and every aspect of the media center and its program affects public relations. Of initial importance is the ambience of the media center. The atmosphere should be one of friendliness and cheer. This feeling may be partly produced by the physical surroundings —which should be inviting and pleasant and should convey warmth and a feeling of hospitality. Center personnel should constantly reassess the center's facilities from the standpoint of other users' entering the media center for the first time. Is the general impression a favorable one? Is the furniture comfortable? Is it attractively arranged? Are browsing and lounge areas provided that are conducive to relaxation and enjoyment? Are all the various parts of the collection clearly marked for easy identification? Are all display areas well used?

Bulletin boards and display cases attract potential users to the media center, publicize its services, and familiarize students with the collection. Although displays are important inside the media center, the display facilities in corridors and classrooms should also be used to advertise and promote the center. Displays can be fitted into a number of places. Conventional bulletin boards and table- or windowtype display cases are most frequently used, but any unused wall space can accommodate a corkboard or pegboard either hooked onto the space, suspended by wires from the ceiling, or displayed on a simple easel setup on the floor. Easels can also be used for direct display of posters or other informational resources. Bare walls can serve as a display area for continuous multimedia shows, and corners of a media center area can be used to exhibit life-size displays of resources and activities in a pop-art manner.

The steps for preparing a display are relatively simple:

1. Decide on the subject—a specific, concrete one is usually better than a general one.

2. Select a caption—make it short, interest-catching, and large enough to be seen at a distance. Where appropriate, present it with a light touch —perhaps with a play on words or some similar device (e.g., "Take me to your reader").

3. Make a rough sketch—show both placement and color of material and backdrop; arrange the parts so that they have a logical form and the eye travels naturally and easily from one section to another. One of the

most common devices is to arrange the parts so that they lead the eye to the center of the display.

4. Produce an interesting balance and keep the display uncluttered.

5. Keep it neat. Lettering is not everyone's forte; if this is the case use commercially manufactured letters.

6. Maintain a file of materials and ideas.

Materials for displays can be easily improvised. Attractive backgrounds can be created with wallpaper, poster paper, burlap, metallic paper, or foil. A variety of simple materials can be used for a three-dimensional effect. Mailing tubes can become large pencils or rocket ships; paper plates can become frames, and cotton batting or steel wool can serve as clouds or hair. Coat hangers make an excellent framework for mobiles.

A few additional pointers: change the display often—in order not to run the risk of losing the audience—and integrate students' projects and community resources with the media center's materials. Copies of the material on display should also be available for circulation in the media center. This will mean using articles that there are duplicate copies of in the center or, in the case of books, using dust jackets obtained from publishers. With a bit of imagination and ingenuity, the media center staff can easily produce attractive, eye-catching displays, but if ideas are slow in coming or time is too pressed to allow for original planning, there are plenty of guide books available on producing displays, and the *Wilson Library Bulletin* conducts monthly a well-illustrated feature article on the subject.

Taking care of the well-being of patrons is a responsibility of every worker in the center—from volunteer students and parents to the media center's full-time staff. It is important that each person be given instructions in how to act toward patrons and how to give patrons proper assistance. In some cases simply referring the patron to a professional staff member might fulfill the person's responsibility. This simple operation, too, should be handled with tact and concern for the patron. All helpers should be aware not only of the established regulations governing the media center's program, but also of the reasons these regulations have been adopted. In this way simple explanations can be given to patrons when particular policies are questioned. The media center staff should also periodically review adopted policies to determine whether they actually promote and facilitate the program or simply act as roadblocks between the patron and the services that are needed.

In promoting media center services and wholesome public relations the center's personnel will work with several different groups inside the school—students, teachers, administrators—and in the community—parents, community groups, local news media, public and other library agencies. Successful communication with one group certainly can affect and influence the other groups. In spite of this interrelationship it is helpful to isolate and study the development of good relations with each.

STUDENTS

There are many special ways for promoting the media center and its services with students. The staff should try to relate the general activities of the school and the current interest and experiences of the students to the media center. For example, a student play or assembly program or an important sport event can form the basis of a display, media bibliography, or some special library program. Also usable are popular television programs, current movies, community activities, world events, or social issues. All available channels of information should be used to disseminate news about the media center. The school's newspaper and public address system are two such channels. Some media centers publish their own bulletins that contain such items as new acquisitions; student reviews; lists of titles that reflect reading, listening, and viewing preferences of different classes or teachers; news on media center events; bibliographies of current popular subjects. In addition to the book talks and story hours offered in the center, visits can be arranged to classrooms or to club meetings to introduce appropriate media center material to the students and teachers.

Student reading, listening, and viewing experiences should be used to promote the media center. Popular with students are informal sharing periods during which they talk about titles they have enjoyed. A separate file drawer of cards containing titles recommended by students (and arranged by students' last names) is often used. Bulletin board displays or printed booklets containing brief reviews written by students can also draw attention to the students' preferences.

The promotion of such special events as National Book Week and Children's Book Week as well as center-sponsored assembly programs, book fairs, and media center bookstores not only furnish valuable services but also help publicize and promote the center's total program. Many centers sponsor group activities, such as reading clubs and film forums, play-reading groups, career programs, or discussion groups on topics of interest to students. Planners of group activities should remember to schedule the meetings on a regular basis and to allow sufficient time before each event to publicize it thoroughly. It is advisable to form a planning group or club council composed chiefly of students to assure potential interest in the program and the actual need for it. A prepared agenda should be drawn up before each meeting. Resource persons and materials for programs may often be found within the community and back-up material from the media center utilized. When appropriate, mention may be made during the meeting of other media center material related to the topic under discussion. Specially prepared bibliographies might also be distributed to teachers.

TEACHERS

Many of the techniques used with students can be employed in developing public relations with teachers. For example, using media center materials in joint displays in the classroom and the center is an excellent way to gain the support of teachers while at the same time promoting the center's collection. Some media centers, particularly those in very large schools where direct communication between the center and its users is difficult, have organized media center advisory committees composed of teachers, students, and representatives from both the central administration and the media center staff. These committees gather information on user needs, supply advice to the center on policy making, and, in turn, publicize and interpret these policies to the general public.

The development of special services involving the professional collection is another useful technique. These services could include routing pertinent articles from professional journals, announcing the arrival of new material, and preparing bibliographies on educational topics of current interest to the faculty. The active participation of the center's staff on faculty committees and in professional organizations and the use of the staff as resource personnel for these groups will help build a liaison between the center and the faculty.

Perhaps the best way to reach the faculty is by supplying each teacher with the personalized attention and professional concern that will aid him or her in preparing, organizing, and presenting his or her instructional program—in short, providing the support that will help the faculty member become a better teacher. Media centers sometimes assign individual staff members to act as advisers to specific grade levels, academic departments, or teaching teams. Staff time is often set aside for conferences with teachers in the center. Other centers prefer to arrange discussions with teachers in the classroom setting. In any case, faculty members should be encouraged to spend part of their classroom preparation periods consulting with the staff, preferably in the media center, and becoming acquainted with the center's resources that are appropriate to their current classroom needs.

ADMINISTRATORS

The same techniques used with the students and teachers (displays, newsletters, etc.) will also make the administration aware of the various facets of the center's resources and programs. Preparing specific reports for administrators has already been discussed. The school administration should always be consulted as well in developing center policies, and members should be invited to participate in any special events held in the center. The resources of the center should be made available to help in those activities that grow out of the administrative function. For example, the center staff might prepare visuals to aid in a budget presentation or to illustrate and interpret a new teaching program before a parent group. The staff should also be available to provide any back-up reference service required by the administration. This might be in supplying specific information, locating material, preparing bibliographies, or routing professional materials. Specifically, the center staff should keep the administration abreast of the latest developments in media and media centers. In addition to furnishing material on these subjects, center personnel should be encouraged to invite administrators to local conferences, workshops, or exhibits where educational media and its uses are presented.

COMMUNITY

Although one of the most essential links in a good public relations program is informing the community about the services of the media center, this is probably the area that is given the least attention. Many parents and school board officials are still not aware of the concept of the media center, let alone the specific activities and programs connected with it. Yet the support that the media center receives from a community helps to determine the media center's success. This support may be directly related to school budgets and building programs or indirectly related to forwarding the school's philosophy. It is therefore essential that the center's professional staff members devote some of their time to explaining and interpreting their program to persons who may not use their services, but who nevertheless sustain the program through financial and moral support.

Here are a few of the techniques to use to reach this hidden public:

1. Prepare a simple slide/tape presentation that illustrates the services given to students by the media center and present this (followed by a discussion period) to various parent and community groups.

2. Utilize local news media to publicize the activities of the center.

3. Schedule a once-a-year Media Night for the school's parent groups to acquaint them with the latest developments at the center.

4. Plan special programs for those occasions—a Back-to-School Night, for example—when parents visit the school.

5. Encourage parents, school board members, and community leaders to visit the media center while school is in session.

6. Utilize community resources for displays and speaking engagements.

7. Make media center resources available for use by school-based parent groups.

8. Attend and participate in community functions.

9. Utilize parents' help for such special functions as book fairs.

10. Prepare and distribute to parents media bibliographies, recommended reading lists, and guides to reference books.

Public Library and Other Local Library Agencies

Building good relations between the media center and other library agencies in the community not only helps promote and publicize the center's program, but more importantly, can result in better library service and more effective use of material by students. An initial step is for the staffs to become acquainted with each other and familiar with the resources and regulations of each other's libraries. In many school districts an Interlibrary Council has been established to discuss mutual problems and concerns in order to develop procedures to help solve or eliminate them. The school media center staff can also serve as a clearinghouse of information about other libraries by publicizing their programs, having their colleagues visit the school to talk before students and teachers, and arranging class visits to other libraries. The center staff should keep in touch with other libraries on a regular basis and notify the library staffs of school assignments, curriculum changes, new acquisitions, and other developments within the school that might affect the students' use of a given library's collection. This line of communication should be maintained particularly with the public library, and in turn the public library can promote special events and services offered by the school media center. To avoid duplication and wasted time and effort, some activities, such as film forums or summer reading programs, might be jointly planned and sponsored by several media centers, together with the public library.

It is necessary for the center's staff to look outside itself and reach all groups affected by the media center's existence. Each situation is unique in some respect and, therefore, will require different solutions. Many of the suggestions made in this chapter might not be applicable or feasible, others might have to be modified, and in some cases totally new approaches may have to be devised. Professionalism, imagination, and an honest desire to supply maximum service with the materials available are the keynotes to utilizing and promoting the resources of the school media center.

4

ASSESSMENT OF MEDIA PROGRAMS

Assessment is an integral part of the instructional services of a school. Its primary purpose is to develop, coordinate, and improve the teaching-learning process. The two most significant factors in assessment are supervision and evaluation; both are important for the success of a media program, whether it is a regional one or a single school program. Leadership and the knowledge of a few fundamental principles form the cornerstone for competent assessment.

This chapter (1) describes the principles and practices of school media supervision on all levels, emphasizing the role of the media specialist as supervisor of the program in the individual school; (2) includes program and support services self-evaluation forms that can be used by the media specialist to evaluate the program in several ways, e.g., for accountability, budget, and program preparation; and (3) offers brief descriptions of programs with one or more aspects that are worthy of note, to highlight the variety of practices employed in media centers throughout the country.

SUPERVISION

The term "coordinator" is used interchangeably with such other descriptive titles as supervisor, director, consultant, or chairman, since the goals and functions of the positions so described and of the coordinator are the same. The modern concept of supervision stresses leadership, coordination, cooperation, creativity, self-direction, and effective public relations. The school media coordinator, as one of the instructional specialists in a school system, regional board of education, or state or Federal department of public instruction, shares the responsibility for the overall educational program.

It is sound practice to delegate the leadership of the program to a school media coordinator. This person should have training as a teacher and a media specialist. Regardless of title, the position should be equal in rank and authority to that of other administrative instructional specialists in the system. This administrative unit, regardless of the level, is the keystone for well-planned, economically sound school library service. School media supervision can exist at all levels, from Federal to local.

SCHOOL MEDIA SUPERVISION AT THE FEDERAL LEVEL

The U.S. Office of Education includes a supervisory position to guide and improve school library service throughout the nation. The two main purposes of this position are: (1) to serve as an informational clearinghouse and (2) to act as liaison between the Federal, state, and local educational agencies.

SCHOOL MEDIA SUPERVISION AT THE STATE LEVEL

In many states, the state supervisor plans and administers the overall school media services. He or she provides leadership and supervisory services to local school authorities. As a part of a state's instructional improvement program and accreditation of library schools, the appropriate bureau or division fosters the concept of the school media center as a unified program for media throughout the school. The state bureau reinforces the Federal supervisory functions by adapting them to the state level of service. In addition, the state supervisors provide services appropriate to their unique position. These services can be classified under the categories listed below.

Guidelines

Develop all regular qualitative and quantitative standards for school media centers.

Appraise and plan media quarters in new school buildings and consult on remodeling.

Supervision

Design a long-range plan for school media development in the state.

Evaluate school media programs in the state.

Guide the development of programs of library education in the state.

Encourage the development of demonstration school media centers throughout the state.

Distribution of Information

Interpret the role and importance of media to the legislature, boards of education, school personnel, and other groups.

Advise and interpret state and Federal legislation and regulations regarding school media centers.

Supply information and publications on school media programs to administrators, teachers, and media specialists.

Prepare annual reports, special reports, and articles.

Statistics and Research

Collect, analyze, and disseminate statistical data on media service in schools.

Initiate and promote research on school media program.

Secure government and private grants to further the development of school media centers within the state.

Certification

Serve as resource centers and advisers on professional qualifications for media specialists.

Aid in the recruitment of media specialists.

Cooperation

Work closely with the chief state school officer.

Coordinate the school media program with other programs within the state education department.

Participate in national, state, regional, and local education and library organizations.

Serve as consultants on school media center and as resource persons with other groups.

Arrange cooperative programs and projects with other professional groups.

Cooperate with governmental agencies, such as state libraries and regional boards.

Cooperate with nongovernmental organizations, such as teachers' associations, PTAs, and so forth.

SCHOOL MEDIA SUPERVISION AT SYSTEM, CITY, AND DISTRICT LEVELS

While each system network or regional cooperative service has its own unique services and activities that are available to the school district, some basic services and activities are offered by most of them as follows:

1. Establishing a union catalog based on the collections of the cooperating schools' libraries.

2. Forming depository collections to supplement the regular school collections.

3. Assigning areas of subject or media specialization to member schools.

4. Sharing operating and maintenance costs of expensive facilities, such as television studios.

5. Computerizing such routines as ordering, preparing, and circulating media.

6. Providing central facilities and consultants for large group meetings and instruction.

7. Coordinating inservice workshops with other groups.

Many cities and districts employ school media coordinators to utilize Federal and state supervisory services and provide effective management. A school system with five or more school buildings should establish the position. The formation of school media centers into a separate administrative unit has proved to be educationally efficient and economically sound. In addition to directing the school district's media program, the coordinator can effect economies by assigning nonprofessional library routines to paraprofessional and nonprofessional staff. Although administering these technical services is important, the primary responsibility of the school media coordinator lies in working with media specialists, teachers, and administrators. In essence, school media supervision involves the development and supervision of a satisfactory school system media program designed to aid teachers in solving their instructional problems, students in participating fully in the learning process, and the community in supporting the program.

A city, county, or large school district media center program usually provides a majority of the following services to its individual schools, either directly or by contractual arrangement with another district agency:

1. Establishing central purchasing, cataloging, and preparation of media.

2. Maintaining additional materials for smaller schools that cannot adequately meet the variety of student and teacher needs.

3. Developing an examination system for the selection of materials and equipment for acquisition.

4. Producing specialized forms of materials, such as slides, audiotapes, video tapes, etc.

5. Maintaining equipment.

6. Establishing printing services.

7. Developing inservice programs for training the entire district faculty (e.g., on the evaluation and use of newer media).

8. Assisting in recruiting and selecting media staff for the district.

9. Coordinating professional collections for teachers and administrators.

10. Initiating the borrowing or renting of costly or infrequently used materials.

11. Establishing a central source for consumable supplies.

12. Developing television services that may include the following types: open circuit, closed circuit, or community antennae.

13. Inaugurating computer services for technical services, information retrieval, and assisting instruction.

Although each local district will have its unique problems, in general, the basic functions of local school media program supervision are similar. The major responsibilities are:

1. Advising local school administrators on the role and management of school media centers.

2. Interpreting school media functions to the board of education, legislature, PTA, citizen groups, and other public bodies.

3. Working with other coordinators and department heads to improve media service.

4. Implementing school media standards.

5. Promoting a media concept in the school by incorporating media services in the center and including media in bibliographies.

6. Assisting in selecting and organizing the media, including equipment.

7. Coordinating the work of all media centers in the school system, including purchasing and technical services.

8. Providing for local production and distribution of instructional aids and materials.

9. Evaluating school media services.

10. Serving on curriculum committees and as a resource person for other specialists.

11. Initiating and directing inservice programs on school media center materials and services, e.g., providing instruction in newer media.

12. Recruiting and directing a qualified staff.

13. Preparing a budget, annual and special reports, and articles.

14. Participating in professional organizations and conferences.

15. Providing a center where educational media can be examined and evaluated.

16. Exploring the use of new technology, such as computers.

17. Fostering research and experimentation with instructional uses

of media and media services arrangements and applying the results of research to the program.

School Media Supervision in the Individual School

In a school media center that has a small staff and lacks a media coordinator on the district level, the media specialist assumes the supervisory role and carries out as many as possible of the district-wide functions that have been enumerated. The media specialists in individual schools may consult directly with the state and Federal school media departments. Other agencies, such as public and college library consortiums, will also give advice and aid to the media specialist. In addition to the important policy-making and program-coordinating functions that the media specialist in this situation will carry out, evaluation is another basic task for the media specialist-coordinator who is trying to run a successful program.

EVALUATION

Evaluation of a program in order to provide accountability and direction for future improvement is increasingly important. A good way to begin is to use the self-evaluation forms shown in Exhibits 3 and 4. These forms suggest the vital areas in the program that may be measured and will give a quantitative and qualitative picture of the existing program. For example, ascertaining the numerical range of people served in each of the audiences will allow the media specialist to view the program realistically and consequently to reorder priorities and institute other services to give a better balance to the media program in the individual school. Each individual may also wish to develop a special measure that relates more closely with the local program.

EXHIBIT 3   SCHOOL MEDIA PROGRAM SELF-EVALUATION FORM

Grades ___ to ___   No. of students _____   No. of teachers _____
High school curriculum: ___% college bound   ___% vocational   ___% handicapped
Elementary curriculum: ___% exceptional   ___% slow learner   ___% handicapped
Attrition rate ___% Average class size ___

Services to Students	Total school	1/2 or more	1/4 or more	less than 1/4
Guidance in reading, viewing, listening				
Reference				
Assistance				
Queries answered				

EXHIBIT 3 (cont.)

Services to Students	Total school	1/2 or more	1/4 or more	less than 1/4
Library orientation				
Once a year				
Periodically				
Library instruction				
Regularly				
Infrequently				
Local production				
Vocational guidance				
Clubs				
Presentations				
Special programs				
Film				
Other				

Services to Teachers	Total faculty	1/2 or more	1/4 or more	less than 1/4
Media examination & selection				
Local production facilities				
Provision of media for developing students' independent study skills				
Coordination of materials with instructional program				
Assistance in planning & presenting instructional skills lessons				
Participation in teaching resource units				
Media for personal needs				
Inservice courses				

Services to Administrators	All info. needed	1/2 or more	1/4 or more	none
Serve as clearinghouse for information on: professional courses, workshops, meetings; community resources				
Media for school programs				
Media for personal needs				
Local production				

Services to Community & Community Groups				
Media for group programs				
Media for personal needs				
Other				

EXHIBIT 3 (cont.)

Accountability Measurements

Instructional Objectives		
Performance level achieved	_____ program 1	_____ program 2 (etc.)
Instruction		
Reference	_____ students	_____ teachers
Information services	_____ students	_____ teachers
Team teaching	_____ courses	_____ hours
Daily circulation		
Materials	_____ school	_____ home
Equipment	_____ school	_____ home
Attendance		
Regular hours	_____ daily	_____ annually
Extended hours	_____ daily	_____ annually

EXHIBIT 4   SUPPORT SERVICES SELF-EVALUATION FORM

BUDGET INFORMATION

Item	Quantity needed	Average cost per item	Total
Books			
Periodicals			
Pamphlets, etc.			
		Print total	_____
Films, purchase			
Films, rental			
Filmstrips			
Slides			
Records			
Tapes			
Cassettes, audio			
Cassettes, video			
Flat pictures			
		Nonprint total	_____
Supplies			
Equipment			
Repairs			
Other			
		Total expenses	_____

STAFF INFORMATION

Job Category	Number	Years in position	Years in district	Salaries
Professional				
Paraprofessional				

EXHIBIT 4 (cont.)

STAFF INFORMATION

Job Category	Number	Years in position	Years in district	Salaries
Nonprofessional				
Clerks				
Technicians				
Volunteers				
Students				
Parents				

FACILITIES INFORMATION

Activities Areas	Size (sq ft)	Seating capacity
Reading, viewing, listening		
Teachers' media prep. room		
Conference room		
Typing room		
Office		
Library classroom		
Workrooms		
Production		
Radio & TV studios		

Storage	Size (sq ft)	Location
Print		
Nonprint		
Equipment		
Magazines		
Darkroom		

Environmental Elements	Type	Number
Acoustics		
Lighting control		
Electrical outlets		
Cables for TV		
Temperature control		
Furniture (wood, metal, etc.)		
Card catalog		
Book catalog		
Circulation desk		
Tables, chairs		
Study carrels, nonelectronic		
Study carrels, electronic		
Pamphlet files		
Displays		
Bulletin boards		

EXHIBIT 4 (cont.)

ACQUISITIONS & ORGANIZATION INFORMATION

Activity	Centralized	Decentralized
Purchasing	_____	_____
Processing	_____	_____
Organization	_____	_____

POLICIES

Public Relations
  Students_____Teachers_____Administrators_____
  Parents_____Community_____Public library_____
  Other agencies_____

Hours open
  Before school_____After school_____Evenings_____
  Saturday_____Summer_____

Communications
  Telephone service_____Delivery service_____

Circulation
  System_____Records_____Fines_____

Records and Reports
  Financial_____Inventory_____Organization manual_____

EXAMPLES OF EXISTING PROGRAMS

There are many excellent media programs in centers throughout the country. Some of them, especially those that were inaugurated with the aid of Federal funds, have been studied and described in the literature. Less has been written about the media programs that have developed slowly as traditional school libraries begin to change into media centers. Visits to both established and emerging media centers across the country indicate that some of the activities and services that together make a media program are noteworthy enough to be used as examples by librarians in individual school buildings to help change traditional school libraries into media centers.

This section highlights a few of the outstanding activities and services that were observed in media centers of all types throughout the country. The programs can be adapted by even the smallest and least affluent school because they depend largely on media specialists serving as facilitators of ideas among people.

McDONALD ELEMENTARY SCHOOL, WARMINSTER, PENNSYLVANIA

McDonald Elementary School has approximately 1,000 students and houses its own library as well as the district Instructional Materials Center. The district, which has a wide economic range, includes 11 elementary schools and two junior and two senior high schools. The library services coordinator's office in the IMC occupies a circular area within one of the four circular structures that together with a rectangular building and connecting passageways constitute the modern architecture of this new school. Directly above the IMC is the Special Experience Room, a spacious dome-shaped room that houses a planetarium and provides facilities for 360° light and sound projection.

Fourteen librarians are employed in the district. The elementary and junior high librarians come to the IMC once every two weeks to evaluate, select, and catalog print and nonprint materials both for the district collection and for their respective building-level media centers. Once a month the secondary and elementary grades librarians meet at the IMC to set policy and discuss issues and problems with the administrators who attend the meetings.

CORONADO JUNIOR-SENIOR HIGH SCHOOL, CORONADO, CALIFORNIA

The Instructional Media Center of the Coronado Junior-Senior High School is housed in a new facility in the Coronado Unified School District. Coronado is a combined residential and resort community of 18,800 persons across the bay from San Diego.

The center is administered by a librarian and two clerks with the help of a district media specialist. The collection includes a wide variety of media from such traditional items as planetary celestial globes to newer instructional equipment such as audiocassette units for use in carrels. The center also has an excellent collection of art reproductions stored in bins. The main room is designed for both individual and large-group use. An interesting part of the center program is the emphasis placed on activities that encourage students to help each other, regardless of age differences.

COUNCIL ROCK HIGH SCHOOL, NEWTOWN, PENNSYLVANIA

Newtown is in Bucks County in a school district that covers 70 square miles of lately rural countryside. Council Rock High School in many ways shows the typical development that has taken place in education over the last decade.

The attractive three-floor school is in one of the greatest growth suburban areas in the county; almost 90 percent of the high school graduates go on to college. It has planned facilities for 2,400 students and serves grades nine to twelve in separate, but connecting buildings for the junior and senior high grades. Shared facilities include the pool, cafeteria, auditorium, and library. The building is wired for both closed-circuit and broadcast TV.

The Library Media Center is on the second floor and operates as a central area for individualized use. The equipment for classroom use is decentralized in 13 areas through the school. Areas contiguous to the main center offer some specialized media services, such as a library classroom for group use, a production room equipped for making materials (e.g., for laminating, for making transparencies and photographic embossed cards, and for video taping) for student and teacher needs, conference rooms for small groups (which double as nonprint collection rooms; the majority of films are rented), a periodicals room, TV studios, a Learning Instrumentation Room with electronic carrels (there are conduits for dial-access instruction [DAI] equipment), a typing room, and the office area for the coordinator of libraries, for the media specialists and technical services, and for circulation of materials. The Library Media Center also has a theft and detection system.

The coordinator spends time in building the collection for the new elementary schools; the media specialist at the high school coordinates the media services and activities. Both have nonprofessional aides for technical services, circulation, media distribution clerical tasks, and production. A teacher conducts a class in broadcasting and develops studio TV and video programs with students as part of the media program. There is an uncataloged paperback collection and a paperback book machine, as well as microfiche and microfilm. One activity that merits particular attention is the community access and resulting goodwill the center gains by staying open on Saturdays and two nights a week.

RIDGEWOOD HIGH SCHOOL, NORRIDGE, ILLINOIS

Norridge's thirteen-year-old Instructional Media Center has a unique claim: it exists in a school that was one of the forerunners in using computerized modular scheduling. This presented problems for the library's free-access reading-room area and the Independent Study (IS) areas attached to the subject areas in the four-year high school. The overlapping time periods for the more than 1,700 students in a school that utilizes independent study arrangements no longer presents a problem for the library area because the traffic pattern is controlled by including the library in the modular scheduling. The obvious lesson, aside from the conflict of "free" library in a modular schedule, is that a traditionally designed and operated media center needs both remodeling and rethinking to provide a media program, e.g., book or card catalogs in the IS together with a system for easy distribution and use of media.

The Ridgewood High IMC has coexisting print and nonprint resources under two coordinators. In a school where there is relative freedom of movement and a great deal of team teaching, the audiovisual coordinator runs a fine program for both teachers and students. Within the scheduling system, there are large group lectures with an attendance of as many as 220 students, for which a range of equipment from boom microphones to slide projectors to video tape equipment is used. There are also small groups and other independent study arrangements in the six-day scheduling cycle. The emphasis in the IMC program is on independent study. There is opportunity for such activities as listening to music for recreation, reading from an extensive print collection, and producing, together with the audiovisual coordinator and graphic artist, slides, transparencies, and tapes.

Two Small City Schools

Each of the small city high schools described here has a district coordinator who administers the media programs in all the district schools.

Grand Haven High School, Michigan

Grand Haven is an example of a separate central media facility that houses the supervising director's office. The director coordinates the media budget and selection for the district, including the technical and printing services for the system. The center's services to the district libraries are well organized and free the librarians from many clerical details. The high school, which serves a population of more than 1,300 students, has media specialists, audiovisual specialists, part-time equipment aides, and several clerks. Adjacent to the main high school media center are conference and dark rooms. The center also houses vocational materials, listening stations for the unscheduled 20-tape audio program capability, a copying machine, and a microfilm reader-printer. The entire area has as many as 800 students in attendance during any day. The unstructured, pleasant atmosphere and the rapport with the personnel permit a wide range of individual and small group activities among the students. The amount of activity devoted to guidance in listening, viewing, and reading is remarkable.

Keene High School, New Hampshire

The Media Distribution Center for the Keene schools is directly adjacent to the Educational Media Center in the high school. The director of the center is in charge of the high school, junior high school, and six elementary schools and supervises the media budget, equipment for classroom and library use, materials, supplies, teachers' production supplies, and library personnel, all of which are maintained on a very nominal budget. The center's support program works with minimal help: a secretary, part-time clerk, student volunteers—as many as 20 who do film booking, photocopying, teacher confirmations, supply lists, etc.—and a part-time aide who daily delivers the centrally housed nonprint, multiuse materials (e.g., films, filmstrips, cassettes) to the other schools. The center's staff serves 285 teachers and about 5,000 students, and the emphasis is on working with some very creative teachers and distributing media well. Each high school classroom makes excellent use of media; the library itself is generally crowded with industrious students. "Yankee ingenuity," according to the director, is a key factor in keeping the program's operating costs reasonable. Filmstrips, films, tapes and discs, transparencies, kits, and study prints, all circulate. Production of media, including photographic work, is also done in satellite production centers.

Special areas in the high school facility show how media is integrated in the curricula. A TV studio is also used by English teachers for courses in film study and for studio programs, cable TV, and video taping. A student Radio Studio also provides career orientation and production facilities. A large reading center, well equipped with carrels, tables, reading scanners, projectors, reading kits, study skills programmings, and remedial- and spced-reading materials and devices, functions for all subject areas; an automobile simulator that records a student driver's responses on a teacher-controlled console is set up in an extra-large classroom for driver education; a Language Laboratory Library in a classroom is supervised by a foreign-language teacher; closed-circuit video cameras are used for microscope display in biology classes. Any of these media-integrated services lead directly to enhanced learning situations for the students.

Two Specially Funded Programs

The following four-year high schools initiated their outstanding media programs as a result of grants.

Waterville High School, Maine

Waterville, the only high school in a town of slightly more than 18,000 persons, received Federal funds to develop a media center that would serve as a demonstration unit for the state of Maine. The Waterville High School Media Center has shown the same perseverance in developing an outstanding program as did the school library when it had to apply twice in 1965 for ESEA Title II and III funds. A state survey has shown that the center has been an influential demonstration for others. Its program has many excellent features, including (1) variety of media, (2) paperbacks to provide multiple copies, (3) extended hours of service, (4) high-quality individual guidance with all media.

Under the direction of a single media specialist, eight staff members, with a ninth for night work, serve 1,200 students. While the spacious corridor that bisects the second-floor library area and leads to stairways at each end has been a handicap in getting the print and nonprint media into reasonable proximity, it serves well as a student-lounge area and passageway between both halves of the center. It houses paperback books, bulletin boards for student work, and art reproductions displayed on movable hangers. In spite of the physical separation, this is truly a center that places equal emphasis on all types of media, both commercially and locally produced. There is a generous production room attended by a versatile artist-photographer paraprofessional who helps students produce their own work, e.g., slide shows. The students are also encouraged to use reproductions of primary source materials, such as "jackdaws," in their research.

In addition to providing guidance in working independently with all media, staff members help with many group projects, such as video taping an original drama or selecting records for sound background on a tape documentary.

Oak Park-River Forest High School, Illinois

This school's long-established and well-known school library received Knapp Foundation money through ALA to become an exemplary media center and a model for national attention. Located in a city of some 62,000 persons that is a suburb of Chicago, the school has been well established since the days when Ernest Hemingway, an alumnus, sat in the oak-panelled-tiled-room-with-a-fireplace that was his senior-year English classroom. Primary credit for the development of the school program must be given to the dynamic librarian, now retired, who used the Knapp grant to turn the facility into a modern, connecting, two-floor installation. The school's computer center, housed in an air-conditioned third-floor room, runs the dial-access installations. The centrally located center is very well integrated into the school through its special depository collections, e.g., the extensive slide collection that is kept in a resource area close to the art department and classrooms.

Eighty-five percent of the approximately 4,500 students in the school go on to college, with 60 percent of those who do enrolling in a four-year school. Working with these students and their teachers is a staff of ten and one-half professionals, four of whom are concerned with audiovisual media. The staff is assigned by subject competency and type of medium. For example, one supervises and gives assistance to students in the foreign-language study area, works with the teachers on foreign-language curriculum needs, handles the selection and routing of notices of these materials, and is also in charge of periodical acquisition, distribution, and circulation; another handles the same tasks for vocational materials and audiovisual equipment. A new director and some new staff will perhaps rearrange this system. The objective had been to create more readers, and accessibility and loan policies were developed to this end; it is probable that a newer objective to create literacy in reading, viewing, and listening will be emphasized. Meanwhile, the provision of subject specialists and people knowledgeable in the medium creates many program opportunities.

Two District Media Services

The two large city school districts described here support materials centers for their schools. Both districts have a long tradition in audiovisual services: the St. Louis, Missouri, district can trace this interest back to 1920; the center at San Diego was founded in 1923.

Library Services Center, St. Louis, Missouri

The Library Services Center in St. Louis serves 85 elementary libraries in 153 schools and a total of 123,000 students in elementary and secondary schools. There are five districts with the one district librarian serving as supervisor. The Library Services Center is housed in a former branch public library under the supervision of a professional librarian with a business management background. He is in charge of planning the budget, planning and implementing experimental programs, providing leadership in media development on the elementary level, working closely with the secondary levels, and making regular visits to local school centers. The center handles more than 100,000 items a year, and its computer program, which is now being developed, will permit greater services for all schools. The program presently includes circulating films and realia. This center installation was one of the forerunners in persuading jobbers to handle all media.

Instructional Media Center, San Diego, California

The Instructional Media Center for the San Diego city schools provides print services, including texts, to 125 grades K–8 centers and 33 grades 7–12 centers as well as all types of nonprint materials, an equipment pool, specialized equipment, and retail facilities for all grade levels. An abundance of material is available: more than 41,000 filmstrips and slides, 18,000 films, 489,000 volumes of pupil reference and science books. The five trucks that cover the five city delivery zones make weekly deliveries to each school. In addition, school personnel make scheduled visits to the center from 8:00 A.M. to 5:30 P.M. daily and Saturdays and personally select their materials using supermarket carts. Films, however, must be booked a month in advance. The well-planned building on the outskirts of town was completed in 1965. Its 70,000 squaue feet provide the space for the IMC and the Education Center. The latter contains the print collection, graphic arts, photo lab, and tape duplication center. The book storage area alone is the size of a football field.

Many activities for teachers go on in these areas: selecting materials; conducting equipment workshops and inservice meetings; evaluating new media and equipment; working with curriculum teams; and producing local materials, such as photography, tape-dubbing, and so forth.

REGIONAL EXAMINATION CENTERS

This type of installation serves as an examination and information center and, perhaps more importantly, as a forum for programs for media specialists. Regularly scheduled after-school workshops are held in print and nonprint evaluation by grade level, equipment handling, curriculum development, and media utilization. These centers offer important professional activities for the media specialists in the area. The Eastern Area Branch of the Division of School Libraries, Department of Education, the Commonwealth of Pennsylvania, is one of the five state regional centers that keeps the Division in close touch with its media centers. The Western Area Branch near Pittsburgh does similar work.

PART 3

MEDIA CENTER MANAGEMENT

5

BUDGET

Accountability is not new to education. Ever since the first sign-in sheet appeared in the principal's office, school personnel have been held accountable for the hours they work. What is new today is the stress on both fiscal and program accountability. While traditionally the budget has been a device for financial accounting, the emphasis has recently shifted to include accountability for program results. The complexities of accountability in this newer sense require an increased understanding of the budgeting process.

The aim in this chapter is to present an overview of budgeting and to explain terminology and processes in order to enable the reader to prepare a budget for a media center. Included is an introduction to PPBS, the Planning, Programming, Budgeting, Evaluating System of evaluating the effectiveness of media programs. All indications are that this program budgeting method will be widely used in the future.

In a broad sense a budget is a chart for a future course of action. It records the outcome of an essentially political process in which alternative plans are examined, preferences are indicated, and decisions are made. In its final form a budget is a statement of policy on which expenditures are based. As every administrator knows, it contains the assigned priorities that are the outcome of bargaining over conflicting goals.

A media center budget is only one part of a school district's total executive budget that includes the operating budget for each school. The media center portion of the overall school budget is sometimes given only minor consideration because of a lack of recognition of the importance of media in instruction and the absence of a well-prepared budget presented by a media specialist. As these factors have changed, however, the media center budget, which represents the direction the program will take in the immediate future, has assumed greater importance. The budget is essentially the philosophy of the center stated in quantitative terms, in the same way that a school district budget expresses the educational philosophy of a community.

COLLECTING BACKGROUND INFORMATION

A prerequisite for budget preparation is collecting background information in several important areas: sources of financial support; standards in the field; inventory of existing collections; community needs; curricula in the schools; and the budget system and accounting code in use in a particular district. Some of these areas will be discussed in relation to the media selection process in chapter 8. Here they are explained specifically as they relate to the budget.

Sources of Financial Support

The monies for education come mainly from local and state taxes. These funds are often the only ones that can be relied upon for budget purposes, and sometimes even these sources are undependable. Nevertheless, the possibility of receiving funds from sources outside the city and state should be investigated.

Since 1958 the Federal government has provided supplementary education monies through the various titles of NDEA (National Defense Education Act) and ESEA (Elementary and Secondary Education Act). Every spring the United States Congress appropriates money for each title. Annual editions of the *Planning Guides* for NDEA and ESEA titles, which give detailed instructions on how to apply for funds, are usually available directly from state education departments through the divisions responsible for statewide school library and media development. These same divisions are often responsible for allocating some of these Federal funds.

In some states unigrants, or special purpose grants that combine specific titles of both acts, are also made. The grants are sometimes described in such special publications as *LAMP* (Library and Multimedia Projects, New York State Education Department, Bureau of School Libraries, Albany; annual) and *Emphasis on Excellence in School Media Programs* (U.S. Office of Education, 1969). In New York State, for example, Federal money has served to develop and strengthen the Board of Cooperative Education Services (BOCES). Governmental units such as BOCES provide contract services to nearby schools that a small school district generally cannot afford, for example teachers' workshops in the uses of media. California has developed similar county and regional agencies that support the development of media programs in schools.

The U.S. Office of Education and the National Institute for Education (NIE) occasionally make funds available and run special programs directly. The Right To Read Program undertaken by the USOE illustrates the selective and innovative character of these efforts. These programs are generally available to districts that will formulate or restructure their existing programs to accord with the purposes of the Federal effort. Although in many states the Federal money is granted through an agency of the state education department, the USOE and the NIE continue to retain the right to fund innovative projects directly to the school. The majority of these funds are awarded to the centers whose media specialists not only keep up with the status of education legislation but also develop projects and apply for the money. Both state and Federal sources should be explored in order to plan the budget.

Regional and special local funds are sometimes available. In California, for example, elementary school libraries rely heavily on unified district or county support for audiovisual material. Contractual arrangements with regional groups for large and expensive services, such as ITV, are common throughout the nation.

Local financial support may be more readily available than is commonly thought. School representatives who are willing to do the necessary public relations work may find business or community groups that will donate money for special media center projects. In Keene, New Hampshire, a media center program received a share of a $5,000 award to the high school that was donated by a local business. This money bought the equipment for a combination TV studio and film-study room for English classes.

Special grants sometimes are available from professional organizations and foundations. The ALA has been the intermediary source for Knapp Foundation money which helped to set up demonstration projects in individual schools. The National Endowment for the Humanities (NEH) is another example of a foundation that has also funded special library projects in the broad area of the humanities.

STANDARDS IN THE FIELD

After possible sources of extra revenue have been explored, and this in itself may prove a continuing project, long-range goals for the media center should be established. Because standards undergo continuous upward revision, it is important to keep abreast of recent changes. It is also important to realize that national standards are ultimate goals for the majority of schools in the nation. They are the pinnacle toward which schools should strive. There has been an increasing trend, as some centers approach the national standards in materials and equipment, to stress the service goals of the center. With the latest budgeting system incorporating program analysis, this emphasis should continue to grow.

Many states have issued suggested standards. Usually these will be less ambitious than the national standards because the state hopes that the school will achieve them sooner. A state's suggested standards should always be considered along with those of the national professional organizations. If there are local or regional associations or governmental units that issue standards, these should also be examined.

Many school officials are likely to be influenced in their decisions about media programs and funding by local standards, that is, how the schools in the immediate area compare. Therefore, a local survey of a few neighboring school districts taken by the media specialist or a recent survey issued to members by a regional professional library or media organization may become a basic consideration in budgeting.

INVENTORY OF EXISTING COLLECTIONS

A quantitative inventory of the existing media center holdings of materials, equipment, and services charted together with the recommendations of national, state, and local standards and projected for multiyear budgeting will give a comprehensive picture of the present status of the media collection and indicate future directions for growth. Exhibit 5, Materials Inventory/Standards Checklist, shows how the quantity of materials available in the center can be contrasted with recommended standards in order to plan the budget in an orderly way for a lengthy period of time. The same form may be used as an Equipment Inventory/Standards Checklist by substituting a list of equipment in the left column, for example, the items listed in Table 1, Equipment Collection for a Basic Media Program (see chapter 2).

The form shown in Exhibit 5 can also be used for measuring available services and equipment against national, state, or local standards. Services and functions are not usually measured in this way, but with program budgeting it is advisable to measure them according to the same system used to measure materials and equipment. Some of the items that would be listed on a Services Inventory/Standards Checklist are:

Printing	Central Cataloging
Duplicating	Cross Reference Cataloging
Tape Duplication	Personnel Training
Graphic Production	Personnel
Photographic Production	Professional
Transparency Reproduction	Technical
Equipment Servicing	Clerical
	Student

EXHIBIT 5   MATERIALS INVENTORY/STANDARDS CHECKLIST

Materials	Total Inventory (in units)	Standards (in units)			Units Needed				Schools (in units)			District Center Collection (in units)
		Local	State	National	Now	3 yr	5 yr	10 yr	Bldg A	Bldg B	Bldg C	
Books												
Paperbacks												
Filmstrips												
Maps												
Charts												
Moving pictures												
16 mm												
8 mm												
8 mm super												
Pamphlets												
Periodicals												
Newspapers												
Microfilm												
Books												
Magazines												
Newspapers												
Slides												
Recordings												
Disc												
Tape												
Cassette												
Video												
EVR												
Flat pictures												
Transparencies												
Kits												
Programmed mat.												

Media specialists in individual schools can adapt the inventory/ standards form for their use by dropping the last two columns, "Schools" and "District Center." A director in a multischool situation would need to use all the columns. A one- to ten-year projection of the needed units of materials, equipment, and services can then be examined, along with other preliminary information, and translated finally into dollar figures in the budget.

COMMUNITY NEEDS

In a democratic society an educational budget should reflect the needs of both the society at large and the local community. This is a difficult task. Legally it is the responsibility of the board of education, but in practice it is often delegated to the school superintendent. A media specialist, along with others in a school, can help in this process by recognizing and understanding local needs; often these are expressed forthrightly by the young people themselves. Defining community priorities is properly a cooperative task and requires a study group, ideally, headed by the superintendent and with representatives from among educators as well as various community groups: business, religious, fraternal, social. The study group should include a proportional mixture of the ethnic, racial, religious, and economic makeup of the community. A socioeconomic community study sponsored by the chamber of commerce, the local Rotary Club, or other group would be a practical first step. Both teachers and media specialists are needed to relate the community and societal needs to the curriculum and media collections. The public librarian should also be included so that the total spectrum of library and media service will be presented to the community. One long-term result of the study group's survey of community educational needs would be information useful in budgeting. However, a media center budget can be framed realistically over a shorter period of time with a fair knowledge of the community supplemented by census information from the district office.

CURRICULA IN THE SCHOOLS

The vitality of a school's curriculum depends directly on continuous revision and updating of the curriculum to align it with societal and community needs. Together with the instruction, a media program designed to enrich the curriculum is perhaps the most important element in the education process. Media specialists have the paradoxical obligation to follow and to lead in the formulation of the curriculum. They must also stay closely in touch with national trends in curricula, especially in the midst of periods of great changes in society.

By relating community needs to curriculum, as shown in Table 2, the

TABLE 2 COMMUNITY NEEDS RELATED TO CURRICULUM
AND MEDIA PROGRAMS

Community needs	Curriculum	Media support program
Lessening of high illiteracy rate	Pre-K–2 Enriched and Remedial Reading Program	A variety of special high-interest reading, viewing, listening collections: books, paperbacks, filmstrips, recordings, films, language masters, storytelling groups.
	Adult Reading Program	Mobile van, with equipment. Easy books for adult readers.
Sex education to fight high VD rate	Units in: Physical Education Health Biology Home Economics Social Studies	Pamphlets, charts, study prints, models, 16mm & 8mm films, filmstrips, magazines, books.
Vocational programs for physically handicapped students	Specialized courses: Tailoring Dress Making Data Processing Paramedical positions	Pamphlets, filmstrips, books, equipment, special demonstrations.

media specialist will be able to plan center support programs that eventually can be translated to quantitative terms in the budget document. This practice *should* be carried out regardless of the budget system used; it is, as will be shown, *essential* in program budgeting.

BUDGET SYSTEM IN DISTRICT USE

Many of the current state and local budget guides for school districts are based on *Financial Accounting for Local and State School Systems* (U.S. Office of Education, 1957). Presently half the states use it, Connecticut with the least modification, New York with the most. The other states are initiating some version of the Planning, Programming, Budgeting, Evaluating System (PPBS).

The financial accounting system in the USOE publications stresses fiscal management of items and functions, but excludes program objectives. USOE's new revision of this system,* however, encourages a more sophisticated managerial approach by providing control over a wider

---

* *Financial Accounting (Classification and Standard Terminology) for Local and State School Systems,* rev. ed. (U.S. Office of Education, 1973), DHEW Publication No. (OE) 73-11800.

range of key educational concerns, especially programs, so that administrators will have a better basis on which to make monetary decisions. The capability of a computer to rearrange and retrieve coded data rapidly is responsible for enlarging the ways in which schooling can be viewed. For example, an administrator can determine exactly how much money is being spent for improving reading, viewing, and listening and where in a school or district it is being spent: for an entire school, for the total district, for any one grade level. The revised *Financial Accounting* also differs from earlier editions in its use of three sets of account codes instead of the traditional one code for expenditures. Expenses, revenues, and balances are kept under separate codes for greater fiscal integrity. This multicoding also provides for an in-depth analysis showing the program that the money was spent for, the department that spent the money, when the money was spent, and in the case of PPBS, why the money was spent. The revised publication stresses keeping the accounting record by the programs that the schools decide to budget.

The public school fiscal year varies according to state law. In many states it runs from July 1 to June 30, and in these cases a media center budget is generally developed in the fall, discussed and integrated into the school executive budget in the winter, and finally adopted in spring or early summer. Budgeting is increasingly becoming a continuous, or year-round task the more complex it becomes.

Some states have a pastiche of cumbersome financial regulations; for example, some may stipulate that unspent funds must be returned to a general account to be used to defray local taxes. Other states have changed this restrictive regulation to permit balances to be spent in a new school year. Another ambiguous area is the definition of the term "capital outlay." Generally, this covers items that have a useful school life of two or more years and an initial cost per unit of at least $25. Tape recorders and 8mm movie cameras, for example, would be considered capital outlay expenditures.

ACCOUNTING CODE IN DISTRICT USE

A final step in gathering information prior to preparing the media center budget is finding out what accounting code the district uses, information that is usually available from the assistant superintendent in charge of business.

School monies, both revenue and expense, have long been categorized under numerical or alphanumeric account codes that permit the business office to keep expenditures for like items together. These accounts also usually have a description title, for example, A220–300, Audiovisual Supplies. Coding has assumed even greater importance in accounting because of the infinite variety of information that can be made rapidly available since the advent of electronic data processing, a computer code system that converts raw information into usable form.

Table 3 illustrates the account codes for a partial media center budget extracted from the total school district budget, while Table 4 gives a more detailed presentation of the audiovisual supplies part of a center budget.

TABLE 3   MEDIA CENTER BUDGET ACCOUNT CODES

Code	Description of account
A212–100	Salary of media center director
	Salaries of clerical personnel
A212–300	Supplies and materials for director's office
A212–400	Travel, conferences, etc., involving director and staff
A220–100	Salaries of media center staff, including specialists, paraprofessionals, and clerks
A220–200	Initial, additional, or replacement of library equipment (furniture, carrels, copying machines, typewriters, shelving, etc.)
	Audiovisual equipment (filmstrip projectors and viewers, record, tape, and cassette players, listening stations, etc.)
A220–300	Instructional supplies (including audiovisual supplies)
A220–310	Library books, pamphlets, other library resources
A220–311	Library supplies, periodicals, replacements, rebinding
A220–400	Repair and maintenance of audiovisual equipment (including projection screens)
	Repair and maintenance of typewriters, adding machines, etc.
	Service contracts for maintenance of library equipment, such as microfilm readers and reader-printers, copying machines
A600–300	Repair, replacement of drapes and shades for audiovisual programs
	Expansion, renovation of media centers

TABLE 4   A220–300 AUDIOVISUAL SUPPLIES (A DETAIL)

Quantity	Description	Unit price	Total
1	Film cleaner, 8 oz.	$ .84	$ .84
10	Film developer, b/w	1.55	15.50
8	Fixer	.69	5.52
2	Film developer, color	12.90	25.80
3	Cords, grounded electrical	5.95	17.85
10	Batteries, C-type	.85	8.50
10	Lamps, projection and photographic	2.46	24.60
60	Mounts, cardboard, 2x2 slides (20/pkg.)	.95	2.85
1	Paper, photographic (100 sheets/pkg.)	12.00	12.00
1	Laminating paper, wide roll	20.00	20.00

BUDGETING LEVELS

Before exploring the major budgeting systems in current use it will be helpful to make a preliminary determination of the level or levels on which the budget is to be constructed and to look at costs and methods of allocating them.

The simplest level of budgeting and the easiest to work with is commonly called *maintenance,* or *continuity budget.* If a program is well established and productive, if the educational goals remain the same, and if no unusual expansion is planned, the same level of expenditures will be maintained and the program will be continued as before. Of course the budget should provide for small increases or decreases in student or faculty numbers as well as the replacement and inflationary costs in goods and labor. Maintenance level budgeting is common in an established media center; it can, however, lead to complacency if the person who is planning neither recognizes nor cares about strengthening programs or reflecting changes.

If there are external and internal changes, such as large increases or decreases in the number of students and staff or a desire to improve or bring a basic program up to advanced goals, these are sometimes reflected in the *incremental budget.* It is common in incremental level budgeting for the cost of larger increases to be distributed over a three- to five-year period.

However, if a major reorganization or important developments are anticipated in the immediate future a third type, the *expansion budget,* is preferred. For example, creative budgeting of this type would be used for initiating programs and in the initial planning for the opening of a new media center, and it would involve expending capital outlay funds. Because capital outlay money represents reserve funds from which interest revenue may be anticipated, it is generally tapped with understandable reluctance. Therefore, extensive preparation must go into expansion level budgeting; needs must be clearly identified and directly related to the additional funds being sought.

A realistic rule of thumb for a media specialist is to determine how much spending is likely to be acceptable to the administration and community and then to frame the budget to reflect this expectation, erring slightly on the side of overestimation. The most important factor, however, is obtaining and maintaining the support and confidence of the media center audience: students, teachers, administrators, and the community.

COST ALLOCATING METHODS

How costs are reported will depend on the budgeting system to be used, but no matter what budgeting system the media specialist uses, costs must be established and direct expenses noted for the materials, equipment, salaries, and services that together constitute the operation and program of a media center.

DIRECT EXPENSES

Each direct expense must be allocated to center use and maintenance, media center activity, or specific program. Direct costs in each category may be determined by multiplying the average price of the physical unit (book, cassette, supplies, etc.) by the number of units needed. The list price is usually used for items in the capital outlay category. If items are bid or let out to state contract, the quoted unit, or bid price is used in the budget. Some useful annual and current sources for estimating direct costs are the *Bowker Annual*; *The Audio-Visual Equipment Directory* (National Audio-Visual Association); *Westinghouse Learning Directory*; *The Booklist*; *LJ/SLJ Previews*; *Media and Methods*; *Audiovisual Instruction*; publisher, distributor, and supply house catalogs.

INDIRECT EXPENSES

Most schools report only the direct expenses for running a school library. However, if a district adopts the newest budgeting system, PPBS, indirect expenses have to be added so that at the district level the budget data can be summarized by program area, e.g., instruction, community service. The total combined direct and indirect expenses represent the real cost of the program.

Indirect expenses include overhead items such as taxes, depreciation, insurance, rent, maintenance, power, heat, accounting charges, etc. Some state education departments are trying to formulate a constant figure for overhead expenses that can be used by schools that use PPBS. Some districts, aided by private accounting firms, have also formulated an overhead constant. A percentage of each of these indirect costs must be added to the direct costs and distributed to each program that the media center is offering or supporting. Following are some useful basic methods for those who need to compute indirect costs:

Time. Prorate expense allocated to a given program in proportion to the time spent on it. For example, persons working one-fourth of their time as media specialists and three-fourths as subject teachers would have 25 percent of their salary charged to the media center, 75 percent to instruction.

Time/Floor Area. Prorate expenses allocated to a given gross floor area and the length of time this floor area is used. For example, assume that $500 would be required for an acoustical ceiling for a listening room area of 2,000 square feet. If 1,000 square feet, or one-half the total, is used in equal amounts of time by music classes and for media center recreational listening, an equal amount of expense ($250) would be distributed to music instruction and to the media center listening program.

Hour Consumption. Prorate a part of an expenditure allocated to a given program in proportion to the length of time the facility is in use for the program. For example, if media center special activity groups use a certain school facility, the expenditures for water, electricity, and heat could be prorated on the basis of the hours the building is used for the media center special program in comparison with the amount of time the building is used for all types of class activities.

Number of Pupils. Prorate expense allocated to a given program in proportion to the actual number of pupils involved in the program. For example, assume that a media specialist gives weekly book talks to 100 pupils in classes for the intellectually gifted in a high school of 2,000 students. In this case, $\frac{1}{100}$ ($\frac{1}{20} \times \frac{1}{5}$) of the specialist's salary would be assigned to the intellectually gifted program.

Quantity Consumed. Prorate expense allocated to a given program in proportion to the actual amount of supplies or commodities consumed. For example, if $500 worth of film is purchased and $\frac{1}{10}$ of it is used by students in English classes, $50 would be charged to the English department.

BUDGETING SYSTEMS IN CURRENT USE

The common and sometimes confusing synonyms for the major budgeting systems reflect the development and changes in the rationale of the budgeting process within this century. Although budgeting on a national level began officially in 1921 with the establishment of an executive budgeting system from the Bureau of the Budget, it already had a history in local government. A major trend in budgeting systems has been a shifting emphasis from solely fiscal accountability to accountability for program results as well. The major budgeting systems are described below in the chronological order in which they were developed, with PPBS, the newest system, discussed in detail in the closing pages of this chapter.

LUMP-SUM BUDGET

Although it was once widely used, this system provides little, if any, accountability and is used today only where costs are not clearly known. Nevertheless, there may be some media center programs in schools without specialists where a principal or department representative may put a lump-sum figure for the media center program in his or her executive budget. This, of course, represents peripheral interest in a center's program and in effect removes the center from serious consideration as a force in education. Defensible uses of lump-sum budgeting are to obtain emergency funds and/or to estimate initial costs.

Line-Item Budget

This historically early type of budget can be extremely detailed and cumbersome, depending on the nature and size of the agency or institution that uses it. It is simply a list that includes items and services, with each notation appearing on a successive line just as it does in a personal checking account. It permits no flexibility and controls only those direct expenses that are funneled into an operation. Programs, however, do not enter into the accounting process. Where a media center operates with either a lump-sum or line-item budget, there is no possibility for program accountability, that is, for determining if a program has achieved its stated objectives. Because of newer and better accounting practices, line-item budgeting is rarely used.

Object of Expenditure Budget

In this type of budget, related expenditures are grouped in categories. Table 5 shows a simplified media center budget in which the items and services that are the foundation of a media center program are listed by category under the proper account codes (see Table 3), and are given a purchase price. A budget constructed in this way can provide careful fiscal management. As shown, each category lists related items. For example, grouped under account A220–200 are the quantity and total cost figures for initial purchase of library furniture and equipment, such as carrels, a copying machine, and projectors; under A220–310 costs are given for library books purchased, with the unit price (average) for each book, and a lump sum is added for pamphlets and other printed material.

Because there is no provision for determining how well the money that is spent on items and services is meeting the educational objectives of the school, the person responsible for this budget will often attempt to justify the costs by appending a written statement briefly describing the way these items will support general objectives. A program using this method can only be superficially described, however. The number of books and other media to be purchased can be indicated, but this type of budget cannot describe how they will be used. Object of expenditure budgeting is popular because it is easy to prepare and understand; it is also effective in fiscal management. As well, the previous year's financial base is readily visible and handy in adjusting and projecting the new base. Object of expenditure budgeting is based on an assumption common to all budgeting systems prior to PPBS, i.e., certain resources are needed to perform certain

TABLE 5   OBJECT OF EXPENDITURE BUDGET

Code	Description	Cost	Totals
A212–300	Supplies for director's office	$ 250	$ 250
A212–400	Travel, conferences	300	300
A220–100	Salaries of media staff		
	professional	14,000	
	paraprofessional	7,000	21,000
A220–200	Initial furniture & equipment		
	carrels (4)	400	
	copying machine (1)	350	
	filmstrip projectors (2)	340	
	16mm projector (1)	800	
	cassette recorder (1)	80	1,970
A220–300	Audiovisual supplies	7,500	7,500
A220–310	Books @ $7.00 ea.	7,000	
	Pamphlets	500	
	Other	300	7,800
A220–311	Library supplies	400	
	Periodicals	450	
	Replacements	1,500	
	Rebinding	500	2,850
A220–400	Repair and maintenance of AV equipment	1,000	
	Other repairs	200	
	Service contract	250	1,450
A600–300	Drapes	300	
	Shades	400	700
	Total expenditures		$43,820

functions, based on the belief that certain activities always produce certain results. Needless to say, this may or may not happen, depending on other factors; the assumption is a poor, if not useless one in education or any endeavor that concerns human behavior.

PERFORMANCE BUDGET

Performance budgeting has its origin and greatest use to date in public libraries. It developed from the desire to relate the achievement of objectives to the resources that were required to carry out a library program. For the first time the results were deemed as important for analysis and control as the resources themselves. It is sometimes called "program" budgeting, unfortunately confusing it with PPBS from which it differs.

In the performance budget library activities, such as cataloging, preparation of materials, and information services are grouped together as functions. After these activities are identified, they are broken down into basic units of work so that a unit cost or work measurement may be applied to the total number of units needed for each activity. Therefore, the number

TABLE 6   PERFORMANCE BUDGET

Activity	Unit	Number of units	Unit cost	Total
Acquisition of materials	Book	3,000	$ 6.00	$ 18,000
Cataloging and preparation of materials	Book	3,000	3.00	9,000
Lending services	Book	25,000	.50	12,500
Information services	Inquiry	30,000	5.00	150,000
Building maintenance	Sq. ft.	3,000	1.50	4,500
Group services	Client contact	400	10.00	4,000
Special programs	Event	10	50.00	500

of units required and the unit cost become the dual focus for both formulating and analyzing the budget. (See Table 6.)

Although it is a major budgeting system, the performance budget has been rare in school media centers because the initial preparation of unit costs and the auditing process are complex, particularly in small, multipurpose media centers where there often is overlapping of activities and functions. Performance budgeting can be related to the traditional object of expenditure budgeting if the media specialist wishes to relate the budget figures to the functions and amount of work that is being carried out in a media center. To do this, the various object code category items are distributed by percent of time, dollar figures, or other appropriate measure among the activities or functions in which they belong (see Exhibit 6). By

EXHIBIT 6   OBJECT—PERFORMANCE LADDER °

Accounts	Acqui-sition	Cata-loging	Lending services	Infor-mation services	Building main-tenance	Group services	Special programs
A220—100 Salaries Specialist Paraprofessional Clerk	*Percentage of time needed for each function converted to dollar salary figures*						
A220—200 Initial library furniture and equipment	*Dollar figures*						
A220—300 Instructional supplies . (including AV)	*Dollar figures*						
A220—310 Books Pamphlets							
A220—311 Supplies							

° Relates account code to library function; see Table 3 for account codes.

looking at an Object–Performance Ladder chart, it is simple to see which and how much of the expenditures are used in each of the center's functions. The process, however, does not provide information about how well the center is meeting educational objectives in terms of student growth and development.

PLANNING, PROGRAMMING, BUDGETING, EVALUATING SYSTEM

The newest type of budgeting is usually referred to as PPBS. Although the letter "E" is dropped from the acronym for greater brevity, "evaluating" is nevertheless an essential part of the system. PPBS is a complex and detailed refinement of the performance budgeting concept, but with the emphasis on human changes rather than on the materials and costs needed to bring changes about. It differs from earlier kinds of budget preparation because it measures the educational products (e.g., how well a child who is given materials can study independently) rather than school characteristics (e.g., how many books should be bought per child or how many projectors should be purchased per teaching station). It is a management technique that seeks to obtain the greatest value for the money spent in terms of satisfying human needs, based on the economic assumption that there are unlimited human needs and limited resources.

This budgeting system has special value for a school system because it tends to focus community and administrative support for programs on the performance of the pupils rather than on the resources or instructional staff and facilities. Although all of these factors are implicit, the programs are measured finally by how well the pupils attain the stated objectives, distributing more equitable shares of responsibility for pupil growth and learning throughout a community. In this way, a community may be asked to scrutinize its expectations more closely in relation to its willingness to give support to its schools.

Planning is the process of determining and projecting educational and instructional objectives and the criteria with which to evaluate the results of the programs developed under PPBS for a period of at least five years in advance of each fiscal year. Projected costs and anticipated results from the expenditures are also included in the planning.

Programming is the process of stipulating activities and devising alternative means of achieving the objective or objectives formulated in the planning stage. PPBS starts each fiscal year at a zero financial base; last year's budget is not necessarily used as a model for preparing the current year's budget. Instead, objectives are reexamined in terms of the year's results by applying program evaluation criteria that are established in the planning stage. The objectives are reshaped as necessary; activities and alternatives undergo the same process. This analysis of programs and alternatives facilitates change and guards against a laissez-faire attitude on the part of both school and community. The program that is finally chosen should prove the more effective way, both qualitatively and quantitatively, of accomplishing the objectives.

Budgeting is the process of systematically recording the planning and programming information in both fiscal and program budget form. Within the U.S. Department of Defense, where PPBS had its origin and first success, an evaluation of the objectives attained based on empirical data was usually possible. In the translation to the educational process, where a product may not be readily visible, precise quantifiable measurements pose a problem. This fact, in addition to a reluctance to change to a complex budgeting system, has made it difficult for schools to adopt PPBS. Nevertheless, a New York accounting firm that conducted a national study for the U.S. Office of Education reported that at least 50 percent of the states had adopted PPBS in some form as the recommended budgeting system for the schools. In preparation for the appearance of the USOE's revised *Financial Accounting* handbook, Dade County, Florida, under the aegis of the Association of School Business Officials (ASBO), undertook a national pilot project to develop a PPBS model that could be replicated in other school districts.

Another indication that PPBS will be in general use is the increasing availability, through electronic data processing, of rapid and accurate financial accounting, because data reported by coded accounts can be manipulated. This capability has shifted an increasing amount of interest to program accounting. One of the more exciting possibilities open to schools through PPBS is the capability for decision makers to discuss the total cost of departments that have overlapping functions, for example, the media center program in its role of providing information to students, teachers, administrators and community, and other departments, such as television studios and radio stations, with a similar role. This is possible for the first time because in PPBS the costs for each area are clustered under broad educational objectives. The aggregate gives the decision maker an opportunity to rearrange the mix of programs to achieve the same objectives at a lower cost, to increase the rate of progress to the objectives, or to do both. It is important to remember that PPBS was not designed to save money but simply to organize and present information in a way that would help people make more rational decisions about how best to attain the objectives and goals of education.

In PPBS, strictly speaking, only programs that originate in the library (e.g., a film festival, storytelling, reader services) and central services given with materials and equipment (e.g., supplying individual filmstrip previewers, video cassettes, light bulbs for projectors) would appear under the media center codes in the executive budget. Most of the other materials and equipment that might be funneled through the library as a central distribution agency would actually be accounted for as part of the curriculum budgets. For example, the materials for a social studies department program in Chinese history (paperbacks, books, films, filmstrips, realia, etc.) or for a third grade anthropological program about other cultures would be charged to the subject or grade-level budget codes. Schools that use PPBS usually have program coordinators who assist, advise, and supervise the formulation of the grade-level or subject programs. Librarians should theoretically serve on as many of the coordination teams as possible so that appropriate media center materials and services can be integrated with final programs.

Evaluating is the process of judging how well the human beings who are the focus of the media program achieve the educational and instructional objectives that are developed in the initial planning stage of PPBS. The evaluative criteria that emerge from the writing of program objectives suggest ways of measuring the effectiveness of media programs, and provide accountability for the money spent on items and services in the center. The evaluation process completes the four stages in the budgeting system and initiates a new cycle by suggesting adjustments and changes that may lead to more effective learning.

PREPARATION AND PRESENTATION OF PPBS

The media specialist should prepare a budget cooperatively with other staff members and persons who will be carrying out the center's programs. PPBS necessitates program analysis and review based on goals and instructional objectives. As noted, evaluative criteria based on the instructional objectives and developed during the planning phase of this type of budgeting will serve as the measurement component. Some school systems have attempted PPBS by initiating the system without either preparation or professional help and as a consequence have had to abandon it, primarily because educators have had little or no training in cost allocation methods and an unwillingness to measure results. The necessity for total staff participation and the large quantity of paper work that accompany this budgeting system also make the adjustment difficult. For example, each program array by grade level or subject area in a school consists of program data sheets, one sheet for each item, service, or staff, coded properly so that the information from the data sheets may be entered in a computer and the data manipulated to give a wide range of fiscal and program information. (Examples of program data sheets are shown in Exhibit 8 at the end of this chapter.)

Programming is the heart of PPBS. It requires time to accomplish and should not be carried out in the deadline atmosphere that seems to be a constant companion to budget preparation. If a district does use or intends to use PPBS or some form of program budgeting, much of the work will eventually become routine. If the district does not use PPBS, a media center can begin to develop its own limited PPBS by adding programming to the traditional budget cycle. It is important, however, that special forms —best prepared in consultation with the business office—be used to encourage and reflect the program process. If the coding has been done to accord with the account codes in use, and particularly if electronic data processing is available, the change in the accounting practice would not be drastic.

The following characteristics are unique to PPBS:

1. Establishment of educational objectives for at least five years.
2. Development of alternative programs that will attempt to reach the same objectives.
3. Identification of activities that can be used to implement the programs.
4. Discovery of the visible and covert factors that may interfere with the success of each program.
5. Analysis and comparison of the alternate programs in relation to both costs and constraints.
6. Decision as to program(s) that will be most likely to accomplish the goals at the lowest cost with the least constraints.
7. Provision of continuous evaluation of the program based on the objectives.

Major Steps in PPBS

1. Prepare guidelines for meeting the nonquantifiable educational goals established by representatives of the community.
2. Formulate measurable objectives: If 75 percent of the teachers in a media production workshop demonstrate proficiency, the program will be successful. Such objectives will help determine the selection of resources to be used in the program and will also serve as criteria for evaluating the results.
3. Set up alternative programs and summarize them on program data sheets that give information, such as time, salaries, cost of space, supplies, and all other resources required, in dollar figures. (See Exhibit 8.)
4. Evaluate each program by identifying constraints and comparing relative costs and results in relation to objectives and goals, for immediate and long-range forecasts.

5. Summarize programs on a multiyear financial chart that shows the costs over a number of years. (See Exhibit 7.)
6. Forecast the impact of each decision on future budgets. (A simulation can be constructed with the help of the business office and a computer.)
7. Select the combination of programs that best matches the resources available in the immediate future.
8. Use a set of codes for each activity in the district as developed by the business office and code the program data sheets.
9. Prepare by code the budget for each activity, collating and adding the dollar amounts under the same code.
10. Evaluate the success of the program: students evaluate teachers; graduates evaluate completed courses; students evaluate programs; achievement measured in cost reduction, etc.
11. Plan for changes and adjustments in objectives, goals, and available resources, depending on yearly evaluations. (*If the yearly updating is neglected, there can be diminishing returns to PPBS.*)

Exhibit 7 is an example of a chart that might be used for summarizing programs and exhibiting the costs over a multiyear period, as stated in step five under "Major Steps in PPBS." This will permit the media specialist to see both long-range costs and program emphases. Multiyear projection, however, must allow for possible changes in emphases depending upon the annual program review and evaluation. Such a chart must therefore be considered flexible and tentative.

Under PPBS, there should be a variety of media center programs:

1. those carried out directly by the center;
2. those planned by other departments or grades to which the media center may contribute media and staff;
3. the program that is the operation of the media center as a library or resource center for independent learning.

EXHIBIT 7   MULTIYEAR COST AND PROGRAM PROJECTIONS

Program categories	Program estimates in dollars					
I. Educational development	1976	1977	1978	1979	1980	Total
A. Intellectual growth						
B. Social development						
C. Personal development						
D. Productive development						
Program I totals per year						

The first program is the easiest to budget under PPBS because it is self-contained. The second is more difficult because the media specialist should properly serve as a consultant to other program array coordinators to help make decisions about costs of supportive help from the center to be added to the programs being planned. With individualized learning as important as group learning, the third, the operation of the center, can also be considered a program. This will mean that some way of measuring the results of the center's activities on the young people—other than by counting the number of items circulated or persons served—will have to be explored. In other words, instructional objectives will have to be established. Depending on the school and its educational philosophy, all three of the possible areas for media center programs should be identified.

EXHIBIT 8   AN EXAMPLE OF THE USE OF PPBS IN ASSESSING A
PROPOSED PROGRAM

PROPOSAL FOR INSERVICE COURSES IN THE USE OF MEDIA

The staff is interested in conducting inservice courses to inform teachers of developments in instructional materials and equipment. The center hopes, through teachers' influence, to increase student use of media. The following two inservice instruction courses have been planned, programmed, and budgeted to originate from the media center.

Educational Goals

1. To introduce and demonstrate the use of new materials and equipment.
2. To arouse interest in new techniques of instruction.
3. To establish rapport between teachers and media center staff.
4. To instruct and aid the teachers in local production of learning materials.
5. To help teachers develop an appreciative acceptance and an enthusiasm toward the media center's potential.
6. To stimulate teachers' motivation to apply their newly gained skills in their classrooms or in the center.

Educational Objectives

1. To help teachers develop skills in using the media center's resources.
   (a) Identify by name the educational tools of the media center.
   (b) Learn the location of the desired tool.
   (c) Interpret catalog information.
   (d) Operate machines properly.
   (e) Produce their own instructional materials.
2. To incorporate new knowledge of resources into their curriculum.

Evaluative Criteria

1. Three out of four teachers, picked at random from those enrolled in the course, will be able to demonstrate proficiency in operating a piece of equipment considered in the course.

EXHIBIT 8 (cont.)

2. The use of audiovisual materials and equipment will increase by at least 50 percent during the two-month period following the completion of the course.
3. The use of materials produced locally by both students and teachers will increase during the two-month period following the completion of the course.

Selection of Teachers

Program 1 will train one teacher from each department; Program 2 provides for two teachers from each department. In each case, staff members who instruct the teachers will benefit from researching, preparing, and presenting the program, and the participating teachers will eventually give guidance to students and other members of the faculty. One person from each department is expected to take on the role of curriculum coordinator for his or her department.

Equipment and Materials

Unless otherwise noted, materials and equipment either are on hand or have been purchased under the ESEA Title II program.

Program 1   Inservice Course — Audiovisual Workshop

1. Teachers will use appropriate materials and tools to produce materials related to their subject area.
   (a) Charts.
   (b) Lettering and printing tools.
   (c) Art stencils.
2. Use 35mm camera.
   (a) Teachers will bring suitable material to class to photograph.
   (b) Each teacher may take camera home for one week to take additional pictures.
3. Use opaque and overhead projectors.
   (a) Practice mechanical operation.
   (b) Produce transparencies.
4. Use 8mm and 16mm projectors.
   (a) Practice mechanical operation.
   (b) Practice using slow-motion projection.
5. Use tape recorder.
   (a) Divide into groups in order to write and produce a tape to be used for self-guided tour of media center.
   (b) Listen to tapes.
6. Filmstrip projector.
   (a) Practice operating the machine.
   (b) Practice projecting slides.
   (c) Use main catalog to choose materials to project.
7. Use testing methods.
   (a) On a spirit master create a written test requiring charts, diagrams, and pictures for answers.
   (b) Practice using spirit duplicator and photocopier.
8. Teachers present lesson plans using audiovisual equipment and materials they themselves have produced or that they have borrowed from the media center.
   (a) Presentations.
   (b) Identify, locate, and interpret research problems.
   (c) General discussion and evaluation of program.

EXHIBIT 8 (cont.)

Constraints

1. Lack of funds.
2. Teachers may be unwilling to spend time involved.
3. Does not provide criteria for selection of media.
4. Omits information on outside resources.
5. Might not provide sufficient motivation to continue using resources of center, because it may not affect attitudes.
6. Trains only 15 teachers.
7. Use of equipment by novices might incur increased repair.
8. Teachers may not be resourceful (lack creativity).

Program 2   Inservice Course—Audiovisual Lecture Demonstration

1. Introduction to center.
   (a) Film *At the Center* (ALA).
   (b) Tour of newly reorganized media center and brief explanation of its resources.
   (c) Outside specialist to further stimulate interest.
   (d) Discussion.
2. Selection criteria.
   (a) Criteria.
   (b) Resources—local, Federal, private.
   (c) Importance of previewing.
3. Idea sources and art aids.
   (a) Layout and design.
   (b) Charting, lettering, and printing.
   (c) Sources of ideas and aids.
4. Demonstration and explanation of operation of opaque and overhead projector.
   (a) Enlarging and reducing visuals.
   (b) Steps in producing transparencies.
5. Slide production and use of 35mm camera.
6. Film and film loops.
   (a) Selection criteria.
   (b) Slow motion.
   (c) Animation.
7. Demonstration and explanation of slides, filmstrips, and projectors; filmstrips and slides are used to explain use of integrated catalog and how to interpret information.
8. Use of tape recorder.
   (a) Sample interview with a resource consultant.
   (b) Dictation and study of noise levels.
   (c) Role playing.
   (d) Self-evaluation.
9. Duplicating processes and equipment.
   (a) Uses and misuses of spirit duplicator and photocopier.
   (b) Suggestions for methods of testing stressing use of pictures, charts, and diagrams for questions and answers.
   (c) Evaluation discussion and survey of research problems.

Constraints

1. Lack of funds.
2. Teachers and instructors may not be resourceful and creative.

EXHIBIT 8 (cont.)

3. Teachers may not be willing to spend time involved.
4. Teachers do not practice operating equipment.
5. Few materials are produced.

Evaluation for Both Programs

1. Instructors' evaluation of teachers enrolled in the program; teachers demonstrate:
   (a) Operation of machines.
   (ʋ) Local production, e.g., the making of a transparency, diagram, or slide.
2. Evaluation by assistant principal in charge of instruction.
   (a) Examination of lesson plans, noting use of media center resources.
   (b) Visits to classrooms, noting use of media center resources.
3. Evaluation of media center coordinator and staff media specialists.
   (a) Measurement of production of local material.
   (b) Measurement of circulation of audiovisual materials: student use related to class assignments; teacher use.

Summary of Alternative Programs

Objective

Develop teachers' skills in using center resources.

Alternative Programs

Program 1: Audiovisual Workshop.
Program 2: Audiovisual Lecture Demonstration.

Evaluative Criteria

1. Three out of four teachers will be able to demonstrate operation of equipment.
2. Teacher-use of center and materials will double in the two months following the program.

Costs

Program 1: $610 for 15-week program; $3,050 for 5 years.
Program 2: $698 for 15-week program; $3,490 for 5 years.

Object Code		Program 1	Program 2
A212–100	Salary of center coordinator	$150	$180
A220–100	Other instructional salaries	280	260
A220–200	AV equipment (available)	—	—
A220–300	Art & AV supplies	15	15
A380–000	Outside specialists	25	75
A600–500	Operation and maintenance	140	168
		$610	$698

Decision

Program 1 is recommended because of the cost benefit and because of the benefits gained by having more materials produced immediately, by offering teachers direct experience in operating equipment, and by the additional personal contact between center personnel and classroom teachers.

EXHIBIT 8 (cont.)

PROGRAM DATA SHEET °

Code: _A212 – 100 Director's salary_

Program Title _Inservice Course_

Program No. _1_   Program Level _Faculty – K-6_   Credit _1_

Program Description _Audiovisual workshop. Teachers will operate equipment, produce and handle materials._

Time _15 hours; 8 sessions after school_

Responsible Individual _Media center coordinator_

Approved by _____

Object Code	Item	Units (hours)	Rate	Amount
A212 – 100	Media center coordinator	15	$ 10	$150
	Total	15	$ 10	$150

° Program data sheets are filled in, one for each account to be used, for all the program alternatives being considered. These illustrate all the sheets needed to budget Program 1, Audiovisual Workshop; they were analyzed against similarly constructed Program 2 data sheets (not shown) before a decision was made.

PROGRAM DATA SHEET

Code: _A220 – 100 Instructional Salaries_

Program Title _Inservice Course_

Program No. _1_   Program Level _Faculty – K-6_   Credit _1_

Program Description _Audiovisual workshop. Teachers will operate equipment, produce and handle materials._

Time _15 hours; 8 sessions after school_

Responsible Individual _Media center coordinator_

Approved by _____

Object Code	Item	Units (hours)	Rate	Amount
A220 – 100	Media center specialist	12	$ 10	$120
A220 – 100	Technician	10	10	100
A220 – 100	Graphic arts teacher	2	10	20
A220 – 100	Business teacher	4	10	40
	Total	28	$10/hr.	$280

EXHIBIT 8 (cont.)

PROGRAM DATA SHEET

Code: _A220 – 200 Audiovisual Equipment_

Program Title _Inservice Course_

Program No. ___1___   Program Level _Faculty – K-6_   Credit ___1___

Program Description _Audiovisual workshop. Teachers will operate equipment, produce and handle materials._

Time _15 hours; 8 sessions after school_

Responsible Individual _Media center coordinator_

Approved by _____

Object Code	Item	Units (hours)	Rate	Amount
A220 – 200	Audiovisual equipment	presently available		
	Total			

PROGRAM DATA SHEET

Code: _A220 – 300 Supplies_

Program Title _Inservice Course_

Program No. ___1___   Program Level _Faculty – K-6_   Credit ___1___

Program Description _Audiovisual workshop. Teachers will operate equipment, produce and handle materials._

Time _15 hours; 8 sessions after school_

Responsible Individual _Media center coordinator_

Approved by _____

Object Code	Item	Units (hours)	Rate	Amount
A220 – 300	Art supplies			$ 15
A220 – 300	Audiovisual materials	presently available		—
	Total			$ 15

EXHIBIT 8 (cont.)

PROGRAM DATA SHEET

Code: *A380 – 000 Instructional Resource Salaries*

Program Title *Inservice Course*

Program No. ___*1*___ Program Level *Faculty – K-6* _____ Credit ___*1*___

Program Description *Audiovisual workshop. Teachers will operate equipment, produce and handle materials.*

Time *15 hours; 8 sessions after school*

Responsible Individual *Media center coordinator*

Approved by _____

Object Code	Item	Units (hours)	Rate	Amount
A380 – 000	*Outside specialist*	*1*	*$ 25*	*$ 25*
	Total	*1*	*$25/hr.*	*$ 25*

PROGRAM DATA SHEET

Code: *A600 – 500 Operation & maintenance* ____

Program Title *Inservice Course*

Program No. ___*1*___ Program Level *Faculty – K-6* _____ Credit ___*1*___

Program Description *Audiovisual workshop. Teachers will operate equipment, produce and handle materials.*

Time *15 hours; 8 sessions after school*

Responsible Individual *Media center coordinator*

Approved by _____

Object Code	Item	Units (hours)	Rate	Amount
A600 – 500	*Operation and maintenance (includes heat and electricity)*	*20*	*$ 7*	*$140*
	Total	*20*	*$7/hr.*	*$140*

6

STAFF

The staff is the foundation of a dynamic and effective center and the mainstay of a school media program. The persons who create and develop the activities are directly responsible for the overall success of the program in each school. Each staff member usually functions in a dual capacity: individually, as a specialist; cooperatively, as a member of the program team. A media center staff should include personnel with a broad range of experience and skills. To promote good personal relations, school administrators should encourage media specialists to participate in the selection of staff in order to insure a well-functioning program.

This chapter's main purpose is to help those who have a responsibility to select staff for a media center in a single school building. It describes the principal categories of personnel and some representative tasks, and presents an overview of certification for media specialists, emphasizing the staff requirements and certification for a media program in a school building.

PERSONNEL CATEGORIES

Studies of staff resources in media centers indicate three broad categories under which the majority of center personnel may be listed: professional, paraprofessional, and nonprofessional.

PROFESSIONAL

Persons educated and certified as media specialists, librarians, or audiovisual specialists by a state or other accrediting agency are considered professionals, regardless of their primary responsibility. School media center directors, assistant librarians, and audiovisual specialists with competency in some specialty within communication technology—for example, television and radio—generally meet these requirements. It is their responsibility to assume leadership in planning, developing, and evaluating a program that meets the needs of the faculty, the students, and the community. They must be interested and knowledgeable in media and the components of media: instructional materials and communications technology. Knowledge of materials in different formats, appreciation of service as resource personnel, ability to operate equipment and aid in the production of material are their important responsibilities. They should also be proficient in the principles of teaching and learning, the program of the school, and the characteristics of the students with whom they work. Because the school media program involves students, teachers, and administrators it is vital that each staff member, especially in a single school situation, be able to work well with people of all ages.

Coordinators

The school media center coordinator usually has training in library service and in audiovisual service and has demonstrable leadership qualities. Those certified as professionals in both services should have the primary responsibility for administrating the media center on either the elementary or secondary level. When two or more professionals are employed in the same center, it is important that one be in charge of and responsible for the program. The coordinator in the school that is establishing a unified media program should have professional-level competency in all media; in addition to administration, he or she shares a common responsibility with other media center staff persons for general services, or all phases of media program work. The coordinator is also in charge of developing in other staff members the necessary knowledge, skill, and competence they need to perform their jobs well. As the program expands, the coordinator also sees to the employment of additional staff who have complementary preparation and subject specialization. In new and developing school media programs with a small-size staff the coordinator performs many of the "100 Representative Tasks" on the list that appears at the end of this section. As staff members are added to expand a successful program and the coordinator spends more time in administration, program planning and implementation, evaluation and media selection, some of these tasks are redistributed, as shown on the list.

Media Specialists

Generally the media specialist has been educated in both the traditional field of librarianship and in audiovisual service, with emphasis on instructional materials. However, both by interest and training, media specialists may work with the equipment or any part of the instructional technology of the media program. This is especially true on a small-size staff that has neither an audiovisual specialist nor a technician.

The main functions of the media specialist cluster around general services and services to students and teachers. Those functions commonly associated with the media specialist are labeled "M" on the "100 Representative Tasks" list. Specifically these are the tasks that contribute to the media center's organization, circulation, instruction, and selection. In addition, the media specialist also helps to develop the program by implementing many of the center's activities. A subject or grade-level specialization, together with some facility with cataloging nonprint materials, is useful. If the media specialist is the only professional on the staff, he or she then assumes as much of the coordinator's and specialist's roles as possible, assigning priority to the most important and immediate demands. The program will grow in direct ratio to the size, qualifications, and imagination of the staff.

Audiovisual Specialists

The audiovisual specialist has certification as a professional in instructional or communications technology by education, by experience, or by both. Increasingly, some education in librarianship is becoming part of the AV specialist's training. The positions of media specialist and audiovisual specialist overlap in many instances, the basic or traditional difference being that the media specialist generally concentrates on the materials services, and the audiovisual specialist's concern is the equipment. Audiovisual specialists are also increasingly concerned with media's instructional applications. Although this has been the typical division for the staff positions, an interesting variation, particularly on larger-size staffs, is the newer role where competencies exist in both materials and equipment or technology, and the person combines them into a subject or grade-level approach that permits the specialist to become part of a team of teachers. This increases the specialist's usefulness to both students and teachers and fits in with the idea of differentiated staffing where educational personnel assume responsibilities based on carefully defined educational functions. For this arrangement to work well, the newer type of specialist must assume the broad tasks of the media and audiovisual specialists and refine them by the curriculum and grade interest.

For the more traditional audiovisual specialist role, however, the primary responsibilities are nonprint materials and equipment services, which at their least sophisticated level are often performed by paraprofessionals or technicians. Audiovisual specialists also take part in the development of the program; selection of media—particularly equipment—and production. The role of the audiovisual specialist in a school media program is in a transitional state and is determined largely by the size of the staff. In a single school with only two or three staff members, one popular and economical pattern uses a professional media specialist, technician, and clerical support. The duties most commonly associated with the audiovisual specialist are labeled "A" on the "100 Representative Tasks" list.

PARAPROFESSIONALS

A person qualified in a special area of media work, e.g., photography, graphics, electronics, but who generally has less than a baccalaureate degree belongs in the paraprofessional category. Usually identified as a technical assistant, he or she is an important staff member in any large-size media center program and, given the wide range of the technical assistant's competencies, a worthwhile member of a small-size staff. Technical assistants are often recruited from industry, community colleges, etc., and their duties are mainly in production, preparation, maintenance, and special services to faculty and students, with whom technical assistants often work directly. Some of the technical assistant's specific tasks are noted under "Paraprofessional Staff" in the "100 Representative Tasks" list. If the post of technical assistant does not exist in the media center program, the duties of the position are assumed by the specialists and other supportive personnel, such as clerks.

NONPROFESSIONALS

Technicians and clerks form the regular nonprofessional staff of the media center program. They may be salaried personnel or unpaid volunteer aides, and they work under the direction of a professional. Their schooling and experience may range from a grade school diploma to training in a technical or clerical institute to graduate college work. Preparation for their work in the media center is acquired by specialized training or practical experience. Rarely, however, do they possess certification as media specialists. In the school media center that has only one nonprofessional, the tasks are combined with those of the professional and paraprofessional staffs.

Technicians

Technicians usually have a high degree of specialization in some aspect of the media program, with special emphasis on the equipment and production tasks, e.g., operating and distributing equipment and producing transparencies or tapes. On a large staff, specialized areas, such as computerized services, display techniques, and television broadcasting, usually require technicians to help the professionals. Technicians are often recruited directly from high school or technical training institutions.

Clerks

Clerks usually have the clerical and secretarial training and experience that makes them especially useful in carrying out the routine, repetitive business operations of a media center program under the supervision of a professional. Their tasks fall into the areas of acquisition, organization, preparation, and circulation of material, along with some production of materials.

Volunteers

Volunteers can be a valuable community liaison. They are usually parents from the school community, students, or both and are often unpaid. In some cases, student assistants receive course credit for their work in the media center, which may be associated with vocational programs for high school technical and business students. The volunteers' work should be creative and rewarding and exploitation of the volunteer aide can be avoided if the volunteer assistant program is formulated and managed with the individual's development as a primary objective. This can be accomplished by:

assigning tedious, boring tasks, such as shelving books, infrequently;
regularly rotating the more desirable jobs, such as circulation desk work;
training in more complex library work, such as helping students locate
    materials;
providing for competencies and availability of volunteers;
continuing instruction and job evaluation;
appropriate incentives and rewards for successful job performance;
opportunities for social and educational activities, such as theater and
    museum trips.

How Big a Staff?

The size of the media staff depends upon several factors: the school enrollment and diversity of student needs, number of grades, nature of the program and instructional pattern, the existence of district level media services, and community support. Many sources recommend staff size, among them the national and individual state standards.

The "Task Analysis Survey Instrument" (*School Library Personnel Task Analysis Survey*, a Special Report of the Research Division, NEA) identifies more than 300 tasks for a media center staff. Well-developed centers with adequate staff will carry out most of the tasks; at least one-third of the tasks are essential in the operation of even the smallest program with the least amount of staff. The following 100 representative tasks are excerpted from the NEA survey. The list is divided among the three main categories of media center personnel: professional, paraprofessional and nonprofessional. All the tasks are interchangeable among the staff, depending on the local situation; as a general rule, however, even with only two or three staff persons these tasks will be covered, albeit some minimally. As the staff size increases in response to an effective program, that is, when an audiovisual specialist, a media specialist, or a clerk is added, the coordinator will increasingly assume the tasks that are starred (*), the media specialist, those designated "M," and the audiovisual specialist and in certain cases a technician, those designated "A." The remaining tasks are chiefly clerical and are assumed by a clerk or technician on a large staff. There is no one way in which these tasks and the many other service-related functions can be specified; the pattern ultimately depends on the nature of the program and the competencies and interests of the staff.

100 REPRESENTATIVE MEDIA CENTER TASKS

The tasks have been selected from the list of 300 in the NEA Research Division's Special Report, *School Library Personnel Task Analysis Survey*. The asterisk and letter symbols in the listing for the professional staff indicate tasks that will be increasingly assumed by certain staff persons as staff size increases in response to an effective program as follows:

* = the coordinator
M = the media specialist
A = the audiovisual specialist and in some cases a technician

PROFESSIONAL STAFF

* Determine educational objectives of library policies.
* Plan school media programs and media center operations and maintenance.
* Help determine overall library policies.
* Assist in selecting media center staff.
* Prepare work schedules for the staff.
* Supervise work of professional and nonprofessional staffs.

* Work with and submit reports to administration.
* Determine records and statistics needed.
* Enlist faculty in writing a materials selection policy.
* Establish cataloging and classification policies.
* Plan for reorganization and relocation of collections.
* Formulate policies and procedures for circulating materials and equipment.

PROFESSIONAL STAFF (cont.)

* Assume responsibility for decisions concerning disciplinary actions.
* Develop a handbook for teachers and for students.
* Work with teachers to establish procedures for group or individual assignments.
* Inform faculty of available inservice courses, workshops, professional meetings, and the community's educational resources.
* Promote use of professional library.
* Plan and participate in community relations activities.
* Visit with other schools and participate in professional meetings.
* Determine policy for accepting gifts.

M/A Schedule use of facilities.
M/A Conduct inservice work.
M/A Participate in curriculum development and review.
M/A Train student aides and volunteers.
M/A Initiate projects and activities relating to media resources.
M/A Originate and conduct special activities for interest groups.
M/A Maintain in the media center schedules of class activities.
M/A Orient students to media center.
M/A Plan sequential programs of instruction in research techniques.
M/A Inform teachers of new services.
M/A Introduce teachers to bibliographic tools in subject and grade-level disciplines.
M/A Outline publicity; write articles, promotional materials, and notices for school and local papers.
M/A Work with teachers and students in reading, viewing, and listening activities.
M/A Plan with faculty members to coordinate materials and media activities.

M/A Observe classroom work to coordinate with media program.
M/A Participate in team-teaching and define staff arrangements.
M/A Enlist faculty participation and recommendations in evaluating or selecting materials.
M/A Develop evaluation forms.
M/A Read books, magazines, professional journals, review services, and local publications for information on selecting materials and equipment.
M/A Evaluate and select materials and equipment.
M/A Organize and maintain reserve and special media collections.
M/A Plan the system for scheduling and delivering materials and equipment.
M/A Compile media lists.
M/A Administer interlibrary loan services.
M/A Perform general reference services.

PARAPROFESSIONAL STAFF

Develop new uses for materials and equipment.
Work with teachers to design innovations in instruction.
Help to determine space for equipment to be purchased.
Develop evaluation forms.
Adapt commercial materials and equipment to meet special needs.

Design publicity materials in all media.
Make simple display devices for use in instruction.
Operate lettering and drawing devices.
Microfilm materials.
Produce specialized materials for school needs (e.g., tapes, record programs, etc.)

PARAPROFESSIONAL STAFF (cont.)

Handle photography and film course and recreation-related media center work.

Maintain dial-access and computer equipment and programs.

Provide for preparation of materials (e.g., laminating, making transparencies, etc.).

Make major repairs of equipment if not in contract.

Evaluate students' special media center projects.

Assist with independent study.

Assist teachers and students in using equipment and materials.

Assist teachers and students in locating and selecting materials and equipment.

Assist teachers and students with taping services.

Assist teachers and students with production techniques.

Answer ready reference questions.

Plan and prepare displays.

Plan and supervise media fairs.

Develop forms for operation of the library in area of specialization.

Maintain materials and equipment evaluation file.

Perform routine print shop activities.

Schedule use of and deliver materials and equipment.

Maintain cumulative records of condition of and maintenance work on equipment.

NONPROFESSIONAL STAFF

Determine, control, order, inventory, and maintain supplies.

Handle clerical and secretarial work of correspondence (e.g., filing, typing, mailing, etc.).

Type notices, requisitions, bulletins, media bibliographies, etc.

Assist in sale of paperback books.

Perform messenger service.

Maintain selection aids for finding new materials.

Check shelf list and other aids to prepare bibliographic data for ordering and duplicating materials.

Transact clerical business operations: file orders and invoices; receive credit memorandum and invoices and transmit them to appropriate office; verify total purchase costs; follow up outstanding orders.

Unpack and check new materials and equipment received, and verify invoices with shipment and order.

Post receipt of periodical and newspaper issues and take care of missing items.

Make items received ready for use.

Stamp ownership mark on all materials.

Place subject headings on vertical file folders.

Adapt commercial catalog cards for local use.

Prepare and file shelf list and catalog cards.

Sort and place materials on shelves or in containers and keep them in reasonable order.

Process records for materials and equipment withdrawn from collections.

Compile and revise media book catalogs.

Compile review files for materials and equipment.

Maintain media inventory records and assist in inventory.

Set up and operate audiovisual equipment, such as projectors and video-readers.

Inspect and make necessary repairs to print and nonprint materials and equipment.

CERTIFICATION

The publication *Standards for School Library Programs* (ALA/NEA, 1969) represents the first national recognition of the need for unified media services in the school. By their agreement on many of the quantitative and qualitative needs in school media programs, the American Association of School Librarians, ALA, and the Association for Educational Communications and Technology, NEA, have fostered the development of the media specialist as a professional with training and experience in both library and audiovisual work. The preparation of professionals in school media work continues increasingly to follow this pattern, as reflected particularly in state requirements for media coordinators. For example, in Illinois the minimum requirement of 20 semester hours of audiovisual and library science hours for a basic certificate is the same as the recommendations of both the State Education Department and the North Central Association (NCA) accrediting agency. Some Illinois districts, however, independently require more: both a master's degree and a special certificate with an endorsement as a teacher that includes 32 semester hours in the subject field. The state requires that 24 of the 32 hours be evenly divided between library science and audiovisual instruction with the remaining eight in either or both. Preparation as a classroom teacher is also stipulated. Although previously issued certificates are honored, as they are in most states under a "grandfather clause," this trend toward more balanced course work occurs more and more frequently in the certification of the media specialist.

A common pattern in certification in the increasingly complex media field generally includes training in five areas: administration and supervision; organization; selection and utilization; production; communications theory and systems; and supporting courses. Many state plans for certification on the level of administration and supervision of media favor the newer combination of fields while remaining flexible enough to permit specialization, particularly in such areas as television, data processing, etc.

AUDIOVISUAL SPECIALIST

Just as the traditional certification as a school librarian with an emphasis solely on print materials still exists in a few states, its counterpart, certification as an audiovisual specialist with a stress on nonprint materials and equipment, does also. Because of the changes and revisions in audiovisual course titles and descriptions, it is difficult to determine the certification requirements for the traditional type of audiovisual work in the schools. Nevertheless, there are about 16 states that still have this type of certification. Some of them are revising certification to accord with the newer trend, while others have plans, some indefinite, to work on it. Six, or half the states that have the dual certification have no plans to change. In spite of the flux in certification standards, some generalizations about the audiovisual certificate are possible. The minimum requirements are a baccalaureate degree, a teaching certificate, and some classroom or directed teaching experience; from 12 to 15 hours of graduate credit in audiovisual courses are usually required. Many states attach these requirements as a "rider" to regular teaching certificates.

SCHOOL MEDIA SPECIALIST

In contrast, certification for school librarians exists in all states and the District of Columbia. The title of the certificate varies from the old-fashioned one, teacher-librarian, to the newer one, media specialist, along with others, such as media generalist or educational media specialist. This confusion reflects clearly the lack of standardization among the states in terminology, grades of certificates, number of required hours, distribution of subjects, and method of certifying. Some general observations are nevertheless possible.

Some states issue more than one grade of certificate with a different number of hours required for each. For example, South Dakota issues a Level II Media Specialist temporary certificate that requires six hours, a permanent one for 10 hours, and a Level I (coordinator) for 15 hours. Other states confer various certificates by level of teaching. California, for example, uses a Standard Teaching Credential with specialization on either the elementary or secondary level, each with 24 hours without directed teaching, 12 with teaching or a masters degree.

The number of hours necessary for certification varies from a low of six, e.g., teacher-librarian (New Hampshire) and limited certification (Delaware), to a high of sixty above the baccalaureate, e.g., coordinator (Florida and Indiana). There are only a few states in either of these extreme categories; the majority mandate 18, 24, or 30 hours. The master's degree and teaching experience are also often a part of the requirements. The conflicts among the states' requirements are generally related to the different grades of certificates, the variety of the certificate labels, and the diversity of course descriptions.

The distribution of course content needed by a media specialist varies among the states. Comparatively few states require a full range of production and audiovisual courses, although some do require the latter. The states that require both are: Illinois, Indiana, Minnesota, Nebraska, North Dakota, and Utah. However, in Utah no provision is made for reference or literature course work. Ohio is an exception among the states because it requires production, but not audiovisual course work.

There are several standard ways of granting certification. A state board of education, a national or regional accrediting body such as the ALA or NCA, or both are the chief agents. Certification can be given directly upon an examination of applicant's records or indirectly by an automatic certification upon the completion of an ALA or state-approved (or both) library school program. The teacher certification board in a state education department evaluates an applicant's record and responds to inquiries about the state's certification requirements. School system superintendents are also able in many instances to obtain temporary certification for their employees. However, a media specialist who wants to work in a state other than the one in which the course work was completed may need to check into the requirements.

Another method of certification is currently being explored by some states. Basic endorsement is given based on an applicant's demonstrated proficiency in such areas as cataloging, selection, utilization and production of media, and administration. For professional media endorsement Utah, for example, requires demonstrated ability in the following areas: human relations, leadership, supervision, and communications theory.

The chaotic state of certification is best seen in the lack of reciprocity among states. Only three have a widespread agreement for recognition of each other's certificates: California has certification reciprocity with 27 states, New York with 26, and Pennsylvania with 30. Some states and national organizations are working on accreditation problems, e.g., Washington. The movement, however slow, indicates that the trend to bring the print, nonprint, and technological component of school media service into a more balanced certification position will continue.

7

FACILITIES

Although school media center facilities vary considerably in size and shape or depending upon the age of the building in which they are housed, they share a common purpose: to provide the physical surroundings in which the media needs of the school can be fulfilled. In a society characterized by change the maxim of an earlier and more stable era "form follows function" is now more realistically "form permits function." A school media program therefore is shaped to some extent by what it can accomplish with the size, shape, and age of its facilities. Well-designed spaces add an important dimension to the media center program and enrich the school community.

This chapter covers the major points that a media specialist should consider in designing or remodeling a school media center facility. Preplanning the facility and planning with various individuals and groups are treated first, followed by a discussion of space requirements for the four major groups of activities that take place in a center. Suggestions are made about environmental elements, such as lighting, the thermal environment, electrical power, acoustics, and color, as well as about furnishings. Also treated briefly are facilities for expensive media services that would normally be handled through a central source, e.g., film libraries. Although the guidelines in the chapter can be used for designing a center in a new school building, the focus is on renovating traditional school library quarters. Media specialists are advised to consult other technical sources for additional sources, and some suggestions are listed in the Selected Readings at the end of the book.

PLANNING

The expression "form permits function" has direct application in planning school media centers whether the goal is designing a new facility with an architect or initiating a simple remodeling project with the help of a principal. In either case, the chief administrator has the prime responsibility and his or her approval is needed. It is essential that a knowledgeable media specialist and consultant work together with the administrator and architect in carefully assessing the desired outcomes of the school media program in order to plan a functional and useful facility. Additional help can come from studying plans of other schools and visiting operating school media centers. Many districts have found it helpful to use special consultants to advise on school media services and facilities. Staff, faculty, students, and other persons who will utilize the facilities should also be involved in the planning. Experience has shown it is vital to have the cooperation of all groups in the school setting, from the administrator to the community users whose support is needed; many designs have failed to function properly due to lack of consultation, especially at the planning stage, with those who would be using the media center facilities for work, study, or recreation.

Some important factors to investigate in the introductory planning phase are the nature of the curriculum and the teaching methods in the school, whom the media center will serve, what routines and services must be accommodated, and the type and quantity of the materials and equipment to be housed. Future projections of the number of students, new services, and the size of collections should also be considered. National and state standards will supply guidelines. Other factors that will influence the facility are the overall design of the school building, the accessibility of community resources, and the number of departmental or decentralized collections available elsewhere in the school or district. The importance of this initial study cannot be stressed enough. If the school media program is carefully examined and written down before any blueprints are drawn, it will be possible to tell the administrator and architect exactly what is needed and why.

Each school media program is unique, as is each facility. No one design can be singled out as the best—each school media center has a character of its own. The conventional rectangle filled with cafeteria-style tables and chairs represents a model that is no longer considered adequate. Today the design of media centers stresses openness and flexibility in dividing space and providing for individual and group use with the inclusion of areas for reading, viewing, and listening.

SPACE

Whether the development of a new center or the remodeling of an old one is undertaken, the first step is usually consideration of the location of the school media center. It should be central and accessible to all who participate in the instructional program. The space requirements depend upon the organizational pattern of the instructional program, the commitment to media services in that program, and the funds available for either new school construction or remodeling. Proximity to such noise-producing areas as bus loading zones or orchestra practice rooms should be avoided. The quarters should be placed where access to the rest of the building can be restricted if necessary. This will facilitate use of the media center in the evenings, on Saturdays, or during the summer months when the rest of the school might be closed. If the original facility has been located with remodeling in mind, it will not be adjacent to stairwells, lavatories, or expensive permanent facilities that require great structural changes. Instead, it will be adjacent to relatively open spaces, such as classrooms, so that walls can be removed and extensive remodeling easily accomplished if necessary. Expansion can also be aided if one of the walls is an exterior one that faces an unused space or an interior court.

Another step in the allocation of space is consideration of size. The school media center is often designed as an activity center that students, teachers, and other persons go to not only for media but also for the experiences of learning. The variety of spaces throughout the facility should accommodate all activities that are helpful in developing and encouraging imagination and inquisitiveness about learning.

Exact figures for the recommended size of a school media center can only serve as guides for individual situations. Such variables as enrollment, size and nature of collections, and the services to be offered are important in determining space needs. Some state education departments suggest figures for square footage. For example, the Maryland State Department of Education recommends that the total media services area have: (1) no less than 7–10 square feet per student; (2) accommodation for approximately 25 percent of the enrollment; (3) not more than 100 seats in any one area. Table 7, Recommended Space for Media Centers, presents other of Maryland's specific suggestions.

Schools that produce their own television and radio programs and have a computerized learning laboratory will also need the following: (1) soundproof 40-by-40-foot television studio and control room with 15-foot ceiling and 14-by-12-foot doors, storage space for television properties, visuals, etc.—800 square feet; (2) office with work space, placed back-to-back with television studio—1,200 square feet; (3) 12-by-12-foot audio

TABLE 7 RECOMMENDED SPACE FOR MEDIA CENTERS [a]

Functions	Area requirements [b]	Area (sq. ft.)
To provide for display and circulation of materials and equipment.	Space for circulation desk, catalogs, indexes, displays, exhibits, and copying equipment.	500
To provide for individual reading, listening, viewing, browsing, and study.	Space for tables and chairs suitable for media services. Thirty to forty percent of seating capacity to be individual carrels equipped with power and capability for electronic-response systems and television outlets; area to be ducted for power and coaxial distributions. Carrels to be 36 in. wide and 24 in. deep and equipped with shelving.	4,500
To provide for small group activities such as committee work, listening, viewing, and individual typing.	Conference rooms 10'x10' each with movable walls; area to be acoustically treated with electrical and television outlets and have a wall screen.	600
To provide for large group activities and instruction.	Equivalent of a classroom area, equipped for instructional purposes.	750
To provide for administrative activities.	Office space for professional staff members for media planning.	300
To provide for production and processing of materials.	Space for media production, mending, etc., with sink, electrical outlets, counter work space, and storage.	600
	Space to include faculty media-preparation area.	100
To provide for storage of equipment, materials, and supplies.	Storage space equipped with temperature and humidity controls.	120
	Stacks for incoming print and nonprint materials.	200
	Space for back issues of periodicals, microfilm, maps, globes, realia, etc.	300
	Space for housing and distribution of audiovisual equipment.	300
To provide for video and audiotape recording.		600
Total space requirement		8,870

[a] Reprinted by permission from *Criteria for Modern School Media Programs,* Maryland State Department of Education, 1971.

[b] Based on 1,000 enrollment.

studio and control space, which may be near the television studio; (4) computerized learning laboratory—900 square feet.

FACILITIES FOR MAJOR FUNCTIONS

In general, areas for four major groups of functions should be worked into a plan for any school media center: (1) reading, listening, and viewing; (2) distributing, organizing, and storing the collections; (3) producing instructional materials; (4) maintaining and repairing equipment. Some statements about the nature of the facilities can be made, based on the activities that occur in each of the four areas.

AREAS FOR READING, LISTENING, VIEWING

These areas should be suitable for use by large groups, small groups, and individuals—teachers as well as students—to reflect the emphasis of instruction in the school. To accommodate these activities, a main study area plus adjoining rooms of various sizes are necessary. The combined areas should be large enough to seat at least 20–25 percent of the school's population.

In the main area, space measuring approximately 10–30 square feet is generally recommended as a comfortable amount for each user; it will provide adequate room for furniture, aisles, etc. It is further recommended that not more than 80–100 seats be located in any one area, with experience suggesting the lesser figure as the maximum. If the reading area is to have a larger seating capacity, it should be arranged into a variety of combinations of space within space; students and teachers often dislike one big room because it tends to be too noisy and too open. Flexibility for individual as well as group needs can be accommodated in the space within space design concept.

In media center planning, and especially in open- or semiopen-plan school media centers, it is vital to visualize the entire area in sound zones, in order to suitably separate somewhat noisy, group activities from quiet, individual activities. For example, flexible folding walls can create an area for large group film viewing; an arrangement of furniture can create a "quiet corner" for persons who need to concentrate.

Seminar rooms or instructional areas are useful for many school activities, including small group work, previewing video tapes, and listening to cassettes. If separate rooms are used, they should be adjacent to or at least near the main area. Flexibility in accommodating groups of varying sizes in a main area is one of the elements of good planning and design. In this type of arrangement modular lighting and ventilation units become a necessity. Ideally each separate room should be soundproof, contain darkening facilities, and be approximately 120–140 square feet in size. Sufficient electrical outlets are also essential. Furnishings may include retractable ceiling or wall screens, tables and chairs, shelving, and display stands. A soundproof typing room is sometimes provided for student use, and is often incorporated into the production area.

A separate classroom is frequently included, especially in renovations. Here, library-related instruction may be given to an entire class, reference work supervised, or other activities carried on. Furniture may include students' desks, a teacher's desk, tables, carrels, bulletin boards, chalkboards, a permanent screen, a book truck, shelving, and any furnishings appropriate to the many purposes of the room. Darkening facilities and numerous electrical outlets are also necessary in such a room.

Sometimes a teachers' seminar room or area is provided for preparation and professional work as well as for teachers' meetings. Increasingly, however, this area is being combined with or placed adjacent to the center facility for the production of material.

In addition to space for reading, viewing, and listening, the main area should have space for circulating, displaying, and housing media collections; this is discussed in the next section.

AREAS FOR DISTRIBUTING, ORGANIZING, AND STORING COLLECTIONS

Space for these functions is usually provided in several places: the main area, workroom, office, and storage locations. In the main area the circulation desk should be large enough to handle all distribution procedures for the media collections. A slot and depressible bin for the return of materials are often desirable additions to a functional circulation desk. If possible, shelving for the temporary housing of materials should be provided close to the main desk. The card catalog and other indexes should also be located near the circulation desk.

The nature and quantity of materials housed in the main area will depend on the amount of storage space available elsewhere. Extremely bulky and infrequently used materials are often housed nearby, but outside the main area. The main collections of media and the current issues of periodicals and newspapers are generally kept in the main area, although they may also be decentralized in departments or grade-level resource areas.

Workroom areas for many supportive functions should also be provided, including an area for materials production (described below under "Facilities for Producing Instructional Materials") and an area for materials preparation where incoming materials are received and checked and where whatever technical services that are unavailable centrally or commercially are performed. Sometimes these two areas are combined. Since workroom access to the library and to an outside corridor is important for the receipt of materials and equipment, adequate entrances should be provided. Workroom size will vary with each school, but 150–200 square feet is suggested. Counter space with sink and running water should be provided, together with cabinets for storage, shelving, worktables, chairs, typewriter, and several strategically placed electrical outlets.

The media specialist will, of course, spend the major portion of the work day involved with the center's audiences, in the center's various activities. Nevertheless, an office for the media specialist, separate from the workroom areas, is essential. Here the specialist may conduct private conferences with teachers and students and deal with the administrative details of the media center. The office should be 150–300 square feet in size and convenient both to the workrooms and the main area, and its equipment should include a desk and several chairs, one legal-size vertical file, shelving, a telephone for outside school communication, and sufficient electrical outlets.

Storage area(s) should also be included in the plan. Three different types of media are sometimes stored nearby, but outside the main area: (1) printed materials; (2) nonprint materials; and (3) instructional equipment. Back issues of periodicals, supplementary library books, and sets of additional texts are common examples of printed materials that are often stored. The storage area should contain an adequate amount of appropriate shelving as well as a working surface and chair or stools.

The types of nonprint materials found in storage areas will depend on what is housed in the main area. No absolute rules are possible; each media specialist will make these decisions based on variable criteria, with accessibility the final criterion. Storage space for bulky nonprint materials, such as 16mm films, video tapes, models, large posters, and maps, is often provided outside the main area.

Because instructional equipment tends to be cumbersome and is often mounted on rolling carts, the storage area for this equipment must be large. Much of the equipment for classroom use may be successfully decentralized throughout the school by department or floor level. Special storage bins can also be constructed in the central area to hold additional film, slide and filmstrip projectors, overhead projectors, tape recorders, screens, TV sets, and record players, for ready accessibility and use in the center.

AREAS FOR PRODUCING INSTRUCTIONAL MATERIALS

The size of the area for producing noncommercial materials and modifying commercial products for curriculum use will depend on the nature of the school's program. A basic list of activities would include: (1) preparation of graphics, such as posters, slides, transparencies, and charts, and (2) duplication of materials for teacher and student use. Equipment for this work would include duplicating machines, a photocopier, a dry-mount press, a large typeface typewriter, work tables and chairs, a paper cutter, and suitable supplies. Some centers have extended the capabilities of the production area to include photographic darkrooms as well as taping and recording studios. Students are increasingly involved in the production processes, often through their curricular as well as recreational interests.

In addition to the workroom areas noted above, the center often provides a separate teachers' study room where the professional library can be housed and teachers can pursue their individual projects and have small group meetings. Equipping the room with appropriate shelving and comfortable seating similar to that in the main area will encourage teacher use of their study facility. Sometimes the larger production area is set up to accommodate the teachers' needs for space to accomplish their many and varied instruction-related activities.

AREAS FOR MAINTAINING AND REPAIRING EQUIPMENT

Work area that can be used for the repair and maintenance of instructional equipment is sometimes provided, especially if a technician is on the staff or available in the school. A workbench and chairs plus adequate outlets and tools should be available. In small schools media specialists frequently rely on a service contract with an audiovisual repair service to keep the equipment in good operating condition. If a work area for equipment maintenance is not required, the space may be combined with the production workroom area or equipment storage areas.

As trends in remodeling and constructing new school media centers develop counter to conventional designs, the process of using space for changing needs becomes more creative. Many schools built before World War II and after restrict the use of newer instructional strategies because of the prominence of self-contained classroom and double-loaded corridor construction. The problem in modernizing school media center facilities is basically one of improving the use of existing space in order to take care of variable groupings of persons pursuing different learning experiences.

"Flexibility" is the word most commonly used to describe the overall attempt to solve this problem, and open planning is one of the newer approaches. In the open-planning concept, the degree and variety of flexibility as well as its purposes have to be clearly stated in planning the facilities. Flexibility can be incorporated in a design in a permanent way with additions, structural changes, and spaces for different-size groups; it can be accomplished in a temporary way with movable partitions or furnishings that can be arranged as spaces within space. Program planning must precede any creative designing of the facility in order to integrate center activities with the total educational program in the school.

ENVIRONMENTAL ELEMENTS

Although the possibility for continuing change is vital in dynamic remodeling and designing, some environmental elements are basic and remain constant. They are: lighting, the thermal environment, electrical power, acoustics, and color.

LIGHTING

A functional school media center environment requires optimal lighting conditions for the eye comfort of its users: an adequate level of lighting for the whole area and local lighting for particular activities. Appropriate lighting should be tailored to the specific need in each space, and even for task-areas within the space. Thirty lumens per square foot plus a 2 percent daylight factor for overall desk-type work is often recommended. Another measurement sometimes given is 35 to 70 footcandles for regular viewing tasks or 100 to 200 footcandles for special work that requires more illumination. Although extensive use of natural light is generally not recommended because of the difficulty in controlling both brightness and heat, some degree of natural light relieves the uniformity of artificial light, makes an interior appear livelier and enriches the environment. As well, a glance at a distant view through a window provides a refreshing look at the out-of-doors that is an easement for tired eyes.

Light sources, especially for independent study areas, should exhibit some of the imaginative possibilities, while adhering to the following general principles of lighting:

1. The angle at which the light strikes the work surface is probably more important than the amount of light.
2. The height of the lighting levels should be appropriate to the age group served.
3. The type of light source should be adapted to the purpose for the space.
4. The type of light fixture should also reflect the area and height needs.
5. The capability for dimming and darkening lights should be present.

It is advisable to avoid highly polished surfaces in a media center. Warm white fluorescent lamps with diffusers, as well as the mercury vapor-type illumination are suggested as light sources. Grid fixtures that move horizontally or vertically along poles or beams, fixtures attached to permanent strips, and portable floor or desk-type fixtures can be used creatively to suit area and height needs in the center. Special polarized lamps that direct the light downward at an angle are also available. Certainly important in a school media center is the provision for darkening some areas for projection, with some means of retaining a minimum illumination for unexpected equipment failure and other problems.

THERMAL ENVIRONMENT

Heating, cooling, and ventilating are the three interdependent factors that are the major considerations in a discussion of the primary problem of what the media center's thermal environment should be. The techniques for controlling these thermal elements are of course available to planners attempting to solve the thermal environment problem. The solution should also take into consideration such external factors as the outside climate and the yearly use of the facility and such internal factors as the location of the main area of the school media center facility (i.e., near a boiler room).

No one thermal factor can be evaluated separately; nor can it be judged without reference to all others. A comfortable thermal environment is a matter of deciding on a proper balance. Appropriate heating, cooling, and ventilating techniques can then be used.

Minimum standards for thermal requirements are generally written into official building codes. In almost all cases, however, media specialists must see that the requirements are not only reached but exceeded, because any extreme temperature or inadequate air exchange generally will impair both physical and mental efficiency. It is recognized that air conditioning is the best solution to the ventilation problem in a school media facility where people need to work as efficiently as possible in a warm, humid climate. The need for heat control is also well accepted in cold climates. However, in many of the less-extreme weather belts in the country, a media specialist may have to emphasize the need for a balance of heating, cooling, and ventilation.

There are several points to watch for in overseeing a thermal environment. Ventilation and heating outlets should be located where they will not reduce shelf space or interfere with furniture arrangements. The rooms that house mechanical equipment and compressors should be isolated from the media center so that both their noise and their vibrations will not intrude into the center.

The use of outside glass will influence the thermal environment and must be taken into account. Sufficient insulation should be used to ensure the maintenance of an appropriate environment. A form of ventilation should be installed that will maintain an even temperature between 70°

and 73° and a humidity reading of approximately 40 percent. Many schools have found that air conditioning is the most efficient and, in the long run, most economical method of ventilation. As with lighting, temperature control facilities should be modular to allow for flexibility in space division.

ELECTRICAL POWER

With the increasing use of projectors, recorders, and other types of electrically operated teaching and learning equipment, electrical outlets must be provided in sufficient number and in a variety of locations to allow flexibility in the use of listening and viewing equipment. Electrical outlets should be placed where they will best serve the center's immediate and future needs: either on the floor, the ceiling, the walls, or all three surface areas. A minimum of four 15-ampere outlets is suggested for each small area.

Another important factor in dealing with electrical power is safety, especially when students and volunteers participate and interact with electrically operated equipment. Conduits for future internal coaxial cables, a master antenna array, and the electrical power throughout the school for a number of receivers are necessary considerations for future planning for television. The following three steps are useful in evaluating the present and future electrical power requirements for the school media center:

1. Evaluate your school's particular needs in relation to activities, such as television, that may be carried out in the center at some future time.

2. Formulate a present and future plan for needed electrical power based on step 1.

3. Gather information on any of the newer kinds of equipment that require electrical power from the following associations: Electronic Industries Association (EIA); National Association of Educational Broadcasters (NAEB); Joint Council on Educational Television (JCET).

Because the costs of rewiring are often prohibitive, it is essential for media specialists to assume that centers in the future will utilize more electrical equipment than present needs call for.

ACOUSTICS

Any school media center that is a focal point for learning activity in a school is faced with problems of sound. Controlling the sounds made by people and machines is an important part of designing or remodeling centers. Because of the emergence of open-plan schools and centers, a newer attitude toward acceptance of background noise is developing as well as a better understanding of the noise that naturally emanates from young people at different ages.

Sound is highly directional in nature; however, unrelated sounds of different types and intensities combine to make noise. Since it is a basic characteristic of sound that it requires more energy of a listener or speaker under poor sound conditions, a good environment gives control of both the sounds that originate within an area and the distracting ones from the outside that combine to produce intolerable noise levels.

There are many ways of dealing with the problems of sound. Some are: room shape, use of acoustical materials, use of sound systems, and improved space dividers. Research suggests that an equal proportion of depth and width in a room will provide the best sound environment. Another way to reduce the sound that reflects from barriers, especially hard surfaces, is to set the walls and ceilings on slightly irregular planes, rather than in the traditional parallel pattern. Materials that are to be used for sound conditioning should be investigated under in-use conditions that are similar in purpose to those being planned. Any soft, absorbent material, such as heat insulation material, will muffle sound, but allow it to be transmitted in some form to adjacent areas. Materials that impede the transmission of sound have a high density, i.e., solid mass or air chamber. Baffles placed in air ventilation ducts will also retard the transmission of sound from one area to another.

As noted in the section on thermal environment, the location of the school media center is important. The vibrations from heavy school equipment, such as printing presses in a vocational education department, or natural, but distracting sounds, from a cafeteria or gymnasium, for example, can rarely be overcome and are best avoided.

Sound systems with electronic amplification are used in many school media center situations. The fidelity of this amplified sound is the most important factor. The quality of the equipment used in the various sound systems determines the fidelity. Therefore in both speaking and hearing with the aid of this equipment, the degree of fidelity becomes an essential ingredient in the sound environment. Finally, because of the increasing trend to open-space centers and areas, the construction and design of space dividers should be considered for the amount of sound control they permit. For example, folding plywood partitions will temporarily change the area arrangement, but they generally permit a level of seepage noise that the media center staff and users may find impossible to live with. Newer research suggests that woven fabrics with an appropriate density and decreased porosity due to the use of special materials and weaving techniques may be one answer to noise problems in an area.

In some school media center areas, such as conference rooms, a certain level of sound from discussion is expected. However, in a main study area, disruptive noise and motion can be kept to a minimum in two ways: (1) by using sound-reducing materials in construction and (2) by arrangement of the facilities. An acoustically treated ceiling will help reduce sound, as will carpeting on the floor and wall surfaces. Studies indicate that excessive use of acoustical tile ceilings is unnecessary, however, and may even add sound problems. One-third of the area to be covered is suggested as the appropriate portion for acoustical treatment.

Before deciding on the appropriate acoustical treatment for a floor surface, the underlying floor construction, the heating system, and the scope of activities intended for the facility must first be determined. Since the floor will not only be walked on but is the work area's base, it should be draft-free and warm enough in winter. If the range of the school media center's audience is from prekindergarten children to ninth grade young people, the floor plan and construction should provide for a series of play and work postures. Acoustic flooring may be satisfactory for specific purposes in certain media center areas. Although higher in initial cost, carpeting is equal in cost to other flooring material over a period of time, chiefly because of the savings on maintenance. It also has the advantage of being inviting and comfortable.

In planning the facilities, large areas should be broken up by furnishings to prevent an uninterrupted traveling path for sound. Noise-producing activities should be isolated from sections where quiet is needed. Shelving should be located away from study areas, as should the circulation desk, entrances, and exits. Arrangements that force students to walk through the main area to get to the shelves or card catalog should be avoided. A preliminary study of traffic patterns will help determine the appropriate placement of areas and furnishings to control sound.

COLOR

A color scheme that provides both variety and harmony can help to make the school media center the pleasant place to work and visit that it should be. Planning for color in the environment is vital because human beings are influenced both negatively and positively by the aesthetics of color. There is color in everything in a school media center environment: in structural materials, walls, woodwork, furnishings, materials, equipment, in the views out-of-doors, and in the ever-changing variety of people themselves. Care should be taken to coordinate this variety of visual sensory experiences into a cohesive, if continuously varying, and harmonious color environment. Two general rules will aid the media specialist who must be the coordinator without the benefit of a color consultant:

1. Study the scientific recommendations on the use of color as it relates to reflectivity and contrast; i.e., white enamel surfaces reflect light

so effectively that they appear much larger in size than a similar object painted a dull black that absorbs light. Each color shade and tone obeys similar rules of reflectivity and contrast and has as well a complicated relationship of harmony value to the shade and tone of other colors.

2. Use these recommendations cautiously, knowing that the students who are surrounded by color will be affected differently by it depending on their age: young children benefit from the stimulation of cheerful, bright areas of color; students in the middle grades or junior high school need less color stimulation; a more sophisticated blend of color to reflect the adult world is appropriate in the high school.

Oversaturation with too many colors or color clashes can produce a visual cacophony that can disturb many. Remember that the materials, the equipment, and the people in a school media center generally provide an abundance of color. A sophisticated and skillful plain background color scheme is often needed to modulate this condition. Carpeting or flooring should be of a plain, unbroken pattern, preferably of a light color. Furniture and walls may vary in color, from traditional pastels to subdued shades of some of the stronger colors, depending on the age of the patrons. With imaginative use of good design, attractive furniture, and inviting colors the center can be an interesting, aesthetically appealing area in which to work and study.

FURNISHINGS

The traditional furnishings in schools and media centers are being replaced today by modular, easy-to-move, compact, multipurpose furniture that answers the current need for flexibility brought about by the changing instructional techniques and the various sizes of instructional groups. The trend in furniture, shelving, display cases, wall hangings, floor coverings is toward comfort and aesthetic appeal that can be found by the imaginative combining of standard and eclectic designs together with objects of little or no commercial value. For example, large electrical cable spools can be painted and used as low tables, heavy shipping crates can be arranged and fixed into a multilevel carpeted reading area, and an old wall unit juke box can be wired with headsets for listening. These are inexpensive, sometimes free ways of furnishing, but even more, they can be exciting and valuable educationally because they match the young people's developmental needs.

Regardless of the type of furniture, some specific selection criteria should apply. The media specialist should make sure that each furnishing is: (1) simple and safe, (2) rugged and durable, (3) useful and comfortable,

(4) eye-pleasing and compact. Not every furnishing can fit all these criteria, but each piece of furniture should be safe and comfortable.

CARRELS

Students indicate that they like movable, versatile furniture with a potential for privacy. They prefer table surfaces to desks in a group situation and carrels to tables for individual study. Carrels provide private places where students may work undisturbed by other individuals or by program activities going on in the center. There are no hard-and-fast rules for locating and placing carrels. Generally, only a few should be distributed among the collections and the rest placed as spatial dividers, singly or in small groups. Large groupings give less privacy to the student and an institutional appearance to any area.

The table surface in a carrel should not be less than 3 feet wide by 2 feet deep. It should also have 18- to 20-inch partitions on three sides, some shelf or storage space, electrical power outlets, and lighting where necessary. Although many different types of carrels are available commercially, the simplest and least expensive type can be set up by using any conventional library table. Movable panel dividers made of acoustical material, i.e., cork or acoustic-fabric-covered fiberboard, can transform a library table into study carrels. Shelves and electrical inputs from a plug strip can be added so that portable equipment can be used in each carrel. A more sophisticated variation uses the same construction principle with the addition of permanent electrical wiring to permit the installation of fixed equipment. There should also be some tables and chairs in each area. Two important considerations for choosing the correct mix of carrels and tables are: (1) the nature and size of the instructional groups in the school and (2) an appropriate mixture of different seating and working arrangements. A combination of round, octagonal, rectangular, and trapezoidal tables will present an attractive variety in a large main area. These tables and chairs, like the carrels, should not be placed in regimented ways. Rather, they should be distributed judiciously within areas to help provide an atmosphere that is conducive to study. Sturdy chairs should be chosen to go with the tables. It is suggested that they have legs that extend at an angle from under the seat. An often beneficial extra is the convenient underseat shelf or basket for the student's books and papers. Some comfortable casual chairs and low tables are also recommended. A large variety of items that can be used for sitting should be investigated. Here the age of the student and the purpose of the seating will be important considerations. Bricks or concrete blocks and boards can make inexpensive and attractive low tables or benches. Inflatable cushions and carpet covered concrete drains can also be used. Almost any large and sturdy cylindrical commercial "throw away" can be adapted for casual seating. Chimney flues (on their sides), discarded computer or round film storage cans (taped together), and foam-filled fabric covered shapes can also be used creatively as furnishings. Informal lounge furniture is often placed close to the magazine and newspaper racks to encourage recreational and informational reading. Microfilm and copying equipment may also be located in the main area.

Other standard furniture items include a circulation desk, separate cabinets for a card catalog and a shelflist, filing cabinets, book and equipment trucks. The circulation desk should be large enough to handle the flow of multimedia and small equipment for home use, while the cabinets for a card catalog and shelflist should each have enough space to hold the cards for both nonprint and print. Sectional units are suggested because they permit easy expansion. The filing cabinets, some of which should accommodate legal or larger-size materials, are important for pamphlets, transparencies, clippings, and small pictures. They come with three or four drawers or open-faced to be used with hanging file folders. A large drawer-like cabinet or bin may also be needed for large pictures and maps. Mobile book and equipment trucks are available from commercial suppliers. The prime requisites are ease of movement, which is determined by the size of the wheels, and sturdiness.

SHELVING

Books and other materials are generally made accessible to the user on standard adjustable library shelves. There are various types of shelving: steel bracket, freestanding sliding shelves; wood cases with metal strips and clips for supporting shelves; sloping wood or metal shelves; stack columns that hold boxes, lockers, and reading tables. They come in three-foot unit lengths with end panels. The use of freestanding double-faced shelving is preferable to wall shelving. The stacks should be close to the circulation area for ease of use and supervision. When arranged, the shelves should not be longer than 15 feet with 4½-foot rows between them, and a 5-foot clearance between the shelves and adjacent furniture. From five to six shelves per section are useful in high school, but fewer fit the elementary school needs better. One good use for counterheight shelving is to define areas within a room. Rows of shelves grouped in blocks facilitate accessibility. Generally, the greater percent of the shelves should be 8 inches wide, the remainder 10–14 inches wide, for oversize material. Reference books and nonprint items, such as films, may require different types of shelving. The amount of shelving should be able to house a minimum of 15 items (books, slide sets, and other materials) per student.

OTHER STORAGE AND DISPLAY FURNISHINGS

Other types of furniture should include bins to store phonograph records, racks to display current magazines and newspapers, and cabinets for filmstrips, slides, and film loops if these are not intershelved. Special multimedia shelving to interfile print and nonprint materials in the same way they appear in a card catalog is beginning to find an audience among media specialists and is a new trend worth investigating. This type of accessibility can be explored initially by using specially constructed or locally produced multimedia shelving for a curriculum unit within one area of the Dewey Decimal Classification System. Legal-size filing cabinets can be provided for difficult-to-shelve pamphlets, pictures, and clippings. Rolling trucks for print and nonprint and combination or separate atlas-dictionary stands are also useful.

Display shelving for magazines, i.e., sloping shelves that are generally 36 inches wide and 16 inches deep, lends itself to the use of imaginative as well as standard ideas. The primary purpose of any display is to make the front cover as visible as possible. This can be achieved by the imaginative use of a clothesline or metal rod strung across one or more areas with colorful clothespins or magnetic clamps to secure the magazines.

Other display facilities, such as bulletin and peg boards, exhibit cases, and various display stands, that may be used in the ways outlined in the promotion and public relations section of chapter 3 should be available in the main study area as well as directly outside the main entrance.

FACILITIES FOR SPECIAL MEDIA SERVICES

Film, radio, and television services in the majority of schools are still too costly to maintain on an individual building basis. The materials and services in each are generally handled on a network basis at either a system, regional, or state level. Films in a school are generally selected, previewed, and rented by the media specialist in consultation with the teachers, the administrators, and in many instances, the students. If the school system is large enough, it may support a centralized facility that maintains a film library. For an individual school that wishes to start a film library, 8mm, both super and standard, offers almost the same potential as 16mm film, and at a lower cost. Although not all 16mm films are available in 8mm, many classic and increasingly newer releases are.

Radio and television are two media that require special facilities. Although radio was once briefly popular in education, it has generally been superceded by the newer medium of television, except in rural or wilderness areas. The use of television in education continues to grow in many different directions. Presently available for educators are several types of television that differ in technical ways. (See the section headed "Television" in Appendix III.) Only the larger school systems or the more forward-looking smaller ones have tried to incorporate the medium of TV and have generally done so from a district or regional level.

The emergence of video cassettes expands the usefulness of closed-circuit television (CCTV) in schools by permitting the taping of broadcast or "off-air" television programs within copyright permission laws and replaying them on the CCTV receivers in any part of a school. Some state departments of public instruction have inaugurated a duplication service of videocassettes for media specialists from a master print of special programs. The usefulness to media centers and schools of video taping, both alone and together with CCTV, are important enough for small schools to explore this development and plan for the needed facilities.

8

MEDIA SELECTION

The media center collection is in many ways like a living organism—it grows and develops; it is dynamic and everchanging, expanding in some areas while contracting in others. To supervise this growth and to regulate these changes is most exciting, taxing, and ultimately one of the most professional tasks performed by the media specialist.

To build a collection wisely and well, the media specialist should develop judgment and good taste along with a thorough knowledge of all the variables that influence selection, like needs of the community and nature of the curriculum. The media specialist must be alert to changes and trends, show impartiality and objectivity, be imaginative, curious, and resourceful, and be dedicated to the public and the schools being served.

This chapter discusses the background body of knowledge necessary for the creation of the selection process as well as information on how to organize it. Other areas treated are: the development of a selection policy, selection aids, practical pointers on selection and general criteria for choosing materials and equipment.

Media selection must be considered an ongoing process; although orders for media are placed only a few times each year, selection occurs daily. The machinery of selection should swing into action each time a reference question raised at the center cannot be answered with the available material on a subject—for example, when a hitherto ignored part of the world suddenly becomes newsworthy or a different fad hits a school population. The arrival of a new issue of a reviewing periodical should also signal the selection process to start.

No two media centers contain—or should contain—the same collections. Each center's collection should reflect the specific needs of the school it serves. Yet while each media center is thus unique, all centers share three basic aims: (1) to help satisfy the needs of students for cur-

riculum related materials; (2) to fulfill students' wishes concerning materials for recreational purposes; (3) to provide teachers with professional
information. In good school programs, as in good educational materials,
the first two aims often become intermingled and indistinguishable.

BACKGROUND KNOWLEDGE

Before beginning the selection process the media specialist must
learn something about the community; the students, faculty, and curriculum; media; bibliographic and reviewing tools; the existing collection;
and budgeting.

KNOWLEDGE OF THE COMMUNITY

Every community has many aspects that must be considered by the
media specialist. To learn the characteristics of the population the specialist must investigate inhabitants' ethnic and religious backgrounds, age
groupings, occupations, general economic status, cultural and recreational interests, and educational levels. Each of these factors will be reflected in the young people attending the schools. The nature of residential buildings, the kinds of businesses, and even transportation routes
provide clues helpful in understanding the community. The media specialist should also become familiar with the community's other libraries
and cultural resources as well as its recreational resources. Does the average
child come from a home where there is at least a basic reference collection?
How numerous and accessible are other public and private collections of
educational materials? How adequate are these collections? Are there art
galleries or other cultural institutions nearby? What provisions are there
for recreational facilities, athletic fields, meeting rooms for clubs and
hobby groups? One device to use in studying a community is to draw a
simple map of the community and locate on it the various community
resources and the school and public bus routes as well as other modes of
transportation.

KNOWLEDGE OF STUDENTS

In addition to knowing the general age and grade levels in the school,
the media specialist should probe deeper into the activities and interests
of the students. He or she should determine the range of abilities and the
degree of concentration of these abilities at various levels—for the whole
school as well as for each class. Reading ability must be determined and
test scores used to help verify range and concentration. Becoming familiar

with the interests and activities of each age group—their hobbies, favorite sports and social interests, popular TV shows, part-time jobs, and size of allowances—will provide the specialist with valuable insights. What are the general social and emotional maturity levels of the students? How sophisticated, independent, and experienced are they at handling social adjustments, emotional problems, concerns about physical growth and maturation, relations with other members of the family, school assignments, and contemporary affairs? Both general and specific reading interests must be analyzed. By general reading interests is meant the common interests of a specific age group. For example, junior high school boys generally enjoy science fiction and stories of true adventure. However, within these general-interest categories, and in addition to them, are specific differentiations and subtleties of tastes that are uniquely characteristic of the individual school. A study of circulation records and comparisons with the experience of others working with the same age group will help bring some of these differences into focus. Although it may seem an impossible task, in order to know more than just names and faces the media specialist should try to collect this mass of information not only for the student body as a whole but also for each actual and potential user of the media center.

KNOWLEDGE OF THE FACULTY

The interests, backgrounds, strengths, and weaknesses of the faculty are reflected in their teaching assignments, their classroom use of media, and the ways in which they and their students use the media center. The media specialist should be aware of the teaching methods employed, the nature of media center use by specific departments and at various grade levels, and areas where inservice work in media use seems needed. Each term he should find out the courses being taken by teachers for continuing education so that additions may be made to the professional collection to assist them.

KNOWLEDGE OF THE CURRICULUM

Knowing about the school's curriculum involves more than just a knowledge of what subjects are taught and when. It also means knowing the objectives of the school and how the media center relates to them. It involves attending curriculum meetings, conferring with teachers about classroom assignments before they are given, becoming thoroughly familiar with the classroom textbooks used, and when possible, visiting classrooms to observe presentation techniques and use of media.

KNOWLEDGE OF MEDIA

The media specialist must become familiar with the various forms of educational materials, their characteristics, strengths and limitations, and their potential for use in various situations. Similar information should be obtained for the accompanying equipment. There is no substitute for firsthand knowledge. Media specialists, at every opportunity, should be reading books, viewing films, using equipment, and engaging in other activities that will continually augment their knowledge of media centers and their contents. This body of knowledge should be applied when considering future acquisitions.

KNOWLEDGE OF BIBLIOGRAPHIC AND REVIEWING TOOLS

Not all material can or should be appraised locally. Opinions of experts outside the immediate school district should be consulted. There are literally hundreds of bibliographies, media lists, and reviewing journals that can help the media specialist in selection. They are issued by professional associations, commercial publishers of reviewing media, government library agencies (Federal, state, and local), producers and publishers of educational media, and many library systems. Details on the types of selection aids and criteria for their evaluation are given later in this chapter and in Appendixes III and IV.

KNOWLEDGE OF THE EXISTING COLLECTION

If a media center has been in existence for some time, the media specialist must determine the size, nature, strengths and weaknesses, age and general physical condition, and basic usefulness of its contents before undertaking new selection. Several methods can be used to gain this knowledge. First, the shelflist and equipment inventory may be examined to determine which areas have been stressed or slighted, amount of duplication, and recency of titles and equipment. Another method is to "read" the shelves, glancing particularly at unfamiliar titles. Another is to check the collection against standard bibliographies to determine what proportion of these basic titles is present. The media specialist can also become acquainted with the media center's holdings by repeated use of the card catalog. In evaluating an existing collection it is important to check outside the media center to find out what the school's holdings are, for example, in textbooks, classroom collections, study centers, and departmental libraries.

KNOWLEDGE OF THE BUDGET

Before beginning to select media, the media specialist should have at hand the budget allotments for the current year and, if at all possible, for the coming year or years. The selector of media must inquire about the share of additional funds that might be available through Federal, state, or local legislation. Long-range planning, particularly for expensive book sets, motion pictures, and audiovisual equipment is necessary. Unfortunately, less expensive substitutes will sometimes have to be found or the purchase of a desired item postponed to insure balance and equality in distribution of budgetary funds.

ORGANIZING THE MEDIA SELECTION PROGRAM

The number and extent of selection services provided by the single school will depend largely on how many related services are available at the district level. The keynote is the development of a systematized process where each supplements the other without unnecessary duplication of effort. Certain services, such as maintaining a book examination center or exhibiting samples of media center furniture, are best handled in a centralized, district-wide agency, but on the other hand, routing of bibliographies to individual faculty members, for example, should logically be administered at the local school level. Patterns of organization will therefore differ considerably from one situation to another, depending on local conditions. However, one trend is becoming apparent: school districts now realize that it is impossible to have firsthand evaluations of all media before purchase recommendations are given. Nor is this necessary. The reviewing sources that are available for many materials (for example, library books) are of sufficient quantity and quality that to ignore these sources in favor of local reviewing not only wastes time and duplicates effort but also fails to utilize the expertise of those knowledgeable critics and subject specialists who review in these publications.

In areas where the reviewing media are inadequate or where the items under consideration are either very costly or highly specialized, some form of local reviewing will take place. The cost of an initial investment, for example, the purchase price of videocassettes or 16mm films, will often mandate previewing sessions for evaluation. In general, one of two methods, or a combination of both, is used to systematize local reviewing. The first is to organize reviewing committees composed chiefly of teachers, with representation from administration and the media center and, when possible, from the student body. At the district level these committees should represent a cross section of the district school personnel and should be organized according to the participants' subject specialties and general grade-level interests. In individual schools the committees may be organized according to academic departments or specific grade levels. In a single school situation there are also many opportunities to arrange for individual teachers or groups representing many curricular interests to review specific materials.

The second method is to have a teacher or teachers use the material in question in a classroom situation similar to that for which the item to be purchased is intended and thus gain an on-the-spot evaluation.

Regardless of the method or methods used, some type of formal reporting of local evaluations should be made. Many schools have developed standardized forms to insure conformity in these reports. Because each media format has distinct and unique characteristics, it is difficult, if not impossible, to produce a single form that can be useful with all types of materials. However, to avoid developing a multitude of reporting forms, materials can be grouped into logical divisions. For example, the same form can be used for films, filmstrips, slides, and transparencies and another for textbooks and other book materials. A rating scale is often used for each criterion on the form—this could be a numerical scale ranging from 5 for excellent to 1 for poor. Spaces should be supplied for: name of the person requesting a review, dates of the request and of the review, kind of material and its subject area and general grade level, an overall priority rating (basic or supplementary), and a space for the evaluator's comments. Other items generally covered in these forms include: (1) bibliographic information, e.g., title, author, producer, vendor, publisher; (2) format or technical aspects, e.g., quality of sound, color, picture, binding; (3) content, e.g., scope of work, limitations of coverage, up-to-dateness, objectivity; (4) organization and presentation, e.g., suitability of length, logic, and clarity of presentation, interest, pacing, amount of review, and repetition; (5) suitability, e.g., appropriateness to the medium as well as to subject and grade levels, special uses; (6) teachers' aids, e.g., manuals, workbooks, other correlated materials.

Similar forms may be devised for equipment evaluation. The general evaluative criteria found in this chapter as well as the specific criteria in Appendixes III and IV may be used. For additional help consult *Selecting Instructional Material for Purchase: Procedural Guidelines* (NEA).

As stated earlier, responsibilities for selection are assigned in various patterns at the district and single school levels. The single school will share some of the duties with the district center, for example, workshops on media evaluation. However, the following selection-related activities should be initiated at the single school level:

1. Organize and administer the reviewing procedures within the school.

2. Obtain, either through the media center or the district office, preview copies of material requested by teachers.

3. Maintain liaison with the central selection agency and jointly coordinate activities.

4. Involve as many people in the school as possible in the selection process.

5. Route bibliographies and other selection aids, asking for purchase suggestions.

6. Attend faculty meetings as well as departmental or grade-level meetings to become acquainted with curriculum changes and to discuss future acquisition plans.

7. Conduct interest inventories with students to determine what topics interest them most and least. These inventories may be arranged alphabetically in checklist form—from "airplanes" to "zoos."

8. Maintain a file of locally reviewed educational materials and basic commercially produced selection aids.

The following list gives some selection activities that seem best suited to be performed at the district level; some might be shared with individual schools or where centralized selection services are nonexistent, initiated within the schools:

1. Organize and administer a district-wide reviewing network for materials that standard reviewing sources seem inadequate for or that need supplementary local appraisal.

2. Print, disseminate, and maintain a permanent file of reviews of the locally reviewed items.

3. Schedule and make provisions for individual and/or faculty group visits to the examination center on a regular basis.

4. Arrange for preview privileges for material when examination copies are unavailable for extended loan.

5. Maintain liaison with other central administrative and curricular agencies or departments to insure coordination of efforts.

6. Establish and develop cooperative acquisition projects between individual schools in the district and with other libraries in the area—public, academic, and special.

7. Act as liaison between public schools and manufacturers' representatives; maintain a file of current commercial catalogs of materials and equipment.

8. Maintain a cataloged permanent collection of basic titles that can be used as a guide in establishing new collections or reevaluating established collections.

9. Provide an exhibit collection of current books and other print and nonprint media representing at least the current and immediate past pub-

lishing seasons. Clip reviews from standard selection aids and insert them in the material on exhibit.

10. Organize a sample collection of audiovisual equipment and media center furniture.

11. Assemble special multimedia displays or media fairs on specific subjects and, when possible, route these to individual schools.

12. Schedule such prepackaged traveling exhibits as "Books on Exhibit" or the "Combined Paperback Exhibit in Schools" and arrange to have them routed to individual schools when possible.

(For information write to: "Combined Paperback Exhibit in Schools," Scarborough Park, Albany Post Road, Briarcliff Manor, N.Y. 10510; "Books on Exhibit," Mount Kisco, N.Y. 10549.)

13. Be a clearinghouse for new bibliographies and selection aids that should be brought to the attention of other media personnel and a dissemination point for the lists produced in individual schools.

14. Purchase and make available expensive or specialized reviewing sources that normally would not be purchased or made available by individual schools.

15. Conduct workshops for teachers and media specialists on the evaluation of media.

Whatever administrative patterns evolve in the selection process, two considerations are paramount: organization and participation. If these can be achieved within a congenial atmosphere conducive to free expression and the development of professional attitudes, a successful program should result.

WRITING A MEDIA SELECTION POLICY STATEMENT

Considering the amount of published material on the necessity for a written media selection policy, it is amazing how many school districts have not adopted such a document. Yet in reality it should be the cornerstone of a media program that gives both shape and direction to the development of that program. A written selection policy can serve several purposes. It can supply a blueprint for future growth and refinement and prevent haphazard collection development. It can also help prevent extended and unnecessary disputes involving controversial material. Besides supplying criteria and selection procedures for the center's staff, it also can help clarify these matters for the rest of the school's personnel and the community.

Before developing a policy statement, the media specialist should become familiar with the basic documents concerning intellectual freedom. The American Library Association's "Freedom to Read Statement" and "Intellectual Freedom Statement" plus "The School Library Bill of

Rights" from the American Association of School Librarians are three such documents. One or more of these documents are often incorporated into the selection policy. For example, "The School Library Bill of Rights" is part of the Greater Anchorage policy statement (see Appendix II). Additional policies and hints on developing them may be found in Calvin Boyer and Nancy Eaton's *Book Selection Policies of American Libraries* and in an excellent booklet from the California Association of School Librarians (now California Association for Educational Media and Technology) called *Instructional Materials: Selection Policies and Procedures*. Other useful material, including the *Intellectual Freedom Newsletter*, are available from ALA's Office of Intellectual Freedom.

The selection policy should not be constructed in a vacuum. It certainly should include broad universal principles, but as well it must reflect unique local conditions. All groups affected by the policy should participate in its formation. This includes representatives from the media center staff, faculty, administration, students, and the community. The policy should be officially accepted by all of those groups, including the district's school board. After adoption, it should be disseminated widely. No policy statement, however, should be considered permanent and all-enduring; instead it should reflect a dynamic stage of growth and be capable of easy amendment or revision when conditions warrant a change. It should also be broad enough to cover many contingencies, but precise enough to prevent ambiguity. Material selection policies often contain the following elements:

1. A statement of the school district and individual school's philosophy, particularly in relation to educational materials and intellectual freedom.

2. A similar statement summarizing the aims and objectives of the library media center in relation to this overall philosophy.

3. A listing of those who participate in selection and of the specific objectives of the selection function.

4. An indication of delegated as well as final responsibility for selection including a definition of the position of the media center's personnel in this operation.

5. A list of the types of media found in the center and of the criteria applied to the selection of each.

6. An enumeration of the selection aids most frequently consulted.

7. A description of the procedures, forms, and practices used in selection.

8. An indication of areas of the collection that will be either stressed or de-emphasized.

9. Additional or modifying criteria for the various clientele served. For example, a different set of standards might apply when buying profes-

sional materials for teachers than the standards for purchasing high-interest material for slow or reluctant readers.

10. Statements concerning the media center's policies toward gifts, sponsored material, weeding, duplication, and replacement.

11. Information concerning any cooperative acquisition projects in which the media center is involved with other schools and libraries.

12. A description of the procedures for handling complaints and a copy of any forms used when a request is made to reevaluate a particular piece of material.

STANDARDS

A variety of published standards specify norms for the quantities of materials in a media center collection and, in some cases, the quality of the center's progress. The historical background on these standards has been discussed in the Introduction to this book.

Standards can fulfill several beneficial functions. They can become a blueprint for future growth for both new and established media centers and serve as a method of evaluating existing collections. They should be seen primarily as a method that can help schools to implement their educational goals. It is often very difficult to state objective standards in certain areas, particularly where the quality of a program is to be measured. Even when quantities of material are specified, standards are hard to formulate because of frequent changes in educational techniques and teaching practices. For these reasons, standards should be under constant review and revised when needed.

In applying standards it is necessary to relate each recommendation to the whole set of standards. A single standard regarding recommended numbers of particular media should be related to other parts of the existing collection, and on a larger scale, the size of the entire collection, actual or recommended, should be seen in terms of the school's educational philosophy and objectives. It must also be noted that quantities of materials do not in themselves indicate a quality program—they merely supply one of the conditions upon which a fine program can be built.

Standards are of two types, *comparative* and *projective*. Comparative standards are usually short range and are based on existing, not optimum, conditions. For example, a school district with a superior materials collection in one school might attempt to bring the collections in other schools up to this level by using the size of the single collection as a standard for the other schools. Projective standards are long range and deal more abstractly with ultimate goals. Most published well-developed standards are projective. Often these standards are stated in terms of phases that represent various stages of growth. There are usually three phases: *basic* (or minimum), *good,* and *advanced* (or excellent). This breakdown can be utilized as a rating scale and can serve also as a guideline for developing short-term or immediate goals. Many state standards are expressed in these terms.

Several agencies have issued standards. The principal ones are at the Federal and state levels, although school districts, too, often develop and adopt local standards. The district standards are usually closely associated with short-term goals and are often comparative in nature and based either on an exemplary program within the district or in a neighboring district. The district standards are easily modified or enlarged to meet changing local conditions. Flexibility is one of the chief advantages of this type of goal.

Individuals have also developed standards for media centers that have appeared in monographs dealing with schools and educational materials. For example, Ralph Ellsworth in his *The School Library* (Educational Facilities Laboratories) states that every school library should have a basic collection of 50,000 books. However, he suggests that if a school's population has access to a strong public or college library, this figure could be adjusted downward to 30,000 volumes.

The school media specialist should become familiar with as many as possible of the various sets of standards, particularly those at the national, state, and local levels that bear directly on the school's media program. It is also the responsibility of the media center's staff to make other interested groups—administrators, faculties, parents, school boards—aware of these standards and their implications for expansion of existing facilities and programs.

SELECTION AIDS

Like the serious researcher, the media specialist in the process of selection has available both primary and secondary sources. By primary sources is meant firsthand examination of the material or equipment before purchase. Media specialists have many opportunities to gain this knowledge. Visiting exhibits at professional conventions is an excellent way. Such displays as the "Combined Media Exhibit" or the "Combined Book Exhibit" are usually part of the national and state library association conferences. Opportunities to see demonstrations of equipment and materials and make on-the-spot comparisons and evaluations are possible at these conferences as well as chances to browse through a publisher's stock of new books. At the local level, previewing prints or on-approval copies can often be secured. Some exhibits, such as "Books On Exhibit" and the "Combined Paperback Exhibit," can be booked into an individual school district. Many jobbers and wholesalers allow media personnel to visit and preview the stock. There are, of course, many functioning media examination centers scattered about the country, some operating at the school district or city-wide level, others at the multidistrict or state level. Many public library systems also have examination centers. Other examination centers, for example the one operated by the Children's Book Council in New York City, exist on private funds. Lastly, there is a very accessible resource that media personnel apparently seldom use—the collections of their colleagues in other media centers and libraries.

The opportunities to examine materials before purchase are available, but with an explosion of information in all media and with the age of specialization upon us, prior examination of all material is neither possible nor practical. Media personnel must depend on the opinions and advice of professional specialists which are often found in the various reviewing media. Commonly called selection aids, these are bibliographies, catalogs, indexes, review periodicals, and "basic" or "best" lists. The proper interpretation, evaluation, and understanding of these aids is one of the essentials for effective selection.

The two major kinds of selection aids are the *retrospective* and the *current*. Retrospective aids list materials that are time-tested and generally recommended for specific needs. They are helpful in building the initial collection and can be used with existing collections to indicate material that has been missed but is still useful and important. Examples of retrospective aids would include *Books for Elementary School Libraries* (ALA), *Senior High School Library Catalog* (Wilson), and *Best Books for Children* (Bowker).

Current aids, such as *The Booklist* (ALA) or *School Library Journal* (Bowker), are primarily intended to report on new material. Many current selection aids must be used to obtain a range of critical opinions. Selecting material on the basis of its recommendation in only one source is extremely unwise. Because less than 50 percent of all material that might be useful in the school is reviewed in the standard tools of the trade, the librarian must also consult reviews in such specialized professional journals as *English Journal* or *Elementary English* (both from National Council of Teachers of English). Through other subdivisions, selection aids are classified further according to the type of media reviewed: general or special subject, single format or multimedia, etc. Regardless of how the aid is classified the would-be-user must explore it thoroughly and become familiar with its contents before it can be utilized effectively. There are many bibliographies that list recommended selection aids. Two examples are *Aids to Choosing Books for Children* (Children's Book Council) and *Guides to Newer Educational Media* (ALA) by Margaret L. Rufsvold and Carolyn Guss.

CRITERIA FOR CHOOSING SELECTION AIDS

The media selector should be aware of the strengths and weaknesses of a bibliography before using it for selection purposes. When there is an understanding of the general nature as well as the specific limitations, shortcomings, and possible areas of utilization of selection tools, then the possibility of using each wisely and effectively increases. The "Criteria for Selecting Media and Equipment" (presented later in this chapter) should be applied, after which the following specific questions should be asked to make certain that all pertinent information has been collected.

Authority

Who are the reviewers and editors and what are their qualifications?

Do the reviewers represent a particular point of view?

Are the reviews signed?

Scope

Is this a selective (such as the "best-of" type) or an all-inclusive bibliography?

What types of material are listed? Are there limitations on inclusion, including format (classes of material), subjects, time periods, age groups, language, and places of origin?

Are adequate directions on how to use the aid provided?

What is the intended audience?

How often does the bibliography appear?

How up-to-date are the reviews?

In general, how much bibliographic data is included?

Arrangement

Is it arranged alphabetically, by classification or subject; chronologically, by format, or by a combination of these?

Is there an index?

Is the index cumulated? How often?

Annotations or Reviews

What is their average length?

Are they descriptive, critical or both?

Is each piece of material reviewed separately?

Does the review include comparisons with other similar material, or with the producer's or author's other works?

Is there some indication, perhaps through a coding system, whether the material is basic or supplemental?

Are each of the reviews generally consistent in length, point of view, scope, and treatment?

Does the review indicate comprehension, suitability, and interest levels and make suggestions for possible use?

Has the reviewer objectively tested the accuracy, reliability and up-to-dateness of the material?

Special Features

Does the aid include any special material, such as a directory of publishers, professional organizations, manufacturers, distributors, selection centers, rental libraries, or depositories?

Are the reviews indexed or excerpted in another publication, such as *Book Review Digest?*

PRACTICAL POINTS TO AID SELECTION

The following is a list of practical hints and guidelines that should be followed to insure the development of useful, well-rounded collections. Some are offshoots and extensions of the general principles stated earlier in the chapter while others introduce new factors into the selection process.

Participation in the Selection Process. As many of the school's population as possible should be involved in selecting materials for the media center. Reviewing periodicals and preview copies of materials may be routed to the faculty for comments and suggestions. School personnel should be invited to special previewing sessions. Students should also become involved. The Canton (Ohio) Public Schools, for example, have successfully used children as book reviewers. Students in elementary schools read and comment on from 25 to 50 new books per school year. The nature of their reactions is an important factor in deciding whether the book is or is not recommended for purchase. Involving others in the selection process not only adds new dimensions to the collection, but better insight is gained into user's tastes and interests and new avenues of communication are opened between the center and its patrons. Media specialists also find that participation of this sort results in increased interest in the general welfare of the media center.

Diversity in Material. Although satisfying the needs of the center's patrons is the major guiding principle behind selection, when building the basic, or core collection the maxim should be: "Get something on everything." This means that the center's collection should contain information in each of the important divisions of human knowledge. In a high school, for example, Greek philosophy may not be a topic of great popularity, yet most certainly the media center should have some material on it.

Diversity in Students. Within classes in any heterogeneously organized classroom there are three basic kinds of students: above-average achievers, average achievers and below-average achievers. Translated specifically into terms of reading ability: there will be those reading above their grade level, those reading at the expected level, and those reading below it. When buying material on a given topic, the media specialist must therefore bear in mind the various ability levels of the students who will be investigating this topic and try to obtain a sufficiently wide range of materials to be useful at each of these levels.

Purchasing for Nonusers. One selection trap that must be avoided is purchasing solely for the teachers and students in the school who use the media center regularly. If the taste and interests of the nonusers are not represented in the collection, appropriate material is not at hand when the opportunity occurs to convert them into center users. Thus a second maxim might be: "There should be something for everybody" in the center.

Input from the Media Specialist. Throughout this section stress has been placed on the involvement of a number of people in the selection process. This does not in any way mean that the media specialist abdicates responsibility in this area. Unlike many college libraries that buy material only on specific requests from faculty members, media center professional personnel should initiate some orders, act as representatives for those who are not involved in selection, and have the final word in approving items for purchase.

Selection, Not Censorship. Selection is a positive process, and in evaluating the contents of materials remember the aim is neither to shock nor to protect. Overprotection can be as harmful as overexposure. Certain guidelines and limitations will be adopted for purchasing center material solely because of the maturity of the center's audience, but emphasis must not be on what "shouldn't" but what "should" be purchased. It should be remembered that, through mass media, young people are much more knowledgeable about social issues and once taboo subjects than their counterparts were a generation ago.

In trying to avoid controversial subjects or shunning basic realities, the media center collection can become so safe that it is deadly dull and out of touch with the students. Where an item is purchased that is a particularly potent target for the censor, a special file should be kept noting reviews or discussions involving it in other censorship battles. The American Library Association's *Intellectual Freedom Newsletter* is a good source of information for this file.

Subjectivity vs. *Objectivity.* There is always present the temptation to buy from the standpoint of one's own interests. If, for example, a burning interest in Greek drama is not shared by members of the faculty and student body, or is not part of the curriculum, purchases in this area will be minimal. On the other hand, the subject of automobiles may appear to be quite dull, but it is usually one of the primary interests of teenage boys. Purchases should be made from the user's point of view—not what the student *should* be reading or using, but rather what students want, need, and are capable of using.

Media and Messages. When selecting materials, match the message with the appropriate media. The question that should be asked is: Is this medium the most appropriate and best suited to convey the contents of the material? As an example, a motion picture that shows how seeds travel would probably be better than a filmstrip, because the idea of movement is such an integral part of this learning experience.

Duplication. User demand is the yardstick that should determine the extent to which duplication of materials takes place. Yet some media specialists associate duplication of titles with wastefulness; they think that buying a second copy uses funds that should be spent on a different title, thus increasing the general scope of the collection. Obviously, however, it is better to have five copies of a book that is constantly in circulation than five different titles, four of which stay unread on the shelves. With books, paperbacks afford an easy and inexpensive way to supply additional copies of a popular title.

Weeding. The term "weeding" means in library terms what it does in gardening: to eliminate the unsuitable or unwanted. Three types of material should be weeded: (1) the out-of-date and no longer authentic. This condition occurs very frequently with science material, but no single subject is immune; (2) the worn-out or badly damaged. Sometimes repairs can be made—for example books can be rebound—but costs should be weighed carefully against the price of a replacement or of a different title; (3) the unpopular or unused. These titles are perhaps the most difficult to throw out because in some cases it is an admittance that an inappropriate purchase has been made; in other cases, however, it simply means that tastes and interests have shifted. Nevertheless, it is useless to have collections clogged with deadwood that obscures media that do attract youngsters. It is recommended that 4–5 percent of a collection should be weeded each year. This, of course, applies only to collections that have been in existence for a few years.

Selection and Space Limitations. If space limitations are interfering with new purchasing, explore more efficient storage systems so that new material can still be added to the collection. Two obvious ways are to "retire" infrequently used items to other parts of the school and to rotate collections of recreational reading materials to various classrooms.

Technical Services and Selection. Media centers that are responsible for their own processing should try to prepare an item for circulation as quickly as possible. This applies particularly to topical materials and materials that have been specifically requested. If rapid processing is not possible, the material should be allowed to circulate for a time uncataloged. The rapidity with which users' requests are answered will be directly reflected in their interest in future acquisitions.

Use of Several Selection Aids. Using only one or two selection aids is restrictive; using many aids will help assure wiser decisions in purchasing materials that add greater depth and more variety of points of view to your collection.

Review of Selection Aids. Tastes and needs are constantly changing; a book considered unsuitable one school year, may be very useful the following year. Therefore, a system of continuous review of selection aids should be organized. The basic retrospective ones should be checked at least once a year.

Cooperative Acquisitions. There are many cooperative acquisition projects presently operating at the university and public library level. One of the most widely publicized was the Farmington Plan involving purchasing of foreign language materials. Schools within a particular area can also band together to formulate mini-Farmington Plans, whereby each school at a particular level is assigned a particular subject specialty or area of concentration (these could be arrived at by thorough examination of curriculum requirements). This method could also be used to insure that at least one cooperating school has a copy of expensive items like a well-reviewed set of sound filmstrips or a new edition of a multivolume reference work.

Out-of-Print Materials. An out-of-print notice from a jobber, publisher, or producer should not be interpreted as meaning complete unavailability. With print materials, if their acquisition is extremely important, check with out-of-print dealers, catalogs of facsimile edition companies, or the book production services of University Microfilms in Ann Arbor, Michigan. These routes are particularly valuable in building up local history collections.

Publisher's and Manufacturer's Catalogs. Extreme care must be exercised in using publisher's or manufacturer's catalogs in the selection process. They should be considered only as descriptive announcements of what is available, not as an indication of quality. Buying on the basis of the blurbs found in these catalogs is dangerous. Quotes from dependable reviewing sources published in these annotations are often misleading; excerpting can turn a panning into what appears to be a rave. An exception should be pointed out: several jobbers and wholesalers have hired reputable media personnel to compile lists of recommended materials, basic book lists, and the like; if the authority that compiled the work is noncommercial and reliable, then the list may be considered a valid selection aid.

Series and Comics. Even the most prestigious of series may vary in quality from one title to the next, and regardless of the standards of quality within a series, in all likelihood not all titles will be suitable for a collection. Each item, whether part of a series or not, should be treated as an individual entity that must be evaluated on its own merits. Educators in general are scornful of such "pulp" series as the Hardy Boys and Nancy Drew. Certainly the literary quality of these books is practically nonexistent. But if this is the only level on which students are reading, inclusion of some of these series books and similar titles should be seriously considered. Here, at least, is a beginning upon which the media center staff can perhaps build through proper reading guidance.

The same policy should apply to comics. Here the question of quality is not quite as important because there are a number of comics of acceptable quality now in paperback format that could easily be included in a media collection. Some examples are: *Peanuts, Pogo, Mad,* and *Ripley's Believe It or Not.*

Book Clubs. Through use of petty cash or similar contingency funds, many media centers join book clubs. They are generally of two main types: those that distribute hardcover editions (for example, the Junior Literary Guild, for ages 5–16, and the adult clubs, Book-of-the-Month and Literary Guild of America) and the paperback clubs (for example, the various Scholastic Book Services and Young Readers Press clubs). While both types of clubs offer carefully selected, appealing titles, the hardcover clubs give subscribers the advantage of getting new books quickly and at a fair discount over publishers' prices (although sometimes not as much as a book jobber might give) and paperback clubs offer very inexpensive reprints of well-received hardcover editions and in some cases original titles that are available only through the clubs.

Gifts and Free Materials. Media centers should welcome gifts as possible additions to the collection. In developing a policy for receiving gifts two points should be stressed: (1) only items appropriate to the collection will be kept; (2) the center may dispose of the remaining material any way it wishes.

A wealth of free material commonly referred to as "sponsored material" is available from various industries, manufacturers, transportation companies and so on. Before accepting items of sponsored material for the collection check to see if there is excessive advertising or proselytizing, distortions of fact to promote products or points of view, or material about one company's wares stated in a way that would prejudice the reader or viewer against a competitor's products. Some school districts have also adopted specific regulations concerning the presence of advertising in the schools. Inquiries should be made on the matter before final decisions are made.

The Professional Library. Faculty members should have available to them a collection of up-to-date, well-selected professional literature. At the single school level, the size and nature of this collection will depend on budgetary limitations and the resources available at the district level or from other agencies. Because the faculty should be largely responsible for selecting the contents of this special collection, a committee made up of teachers and a representative from the media center should be charged with developing acquisition and administrative procedures.

In addition to basic and current books, periodicals, and pamphlets on education, the professional library should contain such items as sample textbooks, workbooks, curriculum guides, indexes to periodicals, media catalogs, as well as local, state, and Federal documents related to education. To insure access to other collections of related materials, the media specialists will have to organize or become part of a network that facilitates borrowing from the district's library, other school systems, neighboring colleges and universities, or perhaps the state's central library agency. *The Teacher's Library* (NEA) is a useful booklet that contains pointers on selection as well as a basic bibliography of books and periodicals in the field of education.

Local History Collections. Each media center should build up a collection on local history and community affairs, whether or not these topics are considered a formal part of the curriculum. The material can be used in a variety of ways: at election time, for background information on community projects, for debating clubs, when classroom discussions turn to topics on public affairs with local implications. In addition to regular printed and pictorial sources, including pertinent community directories, a special file should be maintained of clippings from local newspapers and available material on community industries, clubs, and church and professional organizations. A separate card file should also be maintained on local resources—field trips, speakers, collections of materials, etc.—that are available to the school. Many schools have instituted photography projects and have supplemented their media center's collections on local topics with photographs of key installations, historical landmarks, and persons of local importance. Others have developed oral history collections by taping interviews with prominent residents and storing the tapes in the media center. Particularly important interviews may be transcribed and used in print form.

Reevaluation of the Collection. Like Topsy, collections often just grow. Media selectors should bear in mind that with each new addition or deletion new balances and relationships are created. Continuous reevaluation of the collection is necessary to determine what areas are showing greatest growth, whether the greatest-growth areas are commensurate with users' needs, and that all types of media are being added in proper balance. This kind of watchdog activity can keep the collection balanced, vital, and in line with the school's needs.

Long-Range Planning. To insure continuity, perspective, and orderly progression in collection development, future goals and the steps by which they will be reached should be carefully outlined by the media center personnel in cooperation with faculty and administration. Priorities must be stated and timetables organized that specify the sequential stages for achieving desired growth. This kind of planning is particularly important in respect to major expenditures, such as investing in new equipment or retiring and replacing machines in the existing collection. If possible, a three- to five-year plan should be developed. To ensure the long-range plan's flexibility and use under various circumstances, for each year it should state alternative courses of action that take various levels of funding into consideration. Other aspects of the interrelationship between the selection process and the media center's budget are discussed in chapter 5.

CRITERIA FOR SELECTING MEDIA AND EQUIPMENT

The use of criteria helps objectify an otherwise highly subjective operation. Criteria are necessary on two levels: (1) specific criteria for selecting individual types of educational materials—books, films, filmstrips, etc. (these may be found in Appendix III) and (2) general criteria for selecting all types of educational materials. The following are criteria in the latter category. Such general standards are usually outlined in the school's written selection policy and may be used either when examining or previewing the material firsthand or when selecting through the use of reviewing media. Criteria for selecting related equipment may be found at the end of this section.

If these lists seem formidable, be assured that application of them becomes in time automatic and effortless.

GENERAL CRITERIA FOR SELECTING EDUCATIONAL MATERIALS

Authority. This refers to the qualifications of the people responsible for creating the material (the author; the producer or publisher) and how capable and prepared they are to have undertaken the project in question.

Information on their background, education, experience, reputation and previous works will supply useful clues. Also, a determination of the nature and repute of research sources used is useful. If the item under consideration is an adaptation or revision of another work, the extent and nature of the differences should be determined; often these are so slight that a media center that owns the old work may not wish to purchase the revision.

Scope. Essentially this refers to the overall purpose and coverage of the material. When the breadth and limitation of scope are determined, the work should be compared to others on the same subject to see if it presents a fresh viewpoint or if it displaces, amplifies, or simply repeats existing material in the collection.

Format and Technical Quality. The physical makeup of the material should be appropriate to its content. It should meet acceptable production standards and be of sufficient quality to help promote use. Each form of educational material has distinctive physical characteristics.

Authenticity. The contents should be checked for validity, reliability, completeness, as well as for the degree of bias or objectivity presented. Recency is also extremely important. The copyright date and imprint date should relate favorably; sometimes they are valid guides to the up-to-dateness of the material. However, the contents will usually have to be examined to make a final and accurate determination of currency.

Treatment and Arrangement. The material should be clearly presented in a well-organized fashion. This involves a logical development and the sequence of the content should flow naturally and easily from one section into another. The material should be well balanced and place particular stress on the elements of greatest importance. The arrangement should bear a direct relationship to its potential use and be judged by the degree to which it facilitates that use. The style of the presentation, the general comprehension level, and the nature of the concepts being developed must be appropriate, both to the intended audience and to the nature and depth of coverage intended. The material should be developed in light of sound educational principles and make provision for such elements as review and reinforcement. Finally, the work should catch and hold the user's interest and, hopefully, provide stimulation for further learning.

Aesthetic Considerations. The item must be acceptable artistically, with each separate element combining to form an aesthetically pleasant whole. The material should appeal to the imagination, to the senses, and to the intellect, so that the user's taste and sense of artistic appreciation will be developed.

Price. The acquisition of any piece of material, and particularly expensive ones, must be seen in relation to existing budget limitations. It might be necessary to find out if a satisfactory substitute at a lower price is available. Certainly the initial cost will be weighed against the amount of intended use.

Special Features. The media specialists should try to ascertain the characteristics, if any, that make the item under consideration distinctive or perhaps unique from others of the same type and on the same subject. These might be, for example, an unusual approach to a subject matter, the presence of usage guides, sets of questions and answers, or a list of suggested followup activities.

General Suitability. Having evaluated the material in the preceding general terms, the media specialist now must view the material in light of the school's existing collection. The appropriateness of the material to the school's educational objectives and curriculum is an important factor. Such questions as: Is there sufficient need for the item? How many will use it? Is it suited to the particular needs and abilities of those who will use it? must be answered.

General Criteria for Selecting Audiovisual Equipment

Criteria for selecting audiovisual equipment vary considerably depending on the type of items being selected and the specific use for which each is intended. Some general basic criteria that may be applied regardless of the unique nature of the equipment under consideration follow. Specific lists on individual items (projectors, tape recorders, etc.) are given in Appendix IV.

Safety. This consideration is of particular importance if the equipment is to be used by children. Make sure that there are no rough protruding edges, that the equipment is well balanced and does not topple easily, that dangerous moving parts (e.g., fan blades) are not exposed, and that electrical connections are suitably covered and grounded. Where applicable, simple and direct instructions for use should be included, preferably printed on the machine. It is also important to determine that no further hazards are produced during use—for example, a machine that generates excessive heat during operation can be a potential source of danger for youngsters.

Ease of Use. One frequent stumbling block to the use of audiovisual equipment is the complexity of the procedures necessary for its operation. For example, the bother of setting up a portable roller screen and threading a projector have been formidable deterrents to the use of the 16mm film. The use of permanently installed wall screens and self-threading projectors have now helped change this particular situation.

Factors to be considered in determining ease of use are the number of steps necessary for operation, number of controls (switches, plugs) to be activated, accessibility and ease of use of these controls and any directions for their operation, and the manual dexterity needed. The length and nature of the formal instructions for successfully operating the machine are also important.

Performance. The piece of equipment must operate efficiently and consistently at a high level of performance. Depending on the type of equipment, this "high standard" involves such factors as the nature of the picture or image, fidelity of sound reproduction, presence of speed controls, amount of distracting noise or light produced, and quality of mechanical construction. The published results of field testing (preferably done by someone other than the manufacturer) can serve as guidelines in determining performance levels. Sources that can be checked for this type of information are *Consumer Reports, Educational Product Report* (Educational Products Information Exchange Institute), and *Library Technology Reports* (ALA).

Size, Weight, Design. The physical properties of a piece of equipment often predetermine usage levels. For example, lightness of weight and carrying ease are two essential characteristics of equipment intended for home circulation. Great bulk inhibits use; so does poor or inadequate cases or carrying devices. Not only should the design and exterior be attractive; it should also be capable of withstanding hard usage.

Maintenance and Service. Equipment should be built sturdily enough to hold up under the tough wear of a school situation. Strongly built equipment requires fewer repairs, but if minor ones become necessary, these machines should be constructed so that the repairs can be made quickly and easily. Replacement parts should be accessible, and suitable warranties or guarantees should be issued at the time of purchase. Two additional items for consideration are: (1) the amount of "on-the-spot" repair service available from the manufacturer or distributor as opposed to the time-consuming, costly process of sending an item back to the factory; (2) the availability from the manufacturer of personnel to give inservice training in the operation of the equipment.

Compatibility. Each new piece of equipment under consideration must be seen in relation to the school's entire media inventory to determine whether the acquisition of this new equipment will provide a logical extension of the existing collection. Often only special materials can be used with a particular machine, making the dual investment in both equipment and materials prohibitive. If a new item does essentially the same job as a model already in the collection, perhaps a duplication of existing equipment might be advised over buying the new material and expending valuable inservice-training time in acquainting patrons with its operation. The specifications of each new piece of equipment should be checked to see if spare parts and repair operations are similar to those used with equipment already in the collection.

Versatility. The number and variety of uses that can be made of a piece of equipment should strongly influence selection, particularly when budgetary funds are very restricted. Often the same machine can be used effectively in a variety of teaching situations—for large group and small group instruction, at home and in the classroom, or with primary children and high school students. In other cases, the addition of simple adapters can change some pieces of equipment to accept other types of materials. For example, an attachment may be purchased to convert some filmstrip projector models into slide projectors or microfilm viewers into ones that also accept microfiche.

Availability of Software. There have been incidences of manufacturers marketing equipment for which there has not been a sufficient amount of compatible educational material issued to justify the initial equipment purchase. Promises of greater output often have not been met. As a result, many schools have inventories of expensive equipment and diminishing opportunities for using it. This was particularly true a few years ago with the sudden and alarming development of a variety of teaching machines without the necessary wide accompaniment of programs. The media selector should determine the nature and extent of the materials available suitable for the equipment under consideration. Occasionally, as in the case of Super eight millimeter sound film, for example, an initial delay in purchase of equipment until film production plans for the various systems were announced allowed extra time to weigh the merits of each before final acquisition plans were made.

Cost. The price of each prospective purchase must be evaluated in terms of the school's total equipment budget. Sometimes the purchase of some expensive items will have to be postponed, or less expensive ones substituted, because of budgetary limitations. However, in the selection process the quality of the product should always be emphasized. Price lists can be consulted to find out costs of comparable equipment from other companies, but it should be stressed that when an item is priced higher than that of a competitor, superior performance standards could be the reason.

Need. Finally, all the above factors must be weighed against the answers to questions that probe the long-range usefulness of the acquisition: Is the purpose for which this equipment is being purchased worthy of the expense? What will be the consequences if the equipment is not acquired? Will the equipment be used often enough and by enough people to warrant purchase now?

9

ACQUISITION AND ORGANIZATION

Staff functions and program activities depend not only upon the resources of the center but also upon the organizational patterns adopted by the center. The main goals of this managerial function are to acquire resources and make them available as quickly and efficiently as possible. An efficient processing system is a prerequisite for achieving these goals. Many individual school media centers rely on commercial processing as an important adjunct to organization.

This chapter deals with the general rules that apply to acquisition in school media centers with an emphasis on the minimally staffed center in an individual school building. The system of bidding is discussed. Technical services purchasing, processing, and cataloging are treated, as are considerations involving local production and circulation procedures. An explanation of the types of records and reports that are needed in individual media centers is also included.

When a budget is approved by a board of education, final decisions about expenditures must be made. If the funds are allocated as requested, the procedure is generally predetermined. If the budget requests have been reduced, the media specialist must design a priority system for expenditures. Since reductions affect the entire instructional program, the media specialist should discuss these problems with the principal, department heads, or grade-level coordinators. Once these preliminaries are completed, the media specialist is ready to proceed to the two fundamental steps in the acquisition process, bidding and purchasing.

BIDDING

The Federal government as well as many state education departments and school systems require competitive formal bidding for purchase of materials, supplies, or equipment in excess of specified amounts that vary from state to state—in some, for example, the cutoff figure is $1,000. These agencies also may require a less formalized bidding process for amounts that fall below a specified minimum, for example, $300. State law, city ordinance, school board resolution, or administrative order are some of the regulations that frequently mandate competitive bidding for all types of purchases, including materials and equipment.

The aim of bidding in expending public funds is to get the best goods and services at the lowest possible cost; the bid thus serves as a guard against favoritism to a vendor as well as a device for conserving public funds. The formal bid should also protect the school and media center by the inclusion of penalty provisions and cancellation clauses for substandard or delinquent service on the vendor's part. It is also designed to give the supplier or vendor an opportunity to be considered by a larger buying audience, i.e., an entire state. In practice, however, each media specialist with experience in competitive bidding realizes that bidding raises many problems: the negotiation of the contract through a fiscal agency (usually at the school district level, but sometimes through state or Federal agencies); the possibility of poor service from the vendor; the accuracy of the billing. Vendors, on the other hand, have often encountered problems in dealing with some schools because of delayed payment, a lack of partial payment on merchandise received, and seasonal ordering. Both find that unless the school media center works closely with the business office or school purchasing agency, the lack of coordination complicates the process.

FORMAL BIDDING

The term "formal bidding" usually refers to a system in which sealed bids from vendors for certain items are publicly opened on a given date that has been advertised locally. Firms that meet certain qualifications and have given satisfactory service in the past are often invited to enter a bid. Some nonstandard or monopoly items that there are not enough firms to compete for may be excepted from the bid requirements—for example, a specialized type of equipment or a specific encyclopedia. Another form of formal bidding is the state contract method by which firms negotiate a contract for a period of time with a state education department. As an alternative to local competitive bidding, school media centers can use state contracts. A list of dealers who have a contract with a state education department is generally available from the local district business office. As a typical example of a state that requires formal bidding, the New York State Education Department expects all items to be placed on bid unless they represent either or both of the following categories: (1) an annual total expenditure for one item or type of item within a school district of less than $1,000; (2) a monopoly item (i.e., an item available at a fixed price from only one source).

INFORMAL BIDDING

The term "informal bidding" suggests a less formalized bidding method and usually means that the bid need not be advertised. As few as two or three firms may be asked, even by telephone, for a bid price on the item or items needed. This system is widely used when the expenditure for an item falls between the minimum and maximum figures required for informal and formal bidding, e.g., $100 and $1,000, respectively, in New York.

If neither the competitive bid nor the state contract bid methods is used, the school media center and local business office should agree on a standard bidding practice and set up guidelines. Whatever the procedure, the bidding should: (1) provide satisfactory service to the media center; (2) guarantee fiscal integrity to the business office; and (3) grant realistic specifications on items for the vendors. The following guidelines should be written into the bids:

Specifications. A detailed description of the item, e.g., for binding, saddle-stitching might be requested, or for 16mm projectors, a freeze-frame device might be stipulated.

Ordering frequency. A schedule for anticipated ordering—e.g., large orders in the fall and spring with regular school year biweekly orders.

Time of delivery. A time schedule for delivery expectations—e.g., a 50 percent fulfillment of order within 60 days with a 90–120 day period for completion of order.

Substitutions and changes by suppliers. A definition of what substitutions and changes will be acceptable—e.g., revisions of older titles or newer models of equipment, but not a different filmstrip on the same subject.

Quality and condition of merchandise. A list of unacceptable conditions—e.g., transparencies that differ in definition or color from the samples; prints that are damaged in transit.

Policy on service and returns. A two-part statement on the expectations of (1) the service desired—e.g., a first time service visit to install and put in working condition sophisticated equipment such as dial access—and (2) the conditions under which materials may be returned—e.g., books with missing pages.

Invoices and packing slips. A notice that lists the number and disposition of the shipping and billing statements—e.g., sending duplicate copies of invoices to the media center and guaranteeing the arrival of shipments, with enclosed slips listing the material or equipment delivered.

Bid security. A statement that requires a bond or stipulates penalties in case of default of the agreement. For example, a school may ask a vendor (1) to secure a bond before the school will entertain a bid in excess of $8,000, for instance for 16mm projectors, or (2) to deduct a percentage of the final payment if all materials or equipment have not been received at the agreed upon delivery termination period.

Discounts. A list by type of material or equipment of the acceptable range of discounts—e.g., 10–20 percent for technical or scientific print titles; 33–40 percent for trade print titles; 10 percent off list price for new model equipment, or larger discounts for quantity orders.

Full and partial payments. An agreement to reimburse the vendor within a reasonable time period for both orders delivered in full and in partial shipments—e.g., guarantee payment by school within 30–60 days of completion of either type of order fulfillment.

Exhibit and exhibition merchandise. A written contract form that stipulates such things as the time period between receipt and return of goods; the condition of the materials; the kind and amount of materials and necessary display items; the method and length of payment, if any; if the materials are to be sold, the legal responsibility for the consignment, the insurance coverage, etc.

Services of an area representative. A statement that explains the expectation of ready local help from distant company's field representatives —e.g., the availability of a sales or service person from a national producer of transparencies or manufacturer of photoduplication equipment to adjust claims or advise on use.

Cancellation clause. An enforceable statement that notes the conditions under which either the vendor or school may cancel an order—e.g., if the vendor is not reimbursed after a reasonable period of time; if a delivery is delayed beyond a reasonable period of time; if the titles in an order are substituted for those originally specified, etc.

Consignment privileges. A list of conditions under which materials may be delivered and sold or used under a deferred-payment agreement— e.g., paperbacks for sale in a media-center-operated store or at a materials fair may be purchased on consignment and paid for as they are sold; book clubs often use some form of this method. Time periods and accounting methods are important in the listing of consignment privileges.

Conditions of warranty. A statement that describes the circumstances under which materials or equipment may be repaired or exchanged—e.g., a cassette player may be exchanged or a missing or malfunctioning part repaired free of charge within 90 days of purchase.

No standardized bid form that covers all these guidelines is presently in general use. The forms devised by governing bodies vary from one type for all merchandise to many different types, some of which may contain detailed specifications for a particular commodity. Some agreement among purchasing officials does exist, however, about the importance of the bases on which bids are evaluated; the least bid price in relation to the bidder's responsibility to the vendor. The lowest dollar amount bid price should not be the sole criterion, because the service and the speed with which it is given are also fundamental concerns in the acquisition of media. The responsibility of the bidder, whether manufacturer, producer, dealer, or agent, rests on many factors, including: a sound financial condition; some experience in the work; good past performance. Whenever circumstances permit, the media specialist should consult with the school purchasing officer on these matters.

In dealing with the bidding process, the media specialist should also be aware of the following points:

1. Each item, from pamphlets to video tapes to newspapers, is unique and often requires a different vendor or purchasing method. For example, the materials may be produced privately or commercially, issued by government, societies, universities, or others, or be available on exchange. These factors often serve to exempt school media center materials from a bid requirement.

2. Some state laws and local school system regulations have exempted library materials from a bid requirement.

3. The school district's requirements.

4. The necessity for a solid working relationship in which the school media center's needs may be mutually understood and determined with the school district business office and in which the media specialist participates in the evaluation of the bids.

GENERAL CONSIDERATIONS IN RELATION TO VENDORS

Orders should be placed with reputable business concerns. Some procedures that can help media specialists avoid unsatisfactory service or fraudulent business practices are:

Examine and appraise items on deposit at educational media centers prior to ordering.

Utilize lists of sources in the professional literature.

Seek out other media specialists' recommendations.

Get information about local firms from the Better Business Bureau.

In addition, the media specialist should expect a vendor to fulfill the following criteria:

Maintain adequate physical facilities and a warehouse with a sizeable inventory of items described in the state contract specifications or descriptions of the firm, in order to be able to fill a majority of orders from stock.

Have assets, capital, and a credit rating sufficient to handle potential business.

Have the staff, production, and operating routines necessary to fulfill service requirements, including prompt reporting and follow-up on shipping orders.

Have a satisfactory record in fulfilling similar orders for others.

Each item may be ordered from its originating source—a publisher, producer, or manufacturer—or from wholesalers or jobbers. Many media specialists will order items in a variety of ways, depending on how the format is traditionally distributed. Increasingly, traditionally print-oriented wholesalers are stocking nonprint items in an effort to simplify the media center's acquisition problems. Wholesale distributors of some mix of print and nonprint items to a regional area are best identified through their advertisements in school media and library periodicals, particularly in notices in professional organization bulletins and newsletters. Two important sources for help in identifying suppliers and vendors for specific items are *The Audiovisual Marketplace*, biannual (R. R. Bowker), and *The Audio-Visual Equipment Directory*, annual (National Audio-Visual Association). The first title includes a directory section that identifies under each company's name the print and nonprint items it handles. The second title lists types of equipment as well as vendors.

As single-source service increases, both national and regional suppliers will announce their entry into the field in audiovisual and library periodicals and directories. At this writing, the following five single-source wholesalers handle a variety of media and supplies on a national distribution basis: Alesco (Paramus, New Jersey); Baker and Taylor (Somerville, New Jersey); Bro-Dart (Williamsport, Pennsylvania; or City of Industry, California); Demco Education Corp. (Madison, Wisconsin; or Fresno, California); Gaylord (Syracuse, New York; or Stockton, California).

PURCHASING

Another part of the acquisition process is the preparation of purchase orders. This step lends itself to an organized, routine approach. A network of libraries or a school system with a central administrative unit can avail itself of the purchasing economies afforded by central coordination of orders, and the entire routine of purchasing may be handled by on-line computer processing. Where the ordering is not centralized, the ordering system should be designed by the media specialist in the individual school and approved by the school business office. Two considerations are important: the procedures should eliminate unnecessary duplication and should use simple standardized order forms.

ORDER RECORDS

The following steps for maintaining order records may be used by any media center. Order cards, available commercially from library supply houses, contain appropriate spaces for purchasing information. The cards may also be easily adapted to supply other needed data. The cards may be used early in the selection process by giving them to teachers, administrators, students, and community members, as needed in the particular situation, to note their requests for materials. Because acquisition is a continuous process, the center's patrons should be regularly reminded to turn in their order cards to the media center. This cumulative file can be kept by subject, grade level, or larger curriculum division in order to apportion the funds equitably. When the appropriate fund for purchase of the item is assigned, the card may be filed in a separate, "awaiting purchase" file. Or, two or more files of order cards may also be kept, one for immediate purchase, the others for future acquisition when funds are available. Usually these order files will serve more efficiently if they are subdivided by media format, because they will frequently be sent to vendors who specialize in one type of media, for example, academic games.

Before a purchase order is instituted, a clerk should carefully check the order card against the center's card catalog, shelflist, or "on order" files to determine whether the center already has or has ordered the item. The accuracy of the basic information posted on the order cards should also be checked against indexes and catalogs, such as *Books in Print*, NICEM indexes, *The Booklist*, and *LJ/SLJ Previews*.

Once the order card from the purchase files has been appropriately checked, a multiple-copy requisition form may be typed for each item on the order card. The card may then be placed in the shelflist above the rod in the card catalog drawer to indicate the "on order" nature of the material. Finally, with the addition of the classification number, the order may be used as the shelflist card after the ordered item is received.

ORDER PROCESSING

This section deals with order-processing methods and several steps of physical preparation of material (other than classification and cataloging, which are discussed later in this chapter) that are required to make the item usable in the school media center.

Centralized Ordering and Processing

Processing at the single school level has been unsatisfactory in several respects, not the least of which is the time factor, and experience indicates that some form of centralized processing or use of commercial sources should be established to relieve the individual school of this responsibility.

Much has been written about the advantages of central or commercial processing. In summary the advantages are:

Personnel in the media center are freed to supply increased services to patrons.

Substantial savings in time, labor, and money are produced through larger discounts from jobbers, utilizing clerks for routine jobs, and reducing duplication of effort.

A large-scale, systematized work flow produces greater efficiency and reduces processing time.

Uniformity in cataloging and classification is produced.

Business routines are centralized and simplified.

Union catalogs to facilitate interlibrary loan and prevent unnecessary duplication of expensive materials can be prepared easily.

Some of the larger school systems have developed processing centers that rely heavily on data processing equipment. It is still possible, however, to organize an effective operation when automated devices are not available. For example, the Montgomery County (Maryland) Public Schools have a centralized processing unit that operates efficiently, although most steps are handled manually. Here are the steps by which materials are ordered and processed within the centralized unit.

A school makes out a six-copy, color-coded multiple-order slip, removes one copy for filing at the school and sends the remaining five-part form to the centralized processing center. There the first copy of the five-part form is interfiled by publisher or distributor with orders from other schools. The slips are then arranged by titles and sent to the respective vendors. The second copy of the order slip is used to check the authority file to determine if a master set of catalog cards exists in the center. If so a set of cards is reproduced and pockets and spine labels are printed. The three remaining copies of the order form are placed with these materials until the arrival of the order. If cards are not available, the copies of the order form are held until the material is received. When it is delivered, the purchase price is entered on the three remaining copies of the order form. One copy is then sent to the center's accounting office, another is attached to the invoice, and the third is placed with the material and eventually sent back with the processed material to the school. Media without catalog cards are sent to the catalog section and cataloged before the remaining steps in the process are taken, such as spine lettering and pasting in of pockets. New master sets of cards are sent to the authority file where they are filed by title. The center has a standing order for sets of catalog cards from such outlets as H. W. Wilson Company and the Library of Congress (for filmstrip cards). When the material arrives in the school the media center personnel complete the processing routine by checking for errors and adding necessary information to the shelflist card.

Because the processing center in Montgomery County services about 200 schools, the maintenance of an authority, or master file and a card-production unit is economical. Other centers may wish simply to order sets of cards, or processing kits, from their jobbers and from the manufacturer.

There are several alternative approaches to establishing a central processing center in each school district, and local conditions differ so considerably that in some cases efficiency and economy might suggest other solutions. Commercial cataloging is now available at reasonable prices through several companies. Although their major strength has been in the area of book processing, their coverage for processing of nonbook materials is increasing. It is also possible for schools to contract with other outside agencies for their processing needs. A few states, North Carolina and Rhode Island, for example, have established statewide processing units. Some schools have reached agreements with public library systems, other school districts, or regional educational agencies to handle processing. A key factor is the availability of processing for audiovisual materials. Since many of these agencies do not offer this crucial service, some school districts have found it advisable to rely on the outside agency only for book processing and to create supplementary centers to process their nonprint media. Regardless of the pattern adopted, media should arrive at the school ready for use. In this way processing at the single school level can be confined to those few educational materials produced within the school that cannot be handled by a central agency.

Single School Ordering and Processing

When the media center in the individual school must be responsible for taking care of its own technical services it will need to develop its own appropriate ordering and processing procedures.

Ordering. A six-copy, color-coded order form may also be used, as illustrated in the following example:

1st copy (white original)—for vendor.
2nd copy (blue)—duplicate for vendor.
3rd copy (yellow)—for school business office.
4th copy (pink)—for media center use.
5th copy (green)—for media center use.
6th copy (beige—on index card stock)—punched for shelflist.

As indicated in the example, the set of requisition forms is divided into two sections. The first section, including the original copy, is to go to the school's business office; the second section, including the sixth copy (i.e., on the index card stock) is to be kept by the media center—for example, in an "on order" file, arranged by vendor, awaiting the arrival of the item.

The school's standard purchase order—which contains all the pertinent information, such as vendor, address, total price (if not a bid price, the list price is usually given), special instructions, and the legend, ". . . as per attached forms," should be attached to the first three copies, or first section *for each title or item that is being ordered from that vendor* and then sent to the school's business office for official authorization and mailing to the vendor.

For efficient follow-through in the ordering procedure, the school business office should retain a duplicate copy of each requisition form for its office files and send the original and a duplicate to the vendor with instructions to return one of the slips with each item in an order. The working arrangement should also allow the media specialist to telephone or wire for rush orders as needed on assurance to the vendor of an immediate confirmation purchase order. The media specialist should carefully check the center's expenditure records for the balances in each budget account, as well as the records that are kept in the school business office before using this system of confirmation-purchase-order type of ordering.

Processing Preparations. When shipments are received in the media center they should be opened, checked, and prepared for processing. A clerk or student aide may check the items and the enclosed packing slip against the three copies of the requisitions in the center's "on order" file. These slips, together with any processing element (Library of Congress catalog cards or processing kits from commercial producers), should be put with the item as it is checked in and placed on the processing assembly line. The status of the shipment should be noted by date on the media center's copy of the purchase order. These copies should be filed by vendor or purchase order number, whichever is used in the business office, to give the media specialist a quick-access ready-reference media center file that corresponds to the accounts for the center at the business office.

Upon receipt of the items, there should be three (or four if the vendor returns a copy) requisition slips that may be used in various ways. For example, one of the slips may be returned as a notification to the requesting patron; the index-card-stock copy may be used as an inventory "by format" card to supplement the inventory use of the shelflist card filed by subject or class; a third slip may be sent to department heads or grade-level teachers to provide a supplementary catalog of items especially useful for given areas; the fourth slip may be filed temporarily in the card catalog by title or author, whichever is more useful.

Because of the special characteristics of some of the media that are acquired by a center (e.g., microfilm that can be a monopoly item, film rentals, paperbacks, etc.), the media specialist should strive for the best possible working relationship with the business office in order to stream-line ordering procedures, eliminate unnecessary paperwork, and guarantee the speedy receipt of media. One of the ways to ensure the last, as well as the goodwill of suppliers, is to arrange for prompt payment of invoices for partial shipments of an order. There are several ways to circumvent regulations that an order must be completed before any invoices on a partial shipment can be paid. A simple one requires only that the business office issue a confirming purchase order to cover invoices for the material received.

The media center should receive a copy of the vendor's invoice, either from the vendor or the business office, so that a running statement of the media center account funds can be kept in the center. In this way the media specialist will be able at any time to determine the encumbrances against the account balances. The media specialist should also check regularly with the school business office to verify these amounts.

CLASSIFICATION AND CATALOGING

In organizing a collection a media specialist should keep user con-venience and accessibility uppermost in mind. Materials on the same sub-ject should be integrated and stored together if at all possible. Where physical conditions dictate housing parts of the collection by format, the same criteria involving accessibility should apply equally to all formats. Traffic flow, economical use of space, and user safety are factors of impor-tance in deciding organizational patterns, but these patterns should be sufficiently flexible to allow for some modification and future change.

CLASSIFICATION

Classification is the systematic arrangement of materials into groups according to some predetermined list of criteria. Of the number of classi-fication schemes in existence the one that has been almost universally adopted in media centers is the Dewey Decimal (DDC) Classification, developed by Melvil Dewey after his careful study of several systems used to classify knowledge. Dewey began work on his system in 1872 while a student library assistant at Amherst College. When it was published in 1876 it was greeted unenthusiastically by many librarians, but its growth in popularity paralleled the tremendous library expansion in the twentieth century. Its major rival is the Library of Congress (L.C.) classification system, which was developed in 1897 specifically for the recataloging of the Library of Congress's vast collection. The L.C. system uses both letters and numbers as location devices, and because of the complexity and the minuteness of its breakdown of subject matter, it has been adopted only for use with large or specialized collections. The DDC, on the other hand, has many advantages for use in school media centers:

1. It brings materials on the same subject together in a logical and uniform sequence.

2. It is sufficiently simple to be understood by both staff and patrons without frequent referral to classification schedules.

3. Materials organized by this system can be found and retrieved quickly.

4. Because the system moves from large subject areas to more specialized ones through the addition of numbers, the degree of sophistication of the classification can vary with the size and nature of collections.

5. It is used in most public libraries and other libraries with which the students would be familiar.

6. Commercial cataloging sources as well as standard bibliographies and media reviewing tools extensively utilize this classification system.

The three basic sources on how to catalog using the DDC are: *Dewey Decimal Classification and Relative Index*, 18th edition (Forest Press), *Sears List of Subject Headings*, 10th edition (H. W. Wilson), and *Anglo-American Cataloging Rules* (American Library Association).

Some media centers use the DDC for their print collection, but have devised other classifying arrangements for nonprint items, such as films, filmstrips, and phonograph records. The simplest and most common variation is to assign code names (e.g., F = film) and an accession number to the items and house each type of material separately, arranged by the numerical order in which they were acquired. There are obvious disadvantages to such a system: materials on the same subject are not housed together (nor could they be without extensive reclassification); items are separated by format rather than content; if duplicate copies are added, their call numbers will vary and the possibilities of meaningful browsing are lessened because of the absolute dependence on the card catalog as a locating device. The major obstacle in classifying all materials by DDC is that a standard system for cataloging nonprint media has not yet been officially adopted by the combined professional organizations in the field. The publication *Non-Book Materials: The Organization of Integrated Collections* (ALA) is an important milestone. Another is the Association for Educational Communications and Technology title, *Standards for Cataloging Nonprint Materials*.

Cataloging

The card catalog is an index to the media center's collection and thus is the basic key to the center's resources. Its primary purpose is to indicate the materials that are in the collection and their location. It also provides bibliographic data and a description of content for each item. The single dictionary catalog, which contains all the catalog cards (author, title, subject) in one alphabet, is the most common type found in media centers, although many experiments with divided catalogs have brought an encouraging response from patrons. In some divided catalogs only the subject and subject-related cards are filed separately; in others all three types are dispersed into three distinct alphabets. Much of the traditional confusion in catalog use can be avoided with the divided catalog. Because the locating of nonprint materials is done primarily from the subject approach, the subject file has become the largest and most-used part of the catalog. A separate file that integrates subject cards for all the library holdings would seem advisable, to simplify and, in general, help in locating materials.

Of the several types of cards that may be in the catalog, the three basic types are: main entry (author, artist, composer, issuing agency), title (with many such nonbook materials as transparencies, the title frequently is also the main entry), and subject. Other types of cards are for added entries (joint authors, illustrators), analytical data (specific content), and cross references. Some media centers have also experimented with a separate classified catalog with a single card for each item and arranged solely by call number. This differs from the shelflist in two respects: (1) it is for patrons' use; (2) it integrates the cards of all materials with the same number, regardless of each item's location in the library. This special catalog gives the number and nature of the media center's entire holdings in particular subject areas and is helpful in acquainting patrons quickly with the center's collection.

The media center's holdings will include some materials that do not warrant the expenditure of time and money for cataloging. Usually referred to generically as "ephemeral material" this part of the collection includes clippings and unmounted pictures, which are usually stored in file folders arranged alphabetically by subject. The subject lists used to organize these holdings should correspond to the one used for other materials (i.e., *Sears*). To direct patrons to the ephemeral material, subject cards should be inserted in the card catalog indicating where the additional items on the subject may be found—e.g., vertical file, picture file, map drawer, etc.

In the past some media centers adopted a system of color-coding their catalog cards to identify various kinds of media. For example, a strip of red at the top of a card would indicate the item was a filmstrip; green, a phonograph record, etc. However, the number of distinctive colors is limited, and with the proliferation of kinds of material in media centers various shades of each color have had to be used as designators, which often has only confused the patron. Color coding is now being discouraged, principally because commercial processors and manufacturers of catalog cards and kits have not adopted it. Instead, they issue plain white cards that designate the medium after the title and, quite frequently, at the top left corner above the call number.

Prior to the time that libraries began using catalog cards, the printed (or often handwritten) book catalog was the usual format for listing a library's holdings. This method was abandoned because it was time consuming and because it was difficult to keep the catalog up-to-date unless costly complete versions were issued frequently. The present increased application of computerized data processing in automating many library procedures has brought about a renewal of interest in the book catalog. As prices for computers become more realistic, some school systems are able to purchase them or to contract for the use of computer time and services from commercial firms. A few schools have already converted their traditional card catalog into book format. The book catalog has many advantages. Once the initial catalog has been prepared, multiple copies can be produced inexpensively and placed in classrooms or other important locations, either inside or outside the school. In addition to producing greater accessibility, book catalogs are more compact, require no expensive cabinets, and are easier to read than thumbing through files of cards. Another important advantage is the ease with which recataloging can be done in the book catalog by comparison to making similar changes in the card catalog. The single most important drawback to the book catalog is the initial expense of conversion.

Regardless of the format used—card or book catalog—each entry in the catalog should contain the following information:

Location Device. Usually the call number consisting of the Dewey Decimal number and the first two or three letters of the main entry (in the case of biographies, the name of the person written about is used).

Main Entry. In book materials, the author or person chiefly responsible for the preparation of the work; with nonprint media, frequently the title.

Title (and subtitle).

Medium Identification. E.g., film, filmstrip, etc.

Additional Main-Entry Information. E.g., coauthor, illustrator, or narrator.

Imprint. Name of publisher, producer, manufacturer, and copyright date.

Collation. A description of the physical quality of the material—e.g., number of pages or volumes, frames, sound or silent, length of running time, color or black and white. When applicable, a series note is also included.

Annotation or Contents Summary. Optional.

Tracings. A listing of headings for which additional cards have been prepared, such as subject headings and other added entries. (Found on catalog cards but not in a book catalog.)

Magazines are treated more simply. They are usually processed in the media center by stamping ownership marks in each issue as it arrives and accessioning it in the magazine record card file. A separate card for each magazine is kept in the file. The card contains a space for checking in each issue when it arrives, plus information on the name of the magazine, frequency of publication, and subscription date. This file should be accessible to all patrons, but it is also advisable to prepare lists of the media center's magazine holdings that can be distributed within the school and also placed close to the periodical indexes and magazine or microfilm storage facilities. Current issues of magazines should be displayed in transparent protective covers on shelves or racks. A checking record for daily newspapers is usually unnecessary unless the media center's holdings are very extensive. Weekly newspapers are processed like magazines.

LOCAL PRODUCTION OF MATERIALS

Although the range and variety of commercially prepared educational materials is extensive and increasing at a fast rate, there will always be a need in schools for educational materials that are useful only in a specific local situation and are, therefore, not available for purchase. For years either the chalkboard or the bulletin board was used almost exclusively to meet this need. Today the media center has become the headquarters for the production of a wide variety of educational materials suitable for learning experiences unique in a particular school. The following section describes the major types of local production equipment and supplies found in many media centers and their major uses. Specific equipment items, such as tape recorders, that accept both commercially and locally prepared materials, are described in Appendix IV. The general criteria for selecting equipment developed in chapter 8 may also be applied to equipment for local production. Specific emphasis, however, should be placed on versatility—for example, many laminating machines can also be used to produce color-lift transparencies, and thermocopiers will sometimes make both stencils and transparencies.

Mounting and Laminating Equipment

A number of techniques can be used for mounting flat pictures. The conventional method using rubber cement requires no special equipment, but the process is time consuming and the results can vary considerably in quality. A faster and more professional looking product can be obtained by using the dry-mount technique. Dry-mount tissue is very thin paper coated on each side with adhesive that becomes sticky when heat and pressure are applied. Although a common hand iron may be used, it is suggested for this purpose that a dry-mount press and tacking iron be part of the media center's basic equipment. Large maps or charts that require rolling and folding for convenient storage may also be mounted by this process by using a special backing cloth coated with adhesive on only one side. The center's dry-mount press should be big enough to handle the largest size material that it expects to mount and laminate.

Laminating, or affixing a transparent protective film to the face of a picture, can also be done in the dry-mount press. Several manufacturers produce special laminating film that can be used in their thermocopying machines. Also available are laminating acetates that may be applied by hand or with a cold-process laminating machine.

DUPLICATING AND THERMOCOPYING MACHINES

Multiple copies of printed material for use by teachers and students may be produced in a variety of ways, the simplest and most common being by spirit duplicator, or "ditto" machine. By writing or drawing on the master copy, a carbon impression is left on the underside from the attached dye sheet. Different colored dye sheets may be used. The dye is soluble in methyl alcohol—the "spirit"—placed in the drum of the machine. Although only a limited number of copies can be run from each master, the ease of preparation and operation has made this the most popular form of duplication. The 1969 national standards recommend that there be at least one spirit duplicator in each media center.

Other copying machines should also be available, if not in the center, at least where they are easily accessible to media personnel. The mimeograph machine, which uses stencils and an inking process, is not as versatile as the spirit duplicator, but generally is capable of producing more and higher quality copies per stencil. The gelatin hectographing process was once very popular, perhaps because it requires such a small initial investment—for some hectograph ink or carbon papers, gelatin compound, and a shallow cookie pan. The uncertain quality of the product and the limited number of copies possible (between 15 and 50) has made hectographing less popular recently.

Dittos and stencils as well as single copies may also be produced on thermocopying machines. This process exposes and develops specially coated film or paper through heat generated by an infrared lamp in the machine. Thermocopiers can reproduce only certain types of materials:

typewritten originals and carbons, mimeographed or printed material, and writing done with a soft lead pencil or with India ink. Ditto copies or writing done with most ballpoint, felt tip, or fountain pens cannot be reproduced by thermocopiers.

Other processes suitable for making a few copies at a time are electrostatic (xerography, electrofax), photocopy, and diazo. The diazo process is described below under "Transparency-Making Equipment."

Through their industrial arts classrooms or central printing facilities, many schools also have available to them more sophisticated equipment for producing printed materials, for example, printing machines that use either the letterpress method, which involves typesetting and preparation of plates, or the offset method.

Transparency-Making Equipment

Perhaps the most common locally produced transparencies are those handmade by drawing directly onto acetate sheets. Users of this technique should make sure that their drawing materials work well on acetate. Media center supplies should include a number of suitable felt pens and grease or wax pencils (with various size points), plus a supply of acetate and transparency mounts.

The diazo process (named after the diazo salt found on the acetate) is particularly suitable for the reproduction of colors, and—an added advantage—several copies of the same transparency can be produced easily. This process involves three steps: (1) producing a master on translucent paper (many diazo masters are available commercially), (2) printing the image on the diazo acetate by exposing it and the master to an ultraviolet light source, and (3) developing the image on the acetate by placing it in a bath of ammonium hydroxide fumes. Equipment may be purchased that contains units for both exposing and developing the film. Ultraviolet light printers can also be bought separately and any large-mouthed glass container may be used as the developing unit (the so-called pickle jar method).

Many of the duplicating machines found in the media center or elsewhere in the school can also be used for transparency making. For example, many thermocopying machines and spirit duplicators will accept acetate sheets and produce translucent transparencies.

Laminating equipment (both hot and cold) as well as the dry-mount press can be used to transfer both black and white or color pictures onto transparency acetate. Regardless of the picture-transfer method used, the original must be printed on paper stock that is clay coated. It is also important to remember that the original is destroyed during the process of color lifting.

Photographic Equipment

Increasingly, both teachers and students are utilizing photographic equipment of all types to produce a variety of educational materials—from still photographs and slide presentations to motion pictures and video tapes. To accommodate these needs, the media center should have at least a basic inventory of photographic equipment that includes several still picture cameras. Although fixed-focus and range-finder cameras are generally less expensive and perfectly adequate for long-range shooting, the reflex camera is more versatile and can be easily equipped with close-up lenses for photographing clearly at a distance of only a few inches. Copy stands with lighting attachments, light meters, and tripods are also important adjunct equipment. Many media centers now have darkroom facilities complete with equipment for developing and enlarging their own photographs.

Because of such innovations as cartridge loading and simplified focusing devices, very young children have become expert film makers. The further addition of the zoom lens permits a smooth and easy transition from one field of vision to another. Basic equipment for motion picture making involves an 8mm camera (preferably super 8), a 16mm camera, light meters, tripods, floodlights for special indoor filming, a film viewer, film splicer and scraper, rewinds, and extra reels. Video taping equipment has also recently become much less expensive and sufficiently simple to operate that the purchase is feasible for individual schools. Two essential steps to take before purchasing a major piece of photographic equipment for the media center are: (1) get the advice of knowledgeable persons in the field and (2) request a demonstration at which some of the prospective users can be present.

Lettering and Display Equipment

Within the media center there should be services—principally provided by media technicians—to help teachers and students produce posters, charts, dioramas, and other graphic material and to supply guidance and materials for bulletin boards, exhibits, and other forms of displays. Some of the skills involved in producing these instructional materials are often specialized, but with the use of commercially produced aids and other simplifying techniques, the results can be both attractive and professional looking. There are, for example, many inexpensive ready-to-use lettering devices on the market. A few of these are three dimensional letters (with or without pin backs), gummed punch-out letters, dry-transfer letters, rubber-stamp letters, and stencil lettering guides. The media center should contain not only a generous sampling of these but also a variety of other artist's supplies, including a wide selection of drawing pens, markers, and pencils; a supply of drawing paper and an illustrating board, spray-can paints, T-squares and other simple drafting instruments, and various cutting tools. Equipment should include a drawing board, primary (or bulletin) typewriter, and a paper cutter.

CIRCULATION

The chief aim of any circulation system is to facilitate the use of materials and ensure the accessibility of these materials to the users of the media center. Major criteria in evaluating a circulation system are: ease of use, absence of friction-causing elements, economy, and efficiency. Supplementary considerations involve: the desirability of formalizing registration procedures and issuing borrowers' identification cards, the simplicity of charging and discharging routines, the handling of overdues, the flexibility of the system in accommodating such preferred items as reserve books or vertical-file materials, and the ease of collecting circulation statistics. Some media centers, particularly at the secondary level, have experimented successfully with various mechanical, photographic, and electronic circulation devices. The initial cost of renting or purchasing the requisite equipment may be offset by greater efficiency and savings in staff time, particularly in situations of heavy circulation flow. The major drawback to these systems is that they require issuing user identification cards or plates. If these are kept on file in the center, an extra step—locating the card—is involved in the circulation procedure; if issued directly to the borrower, the cards are frequently lost, misplaced, or forgotten.

Most media centers use some variation of the Newark (N.J.) Circulation System. The essential elements are a book card (similar cards are used for other types of materials and equipment) and a date-due slip. The routines in the Newark System are so simple and so easily learned that its day-to-day operation can be handled by clerical or volunteer help. The user is asked to sign his or her name and homeroom number on the first vacant line of the book card. The date due is stamped next to the user's name on the book card and on the date-due slip. Some centers use a pre-stamped date-due card that replaces the book card in the book pocket. Book cards are placed in the circulation file until the material is returned or discharged. They are usually filed under due date by call number (or alphabetically by author in the case of fiction). Materials may be renewed easily by duplicating the initial procedure: the book card is retrieved from the circulation file and borrower again signs name and homeroom number (or writes "R" under the first signature), and a new date due is stamped on the card and slip.

Simple variations of this system may be used for materials that do not have book cards. For example, cards should be made out for each magazine title to be circulated. To check out a magazine, the borrower writes his or her name and homeroom number and the date of the magazine on the card. The due date is then stamped on the card. Some centers also stamp the date due on a slip pasted in the magazine or attach a date-due slip to the back cover with a paper clip. When the magazine is returned the borrower's name is crossed off the card.

Vertical-file materials may be checked out by having the borrower write his or her name and homeroom number and the number of items checked out and their subject headings on a book card marked "Vertical File." The material is placed in a protective envelope to which a date-due slip is attached. Discharging procedures are the same as with magazines.

When a patron requests material that is currently in circulation, a reserve slip is made out giving call number, main entry, title, name and homeroom number of person making the request. The circulation file is then checked, and a flagging device (usually a metal clip or a transparent, color-coded book card cover) is placed on the card for the title desired. When the item is returned, the reserve slip is located and placed in the material with the book card, and the prospective borrower is notified.

Length of loan periods and the number of items that may be checked out by an individual borrower should be as flexible and liberal as possible. While some curtailment might be necessary when collections are small and demand is heavy, when the collection reaches numerical adequacy, restrictive loan policies should be dropped and replaced with others that more closely match users' needs. A few media centers have been bold enough to adopt a loan period that can be as long as the school year if the material is not wanted by another patron. In these cases, instead of the date due, the check-out date is stamped in the material. Other centers allow items in the general collection to circulate for a semester. Extended loan periods are particularly important for students engaged in long-range independent study projects. Most centers, however, use loan periods of between two to four weeks. To facilitate filing in the circulation file and also to give borrowers an easy way of remembering due dates, some centers have adopted a "fixed" date for returning materials. For example, all materials checked out in a particular week are due on a specified Monday two or three weeks later. Thus Monday (or the first school day after, in case of holidays or vacations) becomes the day each week on which loaned materials are due back in the center.

Although no specific limits should be placed on the number or type of items that may be borrowed from the center, some reasonable and temporary restraints may have to be imposed, as necessitated by demand and curriculum requirements. For example, when duplicate copies of heavily used reference books are not owned in the center, a system of overnight loans might have to be used. The same problem can arise with media placed on reserve by teachers, current issues of periodicals, or pieces of equipment scheduled for use during the school day. Many of these situations can be avoided through judicious duplication of titles and extensive preplanning with the faculty. In inevitable cases, restricted loans should be applied as sparingly as possible and always with the needs of users in mind.

In library jargon, "snag" refers to a situation in which the original book card for a returned item cannot be found. If, after a thorough check of the circulation file, the original card is still missing, duplicate copies of the book on the shelves and cards in the file that represent other circulating duplicate copies should be checked. If the correct original card still cannot be located, a book card marked "DUP" should be typed and the card number, main entry, and title should be added to the list of other materials for which duplicate book cards have been made. Should the original card appear, the replacement card should be destroyed and crossed off the duplicate card list.

How to handle problems related to overdues has plagued librarians since library materials first began to circulate. It often seems that an inordinate amount of time and effort is spent in this area. One traditional recourse has been to impose fines, on the theory that students who lack feelings of obligation toward others will develop them when their (or their parents') finances are tapped. Many centers have abandoned the collection of fines, however, chiefly because they find it doesn't work—students are often quite willing to pay the small amount, as a form of "rent" to keep the material they want. Perhaps more important, fines represent a negative or punitive measure that contradicts the attempt in schools to build attitudes of responsibility and citizenship. Opponents also point out that collecting fines is very time consuming and that excessively repressive regulations create hostility and can lead to increased thefts and mutilation of material. Still other centers compromise and levy fines only on material that is placed on a highly restricted loan schedule, such as overnight books, when the absence of the material from the center can produce great inconvenience for other users.

Regardless of whether fines are collected or not, other procedures are often adopted to remind students (or sometimes faculty) that the material they have on loan should be returned or renewed. The most accepted method is sending out overdue notices to homerooms. These notices may be purchased commercially or printed in the school. Some centers use multicopy overdue notices so that, if necessary, second and third notices can be sent out without filling in new forms. In the case of material on which a reserve has been placed, the overdue notice should be sent out as soon as the item is due. For others, approximately once per week on a regular schedule the preceding week's overdues should be removed from the current circulation file. Overdue notices are then written and the cards returned to a special file marked "1st notice." If within another week (or longer, depending on center policy) the material has not been returned, a second notice is sent out, and so on. Other techniques are sometimes used, such as setting aside certain days during the school year to have overdue or unused materials returned (in centers where fines are collected these are sometimes called "Amnesty Days"). In a few severe cases it is often necessary to take stronger measures—such as sending notices to parents. However, before anything like this is resorted to, a professional staff member should contact the student and inform him or her personally of the items that are still due and the consequences that might occur.

When a student is directly responsible for the loss of an item or damage to it, some form of reimbursement should be made to the media center. However, because some accidents are unavoidable and some losses are not the fault of the borrowers, adjustments might have to be made in order not to inflict unfair penalties. These decisions, as well as decisions involving delinquent borrowers, should be made only by the media center's professional staff.

RECORDS AND REPORTS

Record keeping and preparation of media center reports serve several purposes. Internally, they can reveal to the center's staff otherwise hidden strengths and weaknesses in the program and thus indicate areas for possible change or improvement. Externally they can serve as a communication device to acquaint others with the scope and nature of the program, its needs and future plans, as well as recommendations for rectifying shortcomings.

RECORDS

The maintenance of accurate records is an integral part of a media center's operation. It is an administrative detail that cuts across the areas of acquisition and organization. Each school media center will develop its own system, but certain records are essential. There are basically four kinds of records prepared and maintained in the media center: (1) financial, (2) organizational, (3) service, and (4) archival.

Financial Records

In a well-run media center, the originals of many of the financial records are kept in the business office; copies in the media center. Some examples of financial records are:

Budget requests, annual and special (NDEA, ESEA).

Budget allocations.

Current statements of expenditures.

Shipment receipts and invoices.

Requisitions and purchase orders, with notations on partial-order status and final disposition.

Receipts of any monies collected or expended by the library outside of regular financial procedures.

Petty cash funds.

Organizational Records

The organizational records usually include as priority items the shelf-list and any supplementary inventory system for nonprint materials and equipment.

The shelflist is a classified card file of all the holdings of a media center. The card contains full bibliographic information, the number of copies, and the list price of the item. In centers that keep collections housed separately by format, an additional card file (one of the requisition set slips; see the discussion on "Order Processing" in this chapter) for non-print media arranged by format will be useful for inventory. In addition, a card file for the equipment handled by the media center is useful for both inventory and repair and maintenance records. The appropriate information about the equipment, including vendor, list price, model number, warranty conditions, date of purchase, and repairs, should be noted and the card pulled when the item is being repaired. Other records for material that is out of the center for other reasons, for example, binding, film exchange, or repair should also be kept. Simply keeping the charge cards in separate files will suffice. A list of typical organizational records follows:

Shelflist of materials and equipment.

Inventory records.

Quantitative record of current holdings.

Card and book catalogs (duplicates to departments, grade levels, or resource areas).

Subject authority file, such as *Sear's*.

Want lists.

Record of materials on order.

Records of loans and gifts.

Check list of periodical holdings.

Records of materials and equipment being repaired and serviced.

Manual that outlines the philosophy, program, and routines of the
media center.

Manuals for student assistants.

Files of promotional materials, e.g., successful displays, exhibits, and
programs.

Inventory records are important for many reasons: to indicate missing or lost materials; to reveal numerical strengths and weaknesses in the
collection; to identify materials in need of repair; to serve as a vital part
of the process of weeding the collection.

Although a periodic inventory of the collection is necessary, precau-
tions must be taken to insure that the inventory does not unduly disrupt
the center's normal services. Closing the center for inventory, as is frequently done during the last week of school, can often deprive students
of center use at a time when they need it most. Two possible alternatives
are: (1) scheduling inventory at a time when school is not in session (to
facilitate performing this and other "housekeeping" chores many districts
have placed at least part of the media center's staff on an eleven-, rather
than the conventional ten-month contract); (2) making inventory taking
a continuous process by drawing up a staggered schedule that covers the
entire collection once per year, but in a piecemeal fashion. Inventory procedures are sufficiently simple that they can usually be handled by clerical
personnel or well-trained student assistants.

The steps in taking inventory are:

1. Arrange the material to be inventoried in correct order.

2. Assign two people to work on the inventory—one to check the
shelflist, the other to examine the item to see that the book card, pocket,
and shelflist information are identical. The physical condition of the material is also checked at this time.

3. Remove from the shelf material that needs repair. If there are any
discrepancies in the information on the book card, shelflist, etc., the item
should either be set aside or, in the case of books, turned down on the
shelf for later checking.

4. If the item is missing, place a clip or some other tagging device on
the shelflist card and, in the case of duplicate copies, a lightly penciled
mark next to the missing accession or copy number.

5. Check the missing item in other sources, such as circulation files,
bindery records, reserve collections, materials in the workroom for repair,
and display cases. If the item is located, remove the clip and erase the
shelflist marking.

6. Prepare inventory records giving a numerical count of the items
in the collection and those that are missing.

7. Write a notification on the shelflist, e.g., "missing 9/73," if the item has still not been located after a suitable waiting period. Later, decisions concerning replacement will have to be made.

Service Records

Service records include chiefly statistical material on attendance, circulation, number of classes taught. Some centers also keep records on such items as number of reference questions asked and number of bibliographies prepared by the staff. To prevent statistics collecting from becoming an end in itself, it should always be determined in advance whether the data produced serve a sufficiently worthwhile purpose to warrant the expenditure of time and effort in producing them. It is also necessary to check the reports required by district centers, state departments of education, or accrediting agencies to find out the type of statistics asked for and the form they should take. The use of sampling techniques should be explored. They often produce similar results with greater economy of time and effort. For example, instead of counting attendance or circulation every school day, records might be kept for only a randomly selected number of school days. Library supply houses are good sources for printed forms used in posting both daily and monthly circulation figures. Some modifications might have to be made in these forms, however, if figures are to be broken down by both Dewey Classification and format.

Some examples of service records are:

Job description and analysis of the library staff.
Records of circulation and usage of materials and equipment.
Attendance records.
Library instruction records.
Procedural Manual for Library Instruction.

Circulation statistics are an important part of a media center's organizational record keeping. They are usually kept on a daily basis and cumulated weekly, monthly, and annually and provide one of the common bases for evaluating service. Depending on the objectives of a media center, the media circulation records can be used to evaluate how well they are being met. For example, the material can be recorded by media, subject class, grade level. Finer breakdowns by curriculum or recreation-related areas, e.g., "Weather" or "Science Fiction," may be obtained by including extra information about course work or interest area when the items are charged out. Records may be dispensed with experimentally in special instances, for example, when student participation and performance in library programs is used as a measure for accountability in place of circulation count.

Other records important to media center operation are the schedules for equipment usage, for group use of facilities, for library teaching in the classroom and center. A compilation of these records will be an important part of the monthly and annual reports to the administration. They will also provide statistics for a graphic record, i.e., charts, graphs, etc. In a small center, a large monthly wall calendar will sometimes serve well as a visual record.

Perhaps the overriding considerations for the individual school media specialist with a small staff is to set up the simplest routines possible for the circulation process and to know exactly why and for what purpose any record is kept. A continuous re-evaluation to bring each routine and its desired purpose more closely into line is vital.

Archival Records

The archival file contains a copy of each of the important documents related to the history of the media center. Financial records, administrative announcements, policy statements, media center publications, statistical data are organized (usually by school year) and stored to supply a written record of the center's history. In some media centers, this activity is expanded to include such material as minutes of faculty meetings, student publications, and newspaper clippings related to the school and its program.

REPORTS

Many state departments of education annually distribute to school media centers forms for reporting the center's activities. The information requested is generally statistical in nature and includes such data as attendance figures, number of faculty members, number of classes taught, media center hours, size of collection, number of new acquisitions, circulation statistics, personnel figures, and budget information.

Media centers also usually prepare an annual report for distribution to administrators at various levels and the school faculty that not only chronicles the center's year's activities in narrative form but also supplies guidelines for its future growth. This annual report can also be used to trace and compare developments from year to year. It should cover four areas of information:

The Program. This, the most important section of the report, is a summary of the activities and accomplishments of the center during the preceding year. Information on services supplied to students and teachers should be included, as well as details on such areas as the center's part in curriculum development, reading and study guidance (e.g., bibliography preparation), special projects and programs (e.g., book fairs or assembly programs), and the center's work in promotion and publicity. If the center sponsors special clubs or a student assistant group, material on these should also be present.

Statistics. The raw material for this section may be obtained from figures, already collected, related to such areas as size of collection, attendance, center hours, circulation. When possible the data should be reduced to the most meaningful units. For example, in addition to yearly totals, daily average figures should also be expressed. In this area charts and graphs can be used to good advantage. This part of the report also contains a financial summary on appropriations and gifts as well as expenditures.

Staff Report. This section covers the professional activities of the staff, including activities related to the growth of staff competencies, e.g., participation in professional associations, courses taken, attendance at workshops and conferences, publications.

Recommendations. This section presents a series of recommendations concerning the future of the center, based on the material in the preceding sections of the report. The recommendations should be stated in terms of achieving specific short- and long-term goals, rather than as simple statements of need. It should be indicated that action may not be possible on all of the proposals.

In addition, the center will periodically prepare other types of reports. Decision on the content and treatment of the material in these reports should bear on: (1) why the report is being prepared—its purpose—and (2) the people who will read the report—its audience. For example, a primarily "selling" report—one that is intended to exert influence on a decision involving the center—should be brief, to the point, without extraneous material, and it should carry its message with maximum impact. The use of charts, graphs, or other visuals can help achieve the goal of this type of report.

CONCLUSION

The practices that are discussed in this and the preceding chapters on managing a single school media center point out the differences between the school library of the past and today's media center. The conventional school library was adequate when information was transmitted in traditional ways. Now, however, our electronic environment makes it imperative that educators utilize new sources of information and teach the skills necessary to understand and interpret them.

To some, the media center described in this book might seem unattainable. Nevertheless, there are many schools that have instituted media programs similar to those described here. Although institutional change is often a slow and gradual process, with imagination and perseverance a beginning can be made even in the most limited situation.

It is interesting to speculate on what the scope and contents of a handbook similar to this one will be in the future. If technology continues to practice more sophisticated ways of disseminating information, the organization and management of media centers will change drastically. It may well be that through computer hookups and multiple terminals media centers may well act as intermediaries between worldwide data banks and the homes in the community, thus further satisfying the informational and educational needs of the school children and young adults. Whatever may be the future of public education, it is assured that its school media centers are destined to play an increasingly important role within it.

APPENDIX I

The Davies-Brickell Media Selection Policy

This policy statement appeared in the Davies-Brickell System of Administrative Policies (No. 6134.1 and 6144) copyrighted by Croft Educational Services, Inc., and is reprinted with the permission of the publisher, Croft Educational Services, Inc., New London, Connecticut. Although the statement refers specifically to books and other printed material, it can be easily expanded to include other educational materials.

GUIDELINES

[6134.1] The Regional School District Board of Education, though it is finally responsible for all book purchases, recognizes the student's right to free access to many different types of books. The Board also recognizes the right of teachers and administrators to select books and other materials in accord with current trends in education and to make them available in the schools.

It is therefore the policy of the Regional School District Board of Education to require that materials selected for our schools be in accordance with the following:

1. Books and other reading matter shall be chosen for values of interest and enlightenment of all students in the community. A book shall not be excluded because of the race, nationality, or the political or religious views of the writer or of its style and language.

2. Every effort will be made to provide material that presents all points of view concerning the problems and issues of our times, international, national and local; and books or other reading matter of sound factual authority shall not be prescribed or removed from library shelves or classrooms because of partisan doctrinal approval or disapproval.

3. Censorship of books shall be challenged in order to maintain the school's responsibility to provide information and enlightenment.

In accordance with No. 3 above the Board of Education has adopted the following policy when dealing with censorship of books or other materials.

1. That the final decision for controversial reading matter shall rest with the Board of Education after careful examination and discussion of the book or reading matter with school officials or anyone else the Board may wish to involve.

2. That no parent or group of parents has the right to determine the reading matter for students other than their own children.

3. The Board does, however, recognize the right of an individual parent to request that his child not have to read a given book provided a written request is made to the appropriate building principal.

4. Any parent who wishes to request reconsideration of the use of any book in the school must make such request in writing on forms provided through building principals.

Regulations for Interpreting these Principles in Selection of Reading Material:

1. We believe it is the responsibility and right of teachers and librarians to select reading material which is carefully balanced to include various points of view on any controversial subject.

2. Selection of materials will be assisted by the reading examination and checking of standard evaluation aids: i.e., standard catalogues and book review digests.

3. Two basic factors, truth and art, will be considered in the selection of books and library materials. This first is factual accuracy, authoritativeness, balance, integrity. The second is a quality of stimulating presentation, imagination, vision, creativeness, style appropriate to the idea, vitality, distinction.

4. Books for the school library and classroom use shall be examined to select those in which the presentation and the subject matter are suitable for the grade and the interest level at which they are to be used. They will be considered in relation to both the curriculum and to the personal interest of pupils and teachers.

Criticisms of books that are in the library or in use as a text should be submitted in writing to the Superintendent on a form prescribed by the administration. The Board of Education will be informed. Allegations thus submitted will be considered by a committee among the faculty which will be appointed by the Superintendent. This committee will be in the subject matter field of the book or material challenged, and the challenged book or material will be judged in writing by the committee as to its conformity to the aforementioned principles. Appeals from this decision may be made through the Superintendent to the Board of Education for final decision.

TEACHING CONTROVERSIAL ISSUES

[6144] Training for effective citizenship is accepted as one of the major purposes of the schools of the Regional School District. The instructional program developed to achieve this purpose properly places great emphasis upon teaching about our American heritage, the rights and privileges we enjoy as citizens and the citizenship responsibilities that must be assumed in maintaining our American way of life. In training for effective citizenship, it is frequently necessary for pupils to study issues that are controversial. In considering such issues it shall be the purpose of the schools of the Regional District to recognize the pupil's right—

    A. To study a controversial issue which has political, economic or social significance and concerning which (at his level) he should begin to have an opinion;

    B. To have free access to all relevant information including the materials that circulate freely in the community;

    C. To study under competent instruction in an atmosphere of freedom from bias and prejudice;

    D. To form and express his own opinions on controversial issues without thereby jeopardizing his relation with his teacher or the school.

1. The approach of the teacher to controversial topics must be impartial and objective.
2. Teachers should use the following criteria for determining the appropriateness of certain issues for consideration as a part of the curriculum:
   a. The treatment of the issue in question must be within the range, knowledge, maturity and competence of the students.
   b. There should be study materials and other learning aids available from which a reasonable amount of data pertaining to all aspects of the issue should be obtained.
   c. The consideration of the issue should require only as much time as is needed for satisfactory study by the class, but sufficient time should be provided to cover the issue adequately.
   d. The issue should be current, significant, real and important to the students and teacher. Significant issues are those which in general concern considerable numbers of people, are related to basic principles or at the moment are under consideration by the public, press and mass media.
3. In discussing controversial issues, the teacher should keep in mind that the classroom is a forum and not a committee for producing resolutions or dogmatic pronouncements. The class should feel no responsibility for reaching an agreement.
4. It is the teacher's responsibility to bring out the facts concerning controversial questions. He [or she] has the right to express his [or her] opinions, but in doing so it is important that his [or her] students understand that it is his [or her] opinion and is not to be accepted by them as an authoritative answer.
5. The principal bears a major responsibility for the administration and supervision of the curriculum, including the selection of materials and methods of instruction. He [or she] must be continuously aware of what is being taught in his [or her] school.
6. A teacher who is in doubt concerning the advisability of discussing certain issues in the classroom should confer with his [or her] principal as to the appropriateness of doing so. If the principal and the teacher are unable to agree, the issue should be referred to the Superintendent of Schools.

7. It is recognized that citizens of the community have a right to protest to the school administration when convinced that unfair and prejudiced presentations are being made by any teacher. In considering such protests, the Board of Education shall provide for a hearing if in its judgment such procedure is required. Teachers of subjects involving controversial issues are assured of the Board's support, if it's found that such teachers have been subjected to unfair criticism or partisan pressures from individuals or groups.

APPENDIX II

The Greater Anchorage Area Borough School District Selection Policy

This selection policy from the Greater Anchorage Area Borough School District has been edited slightly for this publication. Note that it includes instructions to the evaluating committee, a request form for re-evaluating materials (see Exhibit 9 shown at the end of this policy), and the *School Library Bill of Rights* (not reprinted).

PHILOSOPHY

1. The school learning resource center implements classroom activity and is an integral part of the curriculum, paralleling it at all points in all departments. The center exists primarily for educational purposes. It offers enrichment for the students and resource material for the faculty. Its materials are selected from all forms of media available for interest, vocabulary, maturity, and ability levels of all students within the school served.

2. The school resource center provides additional materials to attract students to reading, viewing, and listening as sources of pleasure and recreation over and above needed subject content.

3. It attempts to foster reading as a lifelong activity through pleasurable exposure to printed material.

GENERAL POLICY

1. The legal responsibility for materials in the school center rests with the school district governing board. Responsibility for the final selection shall be delegated to professionally trained personnel who know the course of study, the methods of teaching, and the individual differences of the pupils in the schools for which the materials are provided, such selection to be in accordance with the statement of specific policy given below.

2. The selection of school resource materials shall be in accordance with the following objectives: (a) To enrich the curriculum; (b) To further the development of youth intellectually, emotionally, culturally, and spiritually.

3. The school board subscribes in principle to the statements of policy on library philosophy as expressed in the American Association of School Librarians' *School Library Bill of Rights,* a copy of which is appended to and made a part of this policy.

SELECTION

1. Instructional materials selection shall be a cooperative continuing process in which administrators, teachers, librarians, and students should participate. The basic factors influencing selection shall be the curriculum, the reading interests, abilities, and backgrounds of the students using the centers, and the quality and accuracy of available materials.

2. Recommended lists shall be consulted in the selection of materials, but selection is not limited to their listings.

3. Additional suggestions will come from: exchange of materials with neighboring district school libraries; visits to book exhibits and displays; examination of bookstore stock, publishers' samples, reading lists from other school systems, texts and courses of study approved for use within the district; teachers, students, Parent Teacher Associations, other educational organizations, and individuals of the community. All suggestions must be evaluated with special care according to the criteria set forth in paragraph 1 above.

PROCEDURE FOR HANDLING OBJECTIONS

1. The suitability of particular books or other materials may be questioned. All criticism shall be presented to the Assistant Superintendent for Instructional Services on the Citizen's Request Form for Re-evaluation of Materials (see sample at end of Appendix II). He or she will forward duplicate copies to the principal and librarian of the school involved.

2. The material in question shall be reviewed by a committee of five * composed of:

> Assistant Superintendent for Instructional Services;
> Building Principal;
> Teacher from the building involved in the subject field of the questioned material;
> PTA representative appointed by the building organization;
> Lay person interested in school affairs, appointed by the Assistant Superintendent for Instructional Services.

The review committee shall function at the call of the Assistant Superintendent upon receipt of a complaint. The material shall be considered with the specific objections in mind. The majority and minority report of this committee shall be completed as rapidly as possible and submitted directly to the District Superintendent who will in turn submit it for approval to the school district governing

* A school district might also wish to include one or more students on this committee.

board, whose decision shall be sent to the complainant. The committee's report and the action of the board should be sent to all schools in the district.

3. No material shall be removed from use until the governing board has made a final decision.

4. The review of questioned materials shall be treated objectively and as an important matter. Every opportunity shall be afforded those persons or groups questioning school materials to meet with the committee and to present their opinions. The school librarian and any other persons involved in the selection of the questioned material shall have the same opportunity. The best interests of the students, the curriculum, the school, and the community shall be of paramount consideration.

INSTRUCTIONS TO EVALUATING COMMITTEE

". . . free men and free inquiry are inseparable."

—President Lyndon B. Johnson

Bear in mind the principles of the freedom to learn and to read and base your decision on these broad principles rather than on defense of individual material. Freedom of inquiry is vital to education in a democracy.

Study thoroughly all materials referred to you and read available reviews. The general acceptance of the materials should be checked by consulting standard evaluation aids and local holdings in other schools.

Passages or parts should not be pulled out of context. The values and faults should be weighed against each other, and the opinions based on the material as a whole.

Your report, presenting both majority and minority opinions, will be presented to the superintendent who will forward it to the board for action.

188 Appendix II

EXHIBIT 9 CITIZEN'S REQUEST FORM FOR RE-EVALUATION OF
LEARNING RESOURCE CENTER MATERIALS

Initiated by _____

   Telephone _____ Address _____

REPRESENTING

   Self _____ Organization or group _____

                                            (name)

   School _____

MATERIAL QUESTIONED

   BOOK: author _____ title _____

   _____ copyright date _____

   AV MATERIAL: kind of media _____

                               (film, filmstrip, record, etc.)

   title _____

   OTHER MATERIAL: identify _____

Please respond to the following questions. If sufficient space is not provided, please use additional sheet of paper.

1. Have you seen or read this material in its entirety? _____

2. To what do you object? Please cite specific passages, pages, etc. _____

3. What do you believe is the main idea of this material? _____

4. What do you feel might result from use of this material? _____

5. What reviews of this material have you read? _____

6. For what other age group might this be suitable? _____

7. What action do you recommend that the school take on this material? _____

8. In its place, what material do you recommend that would provide adequate information on the subject? _____

_____   _____
Date   Signature

APPENDIX III

Specific Criteria
for Selecting Educational Media

The following criteria are intended to supplement the general criteria for selecting educational materials in chapter 8.

ART REPRODUCTIONS

Like many public libraries, school media centers are now collecting mounted and framed art reproductions for home circulation to both faculty and students. Conventional collections continue to contain unmounted prints either singly or in portfolios. When purchasing art reproductions check, if possible, the fidelity of the copy in terms of color and detail. The degree of size reduction, if any, will depend on intended usage. The quality and durability of the frame and mounting are also important considerations.

AUDIO MATERIALS

Audio learning materials make available a great variety of experiences through sound—drama, music, lectures, foreign languages, readings, actual occurrences, and re-creations of events. They have been found to be particularly effective in curricular areas involving speech, language, and music. Programs to develop reading skills have also used with success such audio techniques as allowing children to follow the text of the book while listening to a recording of it.

Specific listening skills are needed to make maximum use of the medium. It is easy for a student to "tune out," wool-gather, or generally fail to pay attention while supposedly listening to a presentation. It is also often impossible to detect when this inattention sets in. The distraction level is also much higher for audio experiences than for those that involve both sight and sound. Sudden movements or extraneous noises can easily distract the listener. The material that can be presented solely through sound is also limited. For example, the text of a poem or the pronunciation of a foreign phrase are easily conveyed by this medium, but a description of a complex scientific process is not. However, because it lacks the specificity that visual materials present, audio experiences often stimulate the imagination by allowing students to supply their own visual dimensions.

Four types of audio materials are generally used in media centers: (1) disc recordings; (2) tape recordings; (3) audiocards; (4) radio broadcasts.

Discs

Disc recordings are known under a variety of names: phonodiscs, phonograph records, audiodiscs, or simply, recordings. Discs contain sound transcriptions and are manufactured in a variety of diameters and in formats designed to be played at different speeds. The most common format today is the 12-inch, 33⅓rpm (revolutions per minute), lp (long-playing) record. The amount of recorded sound per side on this type of record varies from about ten minutes to over one-half hour. Other diameters for records are 7 inches (for "pop" singles), 10 inches (now not generally available) and 16 inches. The 16-inch record is used for radio station transcriptions. Other speeds are 16¾ rpm (used in talking books), 45rpm (again chiefly for popular music) and 78rpm. (Seventy-eight revolutions per minute was the standard speed of shellac records but recordings have not been manufactured for playing at this speed since the late 1940s when the plastic long-playing disc was developed.) New recordings are now issued solely in some version of stereophonic sound. This means, basically, that each groove on the recording contains two or more separate sound channels.

Disc recordings have several advantages over tape recordings. Most people are familiar with them and know how to operate a record player. The material on a disc is easily retrieved and allows for flexibility in timing. No rewinds or advancing are necessary. The required material is available simply by placing the needle arm at the appropriate spot. Phonograph records are generally less expensive than tapes. Discs also have certain disadvantages: they are much more prone to damage, i.e., they scratch easily and warp under certain conditions; their sound quality deteriorates with frequent playing. These limitations can largely be avoided with care in handling and storage.

Tapes

Basically, tape recording uses a magnetic tape, the nonshiny side of which is capable of carrying recorded sound. Like discs, tapes come in a variety of formats. The standard reel-to-reel tape recorder uses ¼-inch tape on reels 3, 5, or 7 inches in diameter. The speeds at which this tape is used for recording and playing back are 1⅞, 3¾, and 7½ips (inches per second). With slower speed there is usually a corresponding lessening of fidelity. Recording models vary from a single monaural to four-track stereo and in broadcasting, eight-track tape. The ¼-inch-wide tape is also available in cartridge form, with some in closed loop format to allow for continuous playback without rewinding.

Recently the cassette tape has gained in popularity and is now overtaking reel-to-reel and cartridge tapes in usage figures. This tape is ⅛ inch thick, enclosed in a container called a cassette, and played at 1⅞ips. Like the cartridge, cassettes are easily snapped into place in the player without threading. Cassettes vary in the amount of tape they contain. They are classified, therefore, by the amount of playing time each contains—from 10 to 120 minutes.

Unlike discs, tapes can serve as both a listening and recording medium. This is their basic advantage over conventional phonograph records. This element of participation has produced a variety of uses for tapes, particularly in language study. They are also less prone to damage and may be erased and used again and/or played back many times without changing the quality of the sound. While repairing of tapes and rearranging material through splicing is easily accomplished on reel-to-reel tape, if a cassette or cartridge tape should break, it is extremely difficult to pry open either container and make the necessary repairs. In spite of fast-forward and rewind controls, a major drawback in tape use continues to be the difficulty of locating specific material recorded on the tapes.

AUDIOCARDS

An audiocard looks like a data processing card, except that along its bottom edge it has a strip of magnetic tape containing up to 15 seconds of recorded sound. When the card is played in an audiocard player, the student sees what is printed on the card as well as hears the sound track. This device of presenting pictures and words simultaneously has been used successfully in teaching reading.

RADIO BROADCASTS

With the advent of television and the availability of great libraries of tapes and discs, the use of the radio in education has declined. It remains, however, a powerful device for presenting listening experiences, and a number of educational radio stations are still producing excellent broadcasts for the schools. With the advent of the inexpensive tape recorder, one great difficulty in radio broadcast utilization—how to synchronize the radio program with classroom activities—has been minimized. Programs can now be taped for listening at the class's convenience, when permission is granted.

Radio programs, along with many other audiovisual materials including commercially produced tapes and disc records, share one important limitation: they are agents of one-way communication that does not allow for an interchange of ideas with the listener. It is possible to talk back to a radio, but not possible to get an answer.

The general criteria for evaluating educational media apply to audio materials, but because distractions are often encountered in a listening situation, the selector must be especially aware of the quality of the performance as well as the quality of the recorded sound. The material must be appropriate, of suitable length, effectively presented, interesting, and if possible, appealing both to the emotions and to the intellect. Be sure to determine whether the content is best suited to a recorded form. For example, a tape recording of a play rehearsal has some distinct uses, but video taping the same rehearsal might be more effective. In evaluating the technical quality, clear, distortion-free sound is important. Tapes and records should be made of durable material and clearly labeled to indicate titles, performers, times, and playback speed.

BOOKS AND OTHER PRINTED MATERIALS

BOOKS

Regardless of how varied the materials in the school's media center are, books will remain one of the mainstays of the collection. Each center will strike different balances concerning the number of titles found in various subject areas; such factors as differences in curricula and student abilities mandate that such variations in collections should exist from school to school. Table 8 gives a general indication of the average size of various parts of book collections at the elementary and secondary levels. These figures are given only to indicate relative sizes, not necessarily to be used as hard-and-fast buying guides or as a tool to evaluate existing collections, because as has been stated, these figures will and should vary from one media center to another. The figures are arranged, as are the collections they represent, by Dewey Decimal numbers.

In addition to the general criteria for book selection in chapter 8 criteria related to format are also important. The book's size should be appropriate to its audience. The paper should be of good quality and sufficiently opaque to prevent seeing through to the next page. Besides being clear and easy to read the type face should be suitable for the intended user. Adequate spacing between words and the leading between lines are important. The binding must show the necessary durability and strength related to the type of use the book will receive. Interesting page layouts, pleasing use of color, and an eye-catching

TABLE 8 PERCENT OF BOOK COLLECTION PER DEWEY CLASSIFICATION

		Percent of collection	
	Dewey classification	K–6	7–12
000–099	General Works & Reference	2–5 %	6–8 %
100–199	Philosophy, Psychology	.5	1–2
200–299	Religion & Mythology	1–2	1–2
300–399	Social Sciences, Folklore	5–10	10–15
400–499	Language	.5	2–5
500–599	Pure Science	10	5–10
600–699	Applied Science	10	5–10
700–799	Fine Arts, Recreation	5	5–10
800–899	Literature	5	5–10
900–999	History, Geography, Biography	20	20
F	Fiction	20	20–25
E	Easy Books, Picture Books	20–25	

cover help make the book physically attractive. Hardcover books should lie flat when open.

Furthermore, specific types of books require specific criteria.

Fiction

Whenever possible fiction titles should reach acceptable literary standards, although in providing stories for reluctant and retarded readers these standards might have to be modified or altered in some way. Good fiction generally has the characteristics described here.

Characterization. The characters should be believable and constant. Changes in character should arise naturally and convincingly from the plot. Stereotypes should be avoided. The author should use imaginative, but suitable ways to reveal characterization through combinations of direct exposition, dialogue, thoughts and actions.

Plot. This is probably the most important element for young readers. It should be logical, well constructed, move at an active rate, appropriately reflect the central theme or purpose of the novel. The story should advance in a continuous, well-balanced flow.

Setting and Atmosphere. The setting and concomitant creation of atmosphere should be appropriate to the author's purpose and should be emphasized or de-emphasized depending on the nature of the novel.

Style. An author's writing style may vary from the extreme objectivity of writers like Hemingway to the excessive subjectivity of Proust or Joyce. Regardless of its nature, the style should suit the material and theme, be smooth and dynamic, and not be so self-conscious that it intrudes and detracts from the reader's enjoyment of the work.

Theme. Any theme is valid if the author is able to combine the above elements to make the central idea valid, believable, and important. The nature, complexity, and subtlety of themes should vary with the author's purpose and be appropriate for the intended audience.

Picture Books

In picture books and other books that rely heavily on illustrations to convey messages the pictures should be clear, simple, and of suitable size, and they should interpret the story truthfully and be unified with the text. The medium used in the pictures (e.g., water colors, pen and ink drawings, or line blocks) should be appropriate to the setting and the atmosphere created in the story.

Reference Books

Reference books and many other books of general nonfiction can be used effectively and efficiently if they contain the following: running heads (as in dictionaries), thumb indexing, extensive illustrations placed close to the related text, thorough indexes, cross references, and pronunciations of difficult words. In multivolume sets, such as encyclopedias, the media specialist should also explore the revision policy as well as the nature and quality of supplements or yearbooks.

Textbooks

For many years the textbook was the leading teaching tool used by teachers. It still supplies a common body of knowledge for all students and in many ways can help to organize and facilitate instruction. Critics maintain, however, that the single textbook concept stifles inquiry and critical thinking, deals with events superficially, does not allow for the individual student's needs and interests, and tends to lock the curriculum into a fixed sequence, and that the text is often poorly written. For these reasons the single text is being increasingly abandoned and replaced in many schools by a multitextbook concept that uses several texts per course supplemented by a variety of other educational materials.

A school's textbooks are usually chosen by a selection committee. The committee should include at least one representative from the media center, and each of the basic criteria involving authority, scope, treatment, authenticity, and suitability must be vigorously applied. In addition the following questions should be asked when a text is being considered:

Does the content of the textbook relate well to the syllabus of the course?

Are the reading and interest levels within the text suited to the students who will use it?

Is the material presented in a way to encourage further study and critical thinking?

Is the material interestingly presented?

Are illustrations used often and effectively?

Does the author present the material in a fair, unbiased manner?

If differing opinions exist, are all sides of a controversial question presented objectively?

In the area of social studies, is proper balance shown to the contributions of various racial, ethnic, and religious groups?

Are supplementary teaching aids available?

Are extensive multimedia bibliographies provided for further study?

Are such learning aids as a glossary, index, extensive table of contents, pronunciations, summaries, and lists of supplementary activities present?

Can the material be easily reorganized to accommodate the different needs of various teaching situations?

In what way, if any, can the material be updated?

Paperbacks

Many studies have been made that show how effective paperbacks can be to individualize and enrich instruction in the schools. These studies show that young people usually prefer a paperback over its hardcover counterpart. Although the distinction between categories in paperbacks is now frequently blurred, paperbacks are usually classified as *mass market* or *quality*, the differences usually being price, format, and distribution patterns. Mass-market paperbacks are generally less expensive, are presented in substantially different formats than the original hardcover editions, and are available through magazine or paperback wholesalers. Quality paperbacks tend to be a little higher in price, but they are often superior in format. They are available directly from publishers as well as from hardcover and paperback book jobbers.

At one time the question in schools was: Should we use paperbacks? The question now is: How do we use paperbacks? Here are some basic uses: (1) to experiment with exploring new areas of reader interest; (2) to supply a variety of material to special students; (3) to provide multiple copies; (4) to make available more books for the reluctant or retarded reader; (5) to provide ephemeral material that has high, but short-term appeal; (6) to supply material that may rapidly become outdated; (7) to supply material unavailable in any other format; (8) to supply branch collections of books through paperback book fairs; (10) to extend the curriculum; (11) to provide individualized instruction.

MAGAZINES AND NEWSPAPERS

The habit of reading magazines grows during childhood, and by adolescence it is usually preferred over all other kinds of reading. Many reasons have been suggested for this popularity of magazines over other types of reading matter: magazines are easily accessible; their contents cater to a wide variety of interests; the use of color and illustrations makes them attractive (they are, in a sense, the adolescent version of the picture book); and their articles are short, usually in easy-to-read language, and do not demand a great time commitment. Perhaps the most important reason, however, is that they deal with current information and today's events, tastes, and interests. In short, they are up-to-date and help keep their readers that way.

Newspaper reading also increases during the school years. In childhood first the comic strip pages and next (for boys, primarily) the sport sections are important. As the child matures, the quality and quantity of newspaper reading expands. An increased emphasis in the curriculum on current affairs and problems has added even greater importance to the presence of extensive, well-rounded collections of newspapers and magazines in the media center.

Magazines and newspapers purchased by schools should comply with the standards of quality required of other media. The selections should supply a variety of points of view and cater to the students' varied interests. The newspapers in the collection should jointly reflect local, state, and national coverage. Remember also that magazines and newspapers are an excellent base for catching the attention of reluctant or retarded readers and attracting them to the media center.

Whether a magazine or newspaper is indexed by one of the standard services, for example, *Reader's Guide*, or provides its own cumulative index, as does the *New York Times*, is a selection criterion for magazines or newspapers that are to be used primarily for research. Many of the magazines popular for recreational reading are not found in the standard indexes. Availability in microfilm might also be considered before purchase. In any case, subscription lists should be reviewed thoroughly every year, and each title reevaluated at that time.

PAMPHLETS AND CLIPPINGS

The vertical file in a library is the depository for pamphlets, clippings, pictures, student reports, and other ephemeral material. When well organized and kept current, it can be a valuable adjunct to the regular collection. Some of the purposes it can serve are:

To update the regular collection. Pamphlets and clippings often contain much more current information than other media.

To supplement and extend material in the existing collection. A pamphlet might, for example, serve as a source of information on a specific subject for which the media center would not purchase more expensive sources.

To supply information and illustration on subjects not covered elsewhere or not treated elsewhere in similar depth.

To furnish a variety of points of view on a subject. This is of particular value with material on controversial subjects. Whereas a book usually reflects a single attitude, a series of clippings may reveal a great difference and range of opinion on the same subject.

Much of the material that is placed in the vertical file is either free or inexpensive. The major sources for clippings are old magazines and newspapers, as well as discarded books. Pamphlets are available from a variety of sources. Media specialists should familiarize themselves with the many bibliographies of these free and inexpensive materials. To facilitate the acquisition of pamphlets, most media centers develop a form letter (known as a begging letter) or postcard requesting the material and leaving spaces for the address, a title or subjects of the specific materials requested, and the number of copies wanted.

Two points to consider in pamphlet selection are: (1) because much of this material is free, it will have to be checked thoroughly for excessive or misleading advertising and for evidence of propagandizing; (2) the vertical file should be thoroughly and frequently weeded to dispose of materials that have outlived their usefulness.

GOVERNMENT DOCUMENTS

Media centers often tend to overlook the wide and rich storehouse of materials available from the various governmental agencies at local, state, national, and international levels. The materials these sources issue are rather misleadingly called government documents. One tends to think of a government document solely as a published treaty, law, or the like. Instead, the scope of government documents is as wide as the interests and concerns of today's governments. The Government Printing Office in Washington, D.C., for example, is now officially known as the world's largest publisher. The pamphlets, books, maps, film, and phonograph records available from that office alone deal with such diverse subjects as child care, farming, Civil War battles, cooking, crime, and the National Parks. Media centers should avail themselves of this large wealth of materials—much of it is free or extremely inexpensive.

GRAPHICS

The word "graphics" is a broad term that refers to a whole group of educational materials with one characteristic in common—each visualizes information through combinations of words and drawings. Usually the data are presented in a summary, or otherwise condensed form. Graphics include (1) graphs, (2) charts, tables, and diagrams, (3) cartoons, and (4) posters. Regardless of type, graphics share basic criteria for quality. The material should be presented clearly and simply—in an uncluttered way and with nonrelevant elements either de-emphasized or omitted. The graphic should show that attention has been paid to such basic artistic principles as balance and harmony in spatial relationships and an overall unity of presentation. Lettering should be clear and legible and color, if used, should fulfill more than a decorative purpose. The graphic should have impact and demand attention. Lastly, it should not be awkward or unmanageable in size but it should be large enough for its intended use.

GRAPHS

A graph is a pictorial device used to present numerical data and their relationships. Statistics can suddenly become meaningful when presented in graph form. The material should be clear, interestingly organized, and capable of revealing comparisons easily. There are four major types of graphs. The *line* graph, the simplest and most popular type, presents data in a simple continuous line in relation to a horizontal and vertical grid. The *bar* graph is easiest to read; it represents relationships by the length of the bars. The *circle*, or *pie* graph is used to show the relation of the parts to the whole. Lastly, the *pictograph*, or *picture* graph uses symbols rather than lines or bars to present the material. The pictograph, which has gained in popularity in recent times, had its origins in the way in which primitive tribes kept their records.

These terms are often used interchangeably, but charts and tables are,

CHARTS, TABLES, DIAGRAMS

generally speaking, drawings that classify or otherwise analyze data. Some examples of charts are business charts, weather charts, and mariner's charts. Youngsters can draw up their own charts to organize their school work or to trace progress in a particular school subject. Tables are used to list or tabulate data, usually figures. Common examples are airline and bus schedules and railroad timetables. Diagrams are graphics that show relationships, as in a process or device. They do not necessarily have to be realistic in representation. Diagrams include flow sheets or flow charts, used to represent a sequence of operations; time lines, to plot relationships in time and events; family trees, or genealogical diagrams; and flip charts that show sequences or steps on a series of sheets rather than in a single diagram.

CARTOONS

A cartoon is a drawing or series of drawings that tells a story quickly. Cartoons may be used either to instruct or to entertain. Generally, they are so small that some sort of projection device, an opaque projector for example, must be used for group viewing of cartoons. Political and satirical cartoons rely heavily on symbols, which often must be explained to students before a cartoon can be understood.

POSTERS

Posters also tell short stories. Good posters relay a single specific message in a clear, dynamic manner. They have instant appeal and clarity of design and are large enough to be seen at a distance. Some sources of free or inexpensive posters are travel agencies, museums, art galleries, government offices, and industrial concerns.

MULTIMEDIA KITS AND EDUCATIONAL GAMES

Many manufacturers now package together different types of media dealing with the same subject. For example, a kit on a foreign country might contain items of realia, a portfolio of pictures, a film, slides, and perhaps filmstrips. Many schools have assembled their own kits, particularly in areas of local history, industry, and social conditions. Individual components of a kit or multimedia device should be evaluated separately as well as in relation to the rest of the material.

Educational games attempt to involve the learner in an educational situation while at the same time providing interest and amusement. Most games try to simulate a real-life situation. Thus, through projection and role-playing, the student undergoes experiences very similar to reality. Games have already been developed around historical events, social problems, family situations, and political and economic questions. An imaginatively structured game that is accurate in detail can be an exciting way to produce active participation in the learning process.

MAPS AND GLOBES

Maps and globes are to-scale representations of a geographical area or areas. Both media involve sophisticated abstractions and their use therefore requires of students special skills related to the students' comprehension levels and ability to deal with symbols.

Maps and globes may sometimes be used together, but they differ basically in two qualities: dimension and accuracy. Whereas a globe is a three-dimensional model, usually of the world, most maps are flat or two-dimensional. No map can be considered as accurate as a globe. Even raised-surface topographical relief maps cannot usually convey the rounded quality of the total earth's surface, while flat maps of the earth may in fact distort the true nature of the earth's surface (this distortion varies from one projection to another). On the other hand, detail is difficult to portray on a globe, and only one-half of a globe can be seen at one time.

Globes can portray a variety of conditions—geographical, political, economic, or social—but if more than two relationships are shown on a single globe there is a danger of confusion. Globes come in many sizes. A 16-inch diameter is usually the smallest suitable for group viewing. Larger globes are expensive and take up greater amounts of space (some inflatable models are now available, however). Many now have raised surfaces to indicate physical features. Others, usually called slated globes, are constructed of materials that can be written on, but easily erased. Globes should be constructed of a durable material and, except in unusual cases, come in a flexible mounting—that is, one that the globe can be removed from and returned to easily. A popular form of mounting is the cradlemount with a gyro or horizon ring that allows for simulation of the earth's spinning.

Maps, like globes, can also portray a variety of relationships and, by comparison to globes, are much more flexible, versatile, and capable of conveying a greater variety of facts. Again, there is always the danger of overcrowding, of trying to convey too much material within a single map. In their zeal to provide accurate and complete information, cartographers can obscure the essentials through excess detail. This is particularly true on many historical maps that attempt in-depth coverage of great periods of time.

Maps vary in size according to the use for which they are intended. In addition to a degree of simplicity relative to use, a map's symbols should be easy to read, its scales and area markers should be plainly visible, and its colors and type size should be suitable to the contents. Additional considerations for maps are: (1) nature of the projection and its suitability to the material; (2) method of indicating the projection; (3) presence of an index; (4) up-to-dateness or, with historical maps, a cross reference from old place names to those currently in use; (5) number of inserts and their value; (6) inclusion of parallels of latitude and meridians of longitude and their frequency; (7) accuracy of directions, boundaries, and areas; (8) storage facilities necessary (some maps can be folded; others must be stored flat); (9) construction strength and glare-proof qualities.

Maps and globes are available from a variety of sources. In addition to many commercial outlets, travel agencies, transportation and petroleum companies, the U.S. Government, as well as newspapers and periodicals are fine additional sources that may be tapped.

MODELS, DIORAMAS, MOCK-UPS

A model is a recognizable, three-dimensional representation of an object that often involves a change in size relationship with the real thing. Through the use of models an object can be brought into a classroom in replica form that in real life would be too large or too small for convenient viewing. Also, cutaway models can show the inside of an object, for example, the interior of an internal-combustion engine or of human anatomy.

A diorama depicts a scene by using realistic replicas of objects in the foreground and a painted curved backdrop that gives the impression of depth. Thus the illusion of reality is created. Dioramas are often used to portray historical events or distant places.

A mock-up differs from an ordinary model in two ways: (1) it usually has moving parts; (2) it is more abstract and less realistic than the model. Unnecessary details are either eliminated or abridged, and important elements are stressed.

In evaluating models and dioramas and mock-ups make sure that size relationships are made very clear, that parts are suitably labeled, and that colors and composition of the materials help stress important features. The size of the model in relation to the nature of the group using it is also important, and finally, if the model can be taken apart, it should be easy to reassemble.

MOTION PICTURE FILMS

The characteristics of motion present in so-called motion pictures is actually an optical illusion that exploits the eye's inability to distinguish adequately between images that are shown in quick succession. Because the eye retains an image for a fraction of a second after it is shown, this "retention of vision" causes a blending with the next image. If the images are closely related in sequence the effect is one of movement. Sound films are shown at 24 images or frames per second, silent films, usually 16 frames per second. When films are projected at less than these speeds a disjointed or flickering effect occurs.

Motion pictures were first used in education following World War I. Since that time their potential has been thoroughly explored and they have grown in use to the extent that today they are rated among the most powerful and effective presentational devices available to the educator. Like TV, motion pictures are unique in appealing in a variety of ways to several senses simultaneously. Not only can they supply visual images in motion and in color; they also extend their dimension with sound.

On close examination, motion picture film has a dull and a glossy side. It is the dull side that contains the image and sound track, if any.

Motion pictures can be classified by their format and their content. By format the basic classification involves the width of the film: 35mm and wider —used for commercial theatrical viewing; 16mm and 8mm—the two sizes used extensively in education. Sixteen millimeter is most useful if a large picture is required, but in an average classroom, 8mm gives satisfactory results in clarity and picture definition. In cost, size, and ease of transport, 8mm films and equipment have advantages over 16mm.

Sixteen-millimeter films can be either silent (silent films have sprocket holes on both sides of the film) or equipped with sound tracks. Sound films have sprocket holes on one side of the film and the sound track on the other. Sound is recorded on film in one of two ways: optically, through photographing the sound and converting it into bands of light and dark that can be reconverted with the use of a photoelectric cell or magnetically by attaching a continuous narrow strip of magnetic tape to the side of the film. The optical track is more common than the magnetic. Films in 16mm come in the regular reel-that are self-threading and -rewinding, and in closed-loop cartridges sometimes to-reel form that requires conventional threading of the machine, in cassettes called repeating films because the beginning and end of the film are joined in the cartridge to form a continuous loop.

All of these variations (sound, either optical or magnetic, silent, reel-to-reel, cassette, cartridge) are also available in the 8mm field with even further diversifications. A few years ago standard or regular 8mm film was joined by a close relative: Super 8. This format has reduced-size sprocket holes and, therefore, has space on the film to accommodate larger pictures. Super 8 sound film's sprocket holes are on the opposite side from those of regular 8mm film. A slight mixing of film formats has taken place. For example, some longer 16mm films often now have accompanying shorter excerpts or brief related films on 8mm, for more intensive small group or individual viewing. Unfortunately, the inability of the accompanying equipment to accommodate wide diversity of film formats has produced great confusion and, as a result, buyer resistance, particularly to 8mm films and equipment. This lack of compatibility continues to be a major stumbling block to freer use of this medium by the schools.

Films may also be classified by content. Traditionally they have, like books, been considered either educational (curriculum oriented) or recreational (entertainment oriented). Happily, this distinction is breaking down. Films can and should instruct and entertain at the same time. Classification by subject area—for example, science, history, geography—is often used. Other terms used in classifying films are: animated films, travelogs, agency sponsored films, training films, documentaries, and true-life dramas.

Because young people spend such a great deal of time before the TV and film screens, a movement to produce greater visual literacy among the young has grown in American education. People who use films with students should familiarize themselves with the techniques and capabilities of the medium and convey them to their students. One is able to "think" with the eyes the more one is able to appreciate the alternatives available to a director in filming a scene, the variety of effects produced by different types of film shots, the techniques and considerations used for cutting from one sequence to another, and other relationships that exist among the camera, the subject, and the viewer.

Perhaps better than any other medium, motion pictures convey the greatest sense of reality to an audience. The attention of the viewer is easily attained and identification possibilities are numerous. Through the medium of the realistic films, the audience can easily be taken to a distant country to study a foreign culture or transported back in time to witness important events of the past. In addition, film is also capable of conveying "unrealistic" motion. By filming at a very fast rate and then projecting at normal speeds, the effect of slow motion is produced and details perhaps otherwise undetectable become visible. On the other hand, through time-lapse photography—shooting pictures at a slower rate than usual, but projecting them at the normal speed—phenomena that ordinarily might take hours or days to take place can be shown in a matter of seconds. In the variation of time-lapse photography called the stop-motion effect, the cameraman shoots only a single picture at a time and the objects photographed are changed slightly for each picture so that an illusion of motion is produced in the final product. Other forms of animation are also used to produce unrealistic motion. Many projectors are now equipped with a "freeze frame," a mechanism that allows a single frame to remain on the screen without damaging the film.

Besides the advantages of wide range and of types of images that can be carried via motion picture film, there are other, more basic reasons for using it. Tests have shown repeatedly that material, particularly of a factual nature, presented through the motion picture medium is learned faster and retained longer than material presented through a more traditional medium. The skills necessary to absorb information from films are minimal—poor readers can grasp material presented in film far more readily than they can material in a printed format.

Other of film's assets are: new formats and equipment now make it possible for children to operate the machines and for a greater range in the size of the group viewing the film; details are easily presented on film; local production of films is fairly simple and not too costly; a wide variety of films at various levels and in various formats is available for purchase or rental.

There are also some disadvantages to the medium of film. First, compared to other materials, films are more costly. This applies not only to purchasing but also to renting a film. Potential purchasers should bear in mind that a film's time of usefulness will be limited (1) by the degree of recency in its content and (2) by the rate of its physical deterioration. Because single schools usually find it too costly to purchase films of long duration, these films must be secured through other distribution centers, such as a district- or countywide collection or rental libraries. This entails advance bookings—in some cases as much as six months—and sometimes planning that far ahead makes it impossible to ensure correct integration of the film into the curriculum. In addition, for economies in time and money, bookings are often made for only a two- or three-day period, but this limited time frequently is not sufficient for previewing, preparation for the presentation, audience viewing, and, if necessary, re-viewing.

Another limitation placed on the use of film is that some teachers still consider films a form of entertainment—to be used as a "reward" for their students—rather than an important instructional aid. As a result, there has been more misuse of this medium in the classroom than of any other nonprint material. It is hoped that the emphasis on audiovisual materials in teacher training institutions and the development of inservice courses within school districts will change this situation.

Two additional limitations on the use of films involve projection conditions. First, many machines still require manual threading or other, rather complex procedures before projection is possible. Teachers often feel insecure in performing these operations and thus curtail their use of this medium. Second, showing most types of films to large groups still requires a darkened room, which decreases the opportunities for note taking and increases the possibility of behavioral problems.

The general criteria for evaluating educational materials may be used with films. Fortunately most films are available on a preview basis so that these criteria may be applied directly and not solely through reviewing sources. Preview records should be kept for future reference. Specific pointers to remember when selecting films are: (1) the content should be more effectively presented via film than is possible in another, less expensive form; (2) if the film is being considered for purchase, the cost must be weighed heavily against the number of subject areas in which it may be used, the length of time it will have value in the curriculum, and the number of showings anticipated per school year; (3) the quality of the acting, the scenario, the presentation techniques, as well as the nature of the photography, sound, and color should be of acceptable standards or better.

PROGRAMMED MATERIALS

Programmed instruction is a teaching method that breaks down the material to be learned into short, logical steps and presents each step in a separate discrete segment, or "frame." Students must respond by answering a question correctly before moving from one frame to the next. The student is also given immediate feedback on the degree of correctness in his response.

As recently as 1954, B. F. Skinner first proposed the idea that human beings could learn efficiently by the same methods that he utilized with his pigeons at Harvard University. The methods relied heavily on the reinforcement theory of learning, whereby after a correct answer is given, a reward is supplied to strengthen or reinforce the learning. Skinner's studies formed the theoretical basis for programmed instruction. Since that time a variety of commercially prepared programs have appeared in a number of different formats. When the program is presented in conventional book form, it is known as a programmed textbook. In this format each frame takes up part of a page and the correct answers are usually found by turning the page. Other programs involve various combinations of both print and nonprint materials. Sometimes a program is housed in a mechanical device, i.e., a "teaching machine." Teaching machines vary in sophistication—from those operated manually by the student to complex, computer-based response systems. In general, programs— regardless of the method of presentation—are of three types: (1) *linear,* in which each student must work through every frame to complete the program; (2) *branching*—also known as *intrinsic* or *adaptive*—in which students may skip or bypass parts of the program after demonstrating mastery of the contents of those parts (when used in a program textbook, this technique is known as a scrambled text); (3) *combination,* programs that are a mixture of the first two types.

Programs may be used in a variety of ways: (1) to teach new knowledge and skills completely independent of other presentational methods; (2) to enrich or supplement the present teaching program; (3) to complement regular teaching; (4) to review material; (5) to help absentees or poorer students to catch up on the regular classroom work. Proponents of programmed teaching suggest a number of reasons for using this medium in teaching. In summary, programs: (1) allow educators to organize their material into logical, step-by-step presentations; (2) reduce teaching gaps and cheating; (3) offer flexible instructional possibilities for use by groups or by individuals, in classrooms, study carrels, or at home; (4) allow individualization of learning through self-pacing; (5) give teachers a concrete and immediate check on a student's progress; (6) force students to be active learners; (7) give students an immediate check on their progress; (8) reduce student error; (9) contain a "built in" motivation; (10) can free teachers for more professional tasks; (11) are often more efficient in realizing specific knowledge goals than are other forms of instruction; (12) are in some cases inexpensive; (13) are in many cases pretested and revised to insure validity and reliability; (14) can be nonverbal in scope.

Critics of programmed instruction use the following points to bring out the limitations of this method of instruction:

1. Programs lack intrinsic motivation. Motivation in its most effective form is a social phenomenon. Because the learner works in isolation, this form of motivation is missing.

2. The claim of individualized instruction in programs is a myth. Fundamentally, except for differences in pacing, students are learning the same thing —there is basically little provision for the child to develop or to express himself creatively as an individual.

3. Programs compartmentalize knowledge in a way that makes cross-disciplinary approaches to subject matter difficult.

4. Basic principles and concepts are sometimes lost in programmed learning because knowledge is so fragmented into small steps in programs that the broad aspects of a subject may be lost.

5. At present not all educational objectives can be programmed. Successful programs now appear to be limited to areas where mastery of specific information is the chief educational goal.

Perhaps the recent disillusionment in educational circles with programmed instruction came about because the medium was so patently misused in many situations. Instead of adapting programs to specific situations, integrating their use with other teaching methods and materials, and being willing to change traditional classroom organizational patterns concerning timetables and scheduling to accommodate this form of individualized instruction, many school systems began introducing programs before acquiring sufficient knowledge of the concept to implement its use efficiently and effectively.

Some school districts have hired programmers or trained their own personnel to construct programs that are custom-made for their own curriculum. This is a specialized, difficult, and expensive task and unfortunately one that is a luxury for most districts. Most rely on programs that are available for purchase.

Several questions should be kept in mind before choosing commercially produced programs: Does the program (or part of it) contain the information you are trying to convey and is the approach to the knowledge compatible with your teaching goals? Is it logically constructed at a level suitable to your students? Is the material interestingly presented? Is it of suitable length to present the material effectively without inducing boredom? Is it linear or branching? If the former, will it hold the attention of the students using it and still accommodate their range of abilities and skills? Are the groups on which the program was pretested comparable to the ones that will be using it? Is there ample evidence that sufficient field tests have been made with the program to assure its quality? Will the administration of the program create the need for changes in the school's organizational pattern? Are those who will administer the program aware of these problems (for example, what to do with the students who finish first) and able, through preplanning, to cope with them?

PROJECTED STILL PICTURES

Filmstrips

Of all the various formats available in projected audiovisual materials, certainly the filmstrip is the most popular and widely used. Basically a filmstrip is a long strip of 35mm film on which a series of related still pictures called frames are arranged in a fixed order. The number of frames in a filmstrip can and does vary a great deal. A typical filmstrip, though, contains from 30 to 50 frames. Filmstrips are classified as either "silent" or "sound." The silent filmstrips usually have either captions of explanatory text under the pictures or accompanying manuals that contain a printed running commentary. A sound filmstrip generally has packaged with it a phonograph record or audiotape, e.g., a sound cassette. One side of the phonograph records and tapes now packaged in these sets has an audible signal ("beep") to signal the operator to move to the next frame. The other side is used in equipment that moves the filmstrip along automatically on a special electronic nonaudible signal. Some manufacturers are now producing single cartridges that contain both the filmstrip and sound tape. These can be easily dropped into a specially produced projector capable of accepting the single unit. Another manufacturer has developed a filmstrip with an optical sound track on the same film as the pictures. Here again, special equipment is required for its use.

The popularity of the filmstrip is due to several reasons: the strips are comparatively inexpensive; there are thousands available on a wide range of subjects and at a variety of levels; and operation of filmstrip equipment is easy enough even for children. In addition, filmstrips are flexible and adaptable. They can be used with either large or small groups or by individuals. They are also compact and easily stored and have the added advantage of adjustable projection speed. Whole frames may be ignored or passed over quickly whereas others may be lingered over or returned to without great inconvenience.

The filmstrip does have some disadvantages of which media users should be aware. Two principal ones are the filmstrip cannot show motion, and the pictures are locked into a fixed order, which makes changing the sequence difficult. One technical hazard is that with each showing the film is exposed to physical damage, such as scratching or ripping of sprocket holes; another is that for good projection, even though a daylight screen is used, the room must be partially darkened.

There are many aids available to help with the selection of filmstrips for a collection, including—in addition to those that cover many media—some works dealing specifically with filmstrips, such as the NICEM (National Information Center for Educational Media) *Index to 35mm Filmstrips,* and *Educators Guide to Free Filmstrips* (Educators Progress Service). Current reviews are featured in such standard reviewing media as *LJ/SLJ Previews* (Bowker) and *The Booklist* (ALA).

Specific criteria for evaluating filmstrips should start with these questions: Does the subject lend itself to the filmstrip format? If so, are the visuals sufficient in quantity and quality to convey the message adequately? On the technical side, the visuals should be clear, sharp, and interesting. They should show suitable variety in style (e.g., closeups—distance) and presentation (e.g., photos, charts, graphs). Captions on silent filmstrips should be legible, not too lengthy, and as with any running commentary, appropriate to the intended audience. Colors when used should be faithful to the original and be used for educational not just for decorative reasons. Recorded sound tracks should conform to good standards of aural presentation—high fidelity, clarity, lack of distortion, and good use of special effects. The sound and visual image should be well synchronized.

SLIDES

At one time the term "slide" applied exclusively to the larger 3¼- by 4-inch glass-mounted lantern slide. Although the use of this size slide has declined enormously, it is still found to be valuable today, particularly in slides that delineate fine details on complex maps and diagrams. Generally speaking, most people now associate slides with the 2- by 2-inch cardboard-mounted slide made popular through home photography. Commercially produced slides of this variety are frequently mounted on sturdier material than cardboard, and for protection, many are completely covered with glass or a layer of clear plastic. These are more expensive, but they will withstand tough wear for longer periods.

Slides have basically the same advantages as filmstrips, but they may be used with more flexibility because they can be arranged in any sequence that will best suit the presentation; carousel trays make sequencing and projection very easy. Slides may be produced locally and presentation may be varied to meet local and individual class needs. In many cases, such as recording a field trip, this simply means taking photographs in the usual way. For photographing diagrams, flat pictures, or parts of a book, a copy stand must be used, but this is a relatively simple procedure. Duplication of locally produced slides is possible through the use of the negatives, or of commercially produced slides (within copyright restrictions) through special equipment.

The disadvantages of slides are similar to those of filmstrips, with three additions. First, because each is a separate, small entity, sets of them can easily be disarranged, particularly when using a nonautomatic projector that requires slides to be fed into the machine manually. Second, most slides do not have the captions found on filmstrips; therefore, another medium, e.g., an accompanying manual, taped commentary, or teacher's remarks, is often needed to interpret the picture. Last, slides are not subjected to the same bibliographic control as are filmstrips. For example, there are no separate bibliographies of slides as there are with filmstrips, and many multimedia bibliographies ignore slides completely. The current reviewing media, as well, pay much less attention to slides than to other materials. Both the Westinghouse *Learning Directory* and *EPM* (Educator's Purchasing Master) do list them, but these bibliographies are nonevaluative.

Criteria for filmstrips also apply to slides. With slides there should also be an evaluation of the strength of the mounting as well as the continuity and organization present within a set. A more specialized slide format is the stereoscopic slide reel in which two prints of the same picture are projected in a hand-held viewer simultaneously to give a three-dimensional effect. There are many reels available (particularly those containing sight-seeing views of places). They are generally inexpensive and easily shown. However, only one student can use the viewer at a time.

MICROFORMS

"Microform" is a generic term for media that carry printed information in a reduced size. There are two major divisions of microforms: (1) those reproduced on transparent film; (2) those reproduced on opaque cards. All microforms share the same basic advantages, which briefly are:

Space. Because of miniaturization microforms have the highest storage density of any media. Entire libraries can now literally be stored in a few drawers of a card file, and in the case of magazine storage, microfilm takes about 5 percent of the space required to store a comparable number of issues in hard copy.

Completeness. The danger of mutilation and theft is minimal and files are therefore almost guaranteed to remain intact and complete.

Cost. Microforms are less expensive than their hardcover counterpart. For example, a volume of a periodical on microfilm costs less than the price of merely binding the same number of issues in hard copy.

Selection. Hundreds of thousands of books, periodicals, and newspapers are now available on microform, and in most cases it is the only form in which the material is available. Thus, when one of these items is under consideration for purchase—it's either a microform or nothing.

Convertibility. Microforms can be converted into paper copy with the use of a simple printing device. The process per page is inexpensive and takes only a few seconds.

There are also several disadvantages in using microforms in libraries, and ironically two of them involve factors already listed as advantages: cost and space. The initial cost of purchasing microform readers and reader-printers and the space required to house them in the library will reduce the savings from microform use in libraries whose microform collection is small. In addition to the cost disadvantages of purchasing and housing special hardware is the necessity either of teaching all would-be users how to use these machines or of facing a situation in which the library staff is responsible for threading and dismantling the machines each time they are used. Increased availability of microfilm cartridges will help in this area. However, using microforms is generally more time consuming than using printed formats—not only is the reader's time expended in setting up the machine but retrieval time is also slow. In the case of the microfilm spool for example, a reader may have to run through an entire roll before finding the specific document that is being sought.

A certain amount of "reader resistance" on the part of students toward microforms has developed primarily because some microreaders produce difficult-to-read images, particularly around the edges, and because unless the microreader is portable, users generally must remain in one place to use the machine. Frequently after an initial exposure, youngsters have shown that they prefer paper copy. The disadvantages of microforms are greatly outweighed, however, by microforms' many advantages and any library media center truly committed to developing broad-based collections should explore the tremendous wealth of material available in microforms. Most library users are inclined to think of microfilm in terms of the open spool, reel-to-reel format. This is certainly the oldest and most common format for microfilm. Although spools come in two sizes, 16mm and 35mm, the former is encountered primarily where microfilming of documents is done locally, for example, in a business concern where bills and receipts are photographed before they are destroyed. The spools distributed commercially from microfilm producers are usually 35mm and are generally about 100 feet long. Although spools are among the least expensive of microformats, they are the most difficult to use, and as well, they expose the film to greater wear and chance of damage than in other microform formats.

The microfilm cartridge, or magazine, on the other hand, is the microformat that combines the advantages of the spool, yet permits self-threading and eliminates film damage from incorrect winding. While 16mm cartridges have been available for many years, libraries can now convert existing 35mm collections to cartridge format simply by purchasing empty 35mm cartridges, into which spools can be snapped or threaded, and either cartridge readers or, as is possible with many machines, adaptors for standard spool readers to allow automatic threading through cartridge use.

A third microformat, the aperture card, uses a standard (3¼- by 7⅜-inch) data processing card with an open window into which is placed a microfilm chip, usually 35mm. Machine-readable information may be punched into the paper part of the card, while the microfilm part contains pertinent miniaturized documents. Through the use of a processor-camera (see "Microform Equipment" in Appendix IV) a document can be photographed, processed, and mounted in an aperture card in less than a minute after exposure. Not only is speed of production an advantage but, also, these cards can be up-dated easily and afford flexibility in sequencing the material on them. For these reasons many schools have placed students' records on aperture cards, and libraries have used the format to store magazine articles, clippings, and other materials often found in the vertical file. Nova High School, Ft. Lauderdale, Florida, for example, has built into its four resource centers a collection of magazine articles on local history, all on aperture cards. These cards are slightly more expensive to produce than other microforms and are not practical for use with documents over 24 pages in length. Realizing these limitations, the basic use of aperture cards in all types of libraries has been to supplement the use of other microforms.

A microfiche (from the French word *fiche*, meaning index card) is microform that uses a transparent flat sheet of film containing reproductions in rows and columns of many pages of printed material. The standard microfiche is 4 by 6 inches and has a maximum capacity of what was originally 72 8½- by 11-inch pages. There are, however, a great variety of sizes and capacities within the microfiche format. Ultrafiche, or ultramicrofiche (UMF) allows an even greater reduction with a single fiche now able to carry more than 3,000 pages on a 4- by 6-inch sheet of film. Many variations of the UMF are currently available. Recently, for example, Library Resources, Inc., in developing their Microbook Libraries, designed a 3- by 5-inch fiche capable of containing up to 1,000 page images in 50 columns and 50 rows. Microfiche is the least expensive way of publishing material, although to be economical it is not practical for documents of fewer than 24 pages. To give some indication of how inexpensive microfiche is, when bought in large quantities a single volume on microfiche, fully cataloged, averages about $1.00, or ⅓ of a cent per page.

Microforms are often available in either or both of two formats, positive or negative. In a positive image, the reader sees the type and photograph in the same relationship as the usual printed page, black print on a white background. In the negative image the relationship is reversed as in a photographic negative. The debate as to which is easier to read has never been resolved— perhaps it is a question of personal preference. Negative microfilm has been shown to be sturdier, however, and less prone to show scratches and dirt. On the other hand, reproduction of photographs on negative microforms appear unnatural and are often difficult to read. The question of positive versus negative becomes further complicated by the fact that most existing reader-printers reproduce solely in the opposite form to the film, i.e., positive microfilm is printed in hard copy in the negative format and vice versa. Therefore, in addition to evaluating the relative importance of texts and photographs, the media specialist must also determine whether machine-reading or hard-copy printing will represent the greater use of the microform. There is now available a reader-printer that can give positive copy from either positive or negative film.

This dilemma also applies to the second major type of microforms, the opaque or micro-opaque card. The two major subdivisions in this group are microcards and microprints. The microcard is usually 3 by 5 inches and contains pages of print reduced in size and reproduced on an opaque card by a photographic process. The microprint is basically the same, except that it is larger (usually 6 by 9 inches), can contain more text, and is produced by a printing process. Most opaque microforms contain print on both sides. The trend in microform production seems now to be away from opaque card forms to those on transparent film. However, a great body of material is still available on microcards and microprints.

Whatever the type of microforms included in the school, the criteria for selection should be those used for other print media. Curriculum demands and requests from students and teachers will, of course, be extremely important. In the case of periodicals and newspapers on microforms, other considerations will involve the availability of an index, excessive use of pictures, particularly colored ones (some color microfilm for periodicals like *National Geographic* is now available), and the amount of backlog available.

There are some general guides to the materials available on microforms, such as *Guide to Microforms in Print* and its companion *Subject Guide to Microforms in Print* (both published by Microcard Editions, Wash., D.C.). Some of the major producers of microforms are Bell & Howell, Library Resources, Inc., Lost Cause Press, New York Times, 3M-IM Press, Reader Microprint Corp., NCR Microcards, ERIC, General Microfilm Co., and University Microfilms.

Because of spiraling costs associated with traditional publishing, microform publishing should be increasingly popular and useful, and a relatively inexpensive medium. Some developments that would be welcome in this area are: inexpensive and more efficient hardware, standardization of format, particularly in the microfiche area, and development of inexpensive color microforms.

TRANSPARENCIES

Both filmstrips and slides are forms of transparencies, but in the present context the term "transparency" refers to a single sheet or continuous role of clear acetate containing images that are enlarged through viewing with an overhead projector. Of all recent audiovisual innovations introduced into the school, certainly the overhead has received the widest adoption. Perhaps this is because it combines the advantages of an old and trusted teaching tool, the chalkboard, with the capability of projecting pictures. Transparencies may either be purchased commercially or be prepared within the school. The simplest of the latter type is produced by writing on the acetate with a marking pen or grease pencil. Most single-sheet transparencies are 8½ by 11 inches when mounted, but this size has been far from universally adopted. The illuminated surface or size of the overhead projector is usually 10 by 10 inches, and the actual size of the aperture in the transparency mounting is about 7 by 9 inches. overlays, can be placed on top of the original transparency to show complex Transparencies can be quite elaborate; a number of additional sheets, called relationships or progressive stages of development. The overlays are usually hinged to the mounting of the basic transparency. Many commercially produced transparencies come in sets, while others are sequenced and placed in binders. It is also possible to buy transparency masters that may be used locally to produce any desired number of actual transparencies.

A special process has been developed that makes it possible to simulate action on transparencies through the use of specially prepared film and an adaptor attached to the overhead. Thus one is able to give the impression of pistons moving or electricity flowing without using machines with complex moving parts. Undoubtedly, transparencies with sound tracks on their mountings will be a future development.

Transparencies have many other advantages as well. The overhead is mechanically easy to handle and operate and supplies a large, clear image in a normally illuminated room—which allows note-taking in comfort if desired. The overhead can be placed at the front of a class so that the user can face the audience, control attention, and observe student reactions. The transparency is always visible to the teacher, who is free to change it at will. The user also has control over the pacing and sequencing of the presentation. Transparencies are easy to return—which facilitates review of the material. Particularly through the use of overlays, complex subjects may be gradually and logically introduced. Also important to note is that many professionally produced transparencies are correlated for use with other media, chiefly textbooks. The use of the overhead is suited particularly to medium-sized groups, such as the class in a classroom, as well as to large auditorium-sized groups. Transparencies may be produced locally by a variety of methods. The simplest, as noted above, is by handwriting, and this is less time consuming than writing on the chalkboard; more sophisticated methods include diazo, heat transfer, photography, and color lift. (See also "Transparency Making" in chapter 9.)

The disadvantages of transparencies are few, but should be enumerated. First, their use is awkward, though certainly not impossible, for an individual viewer. The simulation of motion in locally produced transparencies is difficult to effect and involves added expense. Typical book or newspaper type is too small to be used in a transparency; a larger type—of the primary typewriter size for example—is needed. Also, only paper with clay content can be used in locally producing transparencies by the color lift process, and even then, the production of the transparency involves the destruction of the original print. A final disadvantage, of the professionally produced transparency, is lack of standardization in both size and packaging.

Commercially available transparencies are listed in dealers' catalogs and multimedia catalogs as well as in the Graflex list *Sources Directory: Prepared Transparencies* and the NICEM *Index to Educational Overhead Transparencies*. Many manufacturers allow previewing privileges on sets of transparencies.

Specific criteria in choosing transparencies include: the quality of the mounting, clarity and sharpness of the picture, suitable definition of details, use of color, omission of irrelevant material, ease of transparency identification by labeling and other devices, logical sequencing and organization if they are in sets, and the durability of the packaging.

OPAQUE PICTURES AND OBJECTS

Opaque projection is one of the oldest and simplest methods of showing materials to a group. It allows projection of still pictures of opaque material without undergoing the preliminary photographic process necessary in the preparation of filmstrips and slides. Its chief asset is its versatility. Materials that may be projected include almost all kinds of printed matter—book pages, pictures, clippings, maps, and students' papers—as well as a wide variety of specimens and objects—such as leaves, rocks, coins, stamps, seashells, and fabrics. Time in preparing materials for projection is almost nil, and the enlarged projections can be easily traced onto a chalkboard for further classroom use. An additional advantage of the opaque projector is its ease of operation.

On the deficit side are several limitations. First, because this mode of projection relies on reflecting, or bouncing light off an object rather than having light pass through it, the source of light must be very strong and, more important, the room kept in total darkness. Second, for best results the projector is usually placed in front of the group; thus the teacher's back is to the audience, the view for students directly behind the projector may be restricted, and opening and closing some projectors results in sudden and distracting periods of intense glare for those close to the machine. Last, opaque projectors are often more bulky and cumbersome than other kinds of projection equipment.

MICROSLIDES

Microslides, or microscope slides, may be produced locally, but more frequently commercially prepared slides are purchased. Microslides can be projected by a microprojector so that a large group may see together what otherwise could be seen by one person using a microscope. The advantages of microprojectors are many: the need for each student to have a microscope is eliminated; the teacher can point out the important aspects of each slide to an entire class at once; time spent in instruction on the use of the microscope, focusing techniques, etc., is reduced or perhaps eliminated. Even slides showing living organisms may be projected in this way, but close care must be taken not to let heat generated from the light of the microprojector damage the slide material.

REALIA

Realia are authentic materials or real objects and include such diverse articles as a leaf, a piece of cloth, an Indian arrowhead, or a frog preserved in formaldehyde. Bringing real objects into the educational process allows students direct, firsthand experiences. They are able, if necessary, to touch, smell, handle, taste, or manipulate the object. There is no language barrier to overcome, and the essential qualities of the material are conveyed much more accurately and clearly than through any type of reproduction.

The need for realia varies with the students' experiential level, availability of objects, and feasibility of incorporating the realia into a media center collection. Many real objects are too large, for example, or too expensive for inclusion. The media center staff should work with faculty, parents, and students to build a collection of objects, particularly those found in the everyday environment. Some examples: stamps; coins; butterflies, leaves, and other examples of flora and fauna; election posters, buttons, and related materials; fabrics; raw materials; and utensils.

Certain problems are inherent in the use of realia. Many objects are too small to be seen by a large group at once, others are too fragile or costly to be handled by students, and still others might create safety problems if not used with care. Nevertheless, the use of realia helps to bridge the gap between classroom teaching and real life and is also an excellent way to attract and hold the attention of students.

TELEVISION

Television is the most powerful communication medium yet invented by man. Virtually no single aspect of American life has remained unchanged since the use of television became widespread. The field of education has conducted so many research studies with television that the conclusion is now obvious: children learn through television as much, if not more, than by conventional classroom presentations. Yet in spite of television's great potential as a teaching tool, its adoption by schools has been amazingly slow. In 1967, for example, a national survey conducted by Richard Mueller at Northern Illinois University showed that fewer than 20 percent of the schools questioned used television as part of their instructional programs. Various reasons have been put forth to explain this condition: teacher apathy, fear and distrust of an eventual take-over by the medium, insufficient funds for receivers and broadcasting equipment, and a dearth of good programs.

To a novice the terminology connected with television can be imposing and at times confusing. Here is a brief glossary of terms with their abbreviations and meanings:

Very High Frequency (VHF). Refers to the broadcast frequencies between 30 and 300 megahertz received in a conventional television receiver on channels 2 through 13.

Ultra High Frequency (UHF). Involves the broadcast frequencies between 300 and 3000 megahertz over 70 possible UHF channels, i.e., channels 14 through 83.

2500 Megahertz Instructional Fixed Service (2500 MH_3 ITFS). A series of 31 channels in the 2500 to 2690 megahertz, or microwave range that has been set aside by the Federal Communications Commission (FCC) for educational broadcasting. Transmitters must be low power and stationary, but repeater stations may relay signals. Each school's television receiver must be equipped with a special converter for this system.

Closed Circuit Television (CCTV). In this transmission system coaxial cable, or microwave relays convey signals directly from broadcaster to receiver. The receiver must be linked directly to the transmitter to receive these signals.

Community Antenna Television (CATV). Also known as cable television, this is a closed circuit system that distributes signals in a particular area and involves the use of a master antenna.

Open Circuit Television (OCTV). In this method of transmission signals are conveyed through the atmosphere to the antenna of the viewers' receivers. The VHF and UHF channels, including commercial channels and PBS (the Public Broadcasting System) use this method.

Instructional Television (ITV). These programs originate in a single school system or often within a single school. They are developed to fulfill local needs and are usually transmitted through closed circuit television.

Educational Television (ETV). These programs are broader in scope and in transmission areas than ITV. They are usually broadcast by an open circuit, through-the-air system, although some are closed circuit. One of the most dramatic examples of ETV is the Midwest Program for Airborne Television Instruction (MPATI) in which broadcasts are transmitted by airplane to schools in sections of six states.

Video Tape Recorder (VTR). A device that allows taping of both the visual and sound elements of an actual occurrence or another television program. The development of ½-inch video tape and inexpensive cameras have opened up the VTR field. Taping allows scheduling of programs for the convenience of teachers and students. Video tape is available in a variety of widths (from ¼ inch to 2 inches) and speeds. Care should be taken when making purchases because of the incompatibility of playback equipment with various kinds of tapes.

Videocassette. A fairly recent development in which the video tape is enclosed in a cartridge. The cassette may contain a commercially produced program or be blank for off-the-air taping. The videocassette is played back in conventional television sets via a special attachment. Each cartridge is only 7 inches in diameter, yet can contain over 50 minutes of color or black and white programming.

Television can do a great deal for education. It can bring the whole world, together with its best teachers and educational materials, into the classroom. Because it is such a high-intensity medium, it can shape attitudes as well as convey factual information. New courses can be offered and existing ones enriched. With the development of videorecorders and the possibility of instant playback, students (and teachers) have opportunities otherwise unavailable for self-evaluation.

Like motion pictures, television supplies a combination of visual and verbal stimuli. In addition it has several distinct advantages. It can reach a number of audiences simultaneously, and it can be both broadcast and received at the same time. Furthermore, no additional equipment, such as screens or separate speakers, are required, nor are special viewing conditions like darkened rooms necessary. It is also capable of supplying eyewitness news items. However, television programs are not able to provide for the great range of student differences; allow for audience reaction, or feedback, or check to see if the material is being understood.

Criteria for television programs are similar to those for motion pictures. The program should show adequate planning and effective presentation. In the case of ETV and ITV programs, this involves cooperation between resource teachers and educators, performers and program production personnel. Each program should attempt to use the potential of the medium and not be simply a filmed lecture. The picture should be clear and undistorted, with details easily discernible, and when possible, it should be employed to clarify and add emphasis. When used with care and with wisdom, television can supply a fascinating new avenue to knowledge.

APPENDIX IV

Specific Criteria for Selecting Audiovisual Equipment

The following discussion concerns the factors involved in selecting and using the major kinds of audiovisual equipment found in a well-stocked media center. The specific criteria presented here are intended to supplement those in chapter 8. The equipment for such systems as Dial Access and Information Retrieval Systems (DAIRS), video taping, and closed-circuit-television transmission are not included here, because they are complex systems that will require special technical knowledge, major expenditures, and district-wide individualized planning before installation can take place.

AUDIO EQUIPMENT

TAPE RECORDERS

Tape recorders are classified by two major types: reel-to-reel (which usually involves some form of manual threading) and cassette recorders. The latter type is more easily loaded and often less costly. Inexpensive playback equipment for cassettes has also become increasingly available.

The speed with which tape passes through the machine is measured in inches per second (ips), and it varies, with 1⅞ ips the standard for cassettes and reel-to-reel recorders usually handling speeds of 3¾ ips and 7½ ips. Quarter- or four-track stereophonic tape is common for reel-to-reel machines, and most prerecorded tapes are in this format. As a rule, the faster the tape speed, the greater the fidelity of sound. The quality of the sound one settles for is an important evaluative criterion and depends primarily on the uses to be made of the machine. For voice reproduction only, inexpensive monophonic recorders and playbacks will usually suffice. Sound quality can be tested simply by recording and playing slow music through the machine. Other criteria include convenience and speed of rewinding, erasing or dubbing mechanisms, ease of threading and operating, type of microphone supplied (most are unidirectional, some are bidirectional or omnidirectional), presence of an automatic level control that adjusts the sound level being recorded and the nature of the power source (AC current, battery, or both). Many tape recorders have a tape footage counter to aid in indexing tapes, several jacks for various kinds of input (radio, phonograph, microphone) and individual listening devices, a monitoring switch, and an automatic shut-off that stops the machine when no tape is going through. Both volume and tone controls should be present. Optional accessories that are often sold with tape recorders are earphones, a foot pedal (a help in transcribing from tape), a microphone stand and carrying case, and remote controls for connecting an automatic slide projector.

Record Players

Record players share many specific criteria with tape recorders, such as the necessity of having both tone and volume controls and the desirability of several jacks (often contained in a separate output box) to allow a number of listeners with headphones to tune in at the same time. Also, as in tape recorders, the quality of the sound reproduction required from your record player should correspond to the uses for which it is intended. Most record players can accommodate several formats—monaural, stereo, or both—at several speeds —measured as revolutions per minute (rpm)—16¾, 33⅓, 45, or 78 rpm records (a separate stylus should be provided for playing 78 rpm records). The cartridge and stylus should be easy to replace and of a standard design. The tracking pressure (the pressure with which the stylus is forced into the groove) should not be overly heavy, because this creates excessive record wear. Manual rather than automatic changers are recommended for schools. In some models the speakers can be separated from the machine and with others a microphone can be attached and the machine used as a public-address system.

Radios

Criteria for choosing radios include many of those used with other audio equipment. Particular attention should be paid to the quality of sound, whether AM, FM, or both are received, and the presence of jacks for taping or earphones.

MICROFORM EQUIPMENT

Equipment associated with microforms fall into three broad categories: (1) readers, (2) reader-printers, and (3) equipment for local production of microforms.

Readers

No readers presently on the market will accept all microform formats, and the choice of a reader should be compatible with the kinds of microforms that are or will be collected by the media specialist. Also, since converting from one form to another generally requires special adaptors, it is often less troublesome to have separate readers for each format.

In addition to the general criteria for choosing equipment (e.g., safety, flexibility, etc.), the following specific criteria should be followed in selecting microform readers:

1. Be aware of the important relationship between the reduction and magnification ratios of material. When this is 1:1, the material is reproduced on the reader screen at the same size as the original. However, sometimes for ease of reading a larger image will be needed, or a ratio increase to 1:2, for example.

2. Carefully check the physical properties of the screen. Some readers have internal rear-view projection onto translucent screens while others have external projection onto opaque screens. In any case, the screen should be of adequate size. Ideally, it should accommodate the entire page, but if this is not possible, a scanning device should be present to easily move the image across the screen. Brightness and contrast should be uniform on all parts of the screen and at a level that promotes comfortable reading. The image should be clear and sharp, but without glare.

3. Carefully examine machine specifications to determine if it is possible to rotate the image (maps and charts are often published vertically rather than horizontally on the page); check the adequacy of the film-advance mechanism and see whether multiple-lens turrets are available to give a choice of several magnifications. The variety of readers is enormous; they come in many sizes, shapes, and weights—from large-screen, tentlike readers to small, hand-held microviewers. Unfortunately, few inexpensive, lightweight microform readers of superior quality are as yet on the market. Media center personnel should avail themselves of the many opportunities to check the quality of a reader, reader-printer, and production equipment before purchase; reports from other users, demonstrations, manufacturer's specifications, and evaluations in the literature should be utilized. Section P, "Microforms and Equipment," *Library Technology Reports* and *The Guide to Microreproduction Equipment* (both ALA publications) will be particularly valuable.

READER-PRINTERS

Reader-printers are designed to perform the function of a microform reader as well as produce hard copy from the microform. Most microprinters only produce negative prints from a positive microform or vice versa. Some machines, however, are capable of producing positive prints from positive forms.

Four basic printing methods are used in these machines: (1) photographic (similar to the darkroom developing process; this is a wet method), (2) electrolytic (another wet process using paper attached to foil), (3) electrostatic (can be either a wet or dry process, depending on the manufacturer; usually uses ordinary paper stock), (4) dry silver (a dry process using heat to effect the developing). Each method is usually associated with a particular manufacturer's line or lines (for example, Xerox uses the electrostatic method). Specific criteria for the microform printer involve (1) print quality (type of print, size, legibility, contrast, permanence, cost) and (2) print mechanism (complexity, paper load, time required).

EQUIPMENT FOR LOCAL PRODUCTION OF MICROFORMS

There are two basic methods of creating microforms: the first, using magnetic tape from a computer, is rarely available to school library media centers; the second, much less rare, involves converting hard copy to master microfilm by photographing the material and processing or developing it. If aperture cards are used, a third step, mounting, is necessary.

The cameras used in microfilming are of two basic types: *planetary* (or flatbed) and *rotary* (or flow). The planetary camera is suspended above the material to be filmed and is manually operated. It is useful for filming books and large documents. The rotary camera films documents in sheet form by feeding them manually or by an automatic feeder through a slot in the front of the machine. Both types of cameras can produce either 16mm or 35mm film. Processors produce as an end product rolls of microfilm that may either be retained in the spool format or cut up and mounted. Some processors require the same darkroom facilities as the usual film-developing process. Because processors can be extremely expensive, school districts will often send their films to commercial processors. Mounting can be done through a simple hand-held device that both inserts and crops the film to the desired size. Also available are many pieces of equipment that can perform more than one of the above steps successfully. Camera-processors are not uncommon, for example, and there is one that can photograph a document, process it, and produce a completed aperture card in less than a minute.

MOTION PICTURE PROJECTORS

Both 16mm and 8mm projectors share many criteria. The number of formats a machine can accept is important with both types. In the 16mm area this involves chiefly silent or sound film (an optical playback system is preferable to a magnetic one) and a cartridge or the usual reel-to-reel format. The 8mm field offers additional choices involving regular versus super-8 films as well as different sized cartridges that range from the short continuous loop, single-concept film cartridges, to larger ones that contain films of conventional length. The nature of the software to be used in a collection will dictate the types of projectors to be purchased.

If the machine must be threaded manually, this should be a simple operation to perform; if threading is automatic, manual dethreading should be possible during the showing. Some machines have a lower loop restorer. Other items to be checked are: quality of sound and light output, the steadiness of the image, the quality of the framing device (to prevent parts of separate pictures appearing at the same time), amount of machine noise during operation, ease of focusing and speed of the rewind process. The use of sprocket guards on some machines has cut the wear on film. Other machines are able to accept old or damaged film without causing the projector to malfunction. Additional controls found on some models allow for projecting still frames and a single-frame advance, while others have an automatic stop and shut-off switch. Remote controls are often available. Optional accessories may include a microphone, reel arm extension, rear-view projection mirror, zoom or wide-angle lenses, spare takeup reels, and a built-in screen.

STILL PICTURE PROJECTORS

FILMSTRIP, SLIDE, AND COMBINATION FILMSTRIP/SLIDE PROJECTORS

Simplicity of use and built-in safeguards against misuse are two important criteria for evaluating these projectors. With filmstrip projectors the film slot should be designed to prevent improper threading. Whether manually or automatically operated, the smoothness of the film feed into the projector is also important. The ease of use of the framing device, film take-up and rewind provisions, and safety features to prevent scratching of the film should also be checked.

In a slide-only projector the following should be determined: the number of slide sizes it accepts, amount of storage in slide carriers, whether a single slide can be used in a tray, provisions for skipping or holding slides, and in an automatic projector, the method for controlling the time interval between slides.

In both slide and filmstrip projectors investigate the number and nature of remote controls available; amount of stray light, noise, and heat during projection; the brilliance and sharpness of the image; availability of lenses in various focal lengths, and hold controls for automatic machines. Such special accessories as dust covers, projector stands, and extension cords are often available.

The ease of converting from slide to filmstrip projection should also be considered in combination machines. For individual filmstrip and slide viewers the power source (AC, battery, or both) and the size of the viewing screen are also important.

OPAQUE PROJECTORS

Size, weight, and overall bulk have always been important evaluation points for opaque projectors. The size of the aperture and the maximum thickness of objects that can be projected should also be determined. The necessary amount of light should be produced without excessive heat or undue glare when the aperture is opened during operation. Some opaque projectors come equipped with built-in pointers to indicate particular parts of a picture as well as with additional lenses.

OVERHEAD PROJECTORS

The overhead projector has, for reasons chiefly involving ease of use and versatility, become one of the most frequently found pieces of AV equipment in today's schools. Before choosing an overhead, apply the general equipment criteria as well as the following points: The projection stage or aperture should be able to accommodate various sizes of transparent material for both vertical and horizontal projection (the standard stage size is 10 by 10 inches, and commercially produced transparencies are usually 7½ by 9½ inches). Some heat buildup in the stage is inevitable, but check, by operating the machine for about 30 minutes, to see if this buildup is so excessive that it melts grease markings or makes the stage difficult to touch.

The projector should be easily focused. For example, closeup projection on a small screen requires that the lens must be moved away from the transparency; this adjustment, as well as those necessary for tilting the head (preferable to tilting the entire machine) should be easily accomplished. Note that if a line drawn from the lens of the projector to the center of the screen does not form a right angle, a keystoned or wedge-shaped image will be projected. This distortion will be particularly noticeable if the projector is placed below and close to the screen. (Motion pictures are generally projected at a greater distance from the screen and keystoning is therefore not as great a problem with this medium.) To minimize this effect the top of the projection screen should be tilted toward the overhead projector. On some models additional lenses are available, such as wide lenses for use close to the screen and long lenses for auditoriums.

The image should be bright and consistently sharp and clear at both the center and the edges. Absence of glare and extraneous light is desirable—some models are equipped with glare shields. Most overheads are cooled by a blower controlled by some variation on a thermostatic control. The blower should be quiet and vibration free. The machine should have an attachment to enable the use of blank rolls of transparent material, such as acetate.

The low maintenance cost is an established asset for the overhead. Few moving parts and simplicity of operation help reduce this cost. Related to overall ease of operation is the ease of changing the projection lamp (the average life of a lamp is usually about 75 hours); some machines offer, as an option, replacement attachments that involve only switching a knob or pressing a lever to make a change when a lamp burns out. Other maintenance features include convenience of fuse replacement, ease of cleaning, and simplicity of control switches. The outlet cord should be attached to the machine to prevent its loss. The standard length of the cord is 15 feet. On portable machines a storage space should be provided for the cord.

Many models have unusual features and accessories. For example, some machines are turned on or off simply by placing a transparency on the stage, others have attachments for slide projection. Now on the market are remote-controlled, automatic overhead projectors operated by a push-button switch similar to that on an automatic slide projector. Transparencies used in these machines are generally smaller than those used on conventional models. Overheads with sound attachments have also been developed and are currently being produced.

TELEVISION RECEIVERS

For use with groups, a television receiver should have a minimum screen size of 23 inches. Controls for brightness, contrast, and vertical and horizontal hold should be easily operated. The presence of jacks for a tape recorder, a video tape recorder, and/or headphones increases the versatility of the receiver. Other criteria concern loudspeaker size and quality of sound, whether both UHF and VHF are received, and whether the set may be easily adjusted for closed-circuit television.

Selected Readings

American Library Association. *Board of Education for Librarianship: Standards for Accreditation;* presented by the A.L.A. Board of Education for Librarianship and adopted by the A.L.A. Council, Chicago, July 13, 1951. *A.L.A. Bulletin,* February 1952, pp. 48, 49.

American Library Association. Committee on Post-War Planning. *School Libraries for Today and Tomorrow.* Chicago: A.L.A., 1945.

American Library Association. Library Technology Program. *Library Technology Report.* Chicago: A.L.A., 1971.

American Library Association. *Standards for School Library Programs.* Chicago: A.L.A., 1960.

American Library Association. *Standards for School Media Programs.* Chicago: A.L.A., 1969.

Association of Educational Communications and Technology, Information Science Committee. *Standards for Cataloging Nonprint Material,* 3rd ed. Washington, D.C.: A.E.C.T., 1972.

Bloodworth, Mickey, and Wedberg, Desmond. *Highlights of Schools Using Educational Media.* Washington, D.C.: Association for Educational Communications and Technology, 1972.

Boula, James A. "State Teacher Certification and Recognition of Teaching Media Specialists." *Illinois Libraries,* September 1970, pp. 656–660.

Bromberg, Erik. "Simplified PPBS for the Librarian." Prepared for a Pre-Conference Institute, sponsored by the Library Administration Division at the American Library Association at Dallas, Texas, June 17–19, 1971.

Brown, James W., ed. *Educational Media Yearbook.* New York: Bowker, 1973.

Brown, James W., and Lewis, Richard B. *AV Instructional Technology Manual for Independent Study.* New York: McGraw-Hill, 1973.

Brown, James W., Lewis, Richard B., and Harcleroad, Fred F. *AV Instruction: Technology, Media and Methods.* New York: McGraw-Hill, 1973.

Brown, James W., and Norberg, Kenneth. *Administering Educational Media.* New York: McGraw-Hill, 1972.

Brubaker, Charles William, and Leggett, Stanton. "How to Create Territory for Learning in the Secondary School . . ." *Nations Schools,* n.d.

BSIC/EFL Newsletter. New York: Educ. Facilities Labs.

Case, Robert N. "Criteria of Excellence: The School Library Manpower Project Identifies Outstanding School Library Centers." *ALA Bulletin,* February 1969, pp. 247, 248.

Cecil, Henry L., and Heaps, Willard A. *School Library Service in the United States.* New York: H. W. Wilson Company, 1940.

Corbin, John B. *A Technical Services Manual for Small Libraries.* Metuchen, N.J.: The Scarecrow Press, Inc., 1971.

Crossman, David M. *The Electronic Classroom: A Guide for Planning.* Albany: State University of New York, The State Education Department, 1964.

Dale, Edgar. *Audiovisual Methods in Teaching*, 3rd ed. New York: Holt, Rinehart & Winston, 1969.

Darling, Richard L. *Survey of School Library Standards*. Washington, D.C.: Government Printing Office, 1964.

Davies, Ruth Ann. *The School Library Media Center: A Force for Educational Excellence*. New York: Bowker, 1973.

Department of Audiovisual Instruction. *Quantitative Standards for Audiovisual Personnel, Equipment and Materials*. Washington, D.C.: National Education Association, 1966.

Deutsch, Herbert. *Library Technical Assistant*. Washington, D.C.: U.S. Office of Education, Bureau of Libraries and Learning Resources, 1972.

Dorsey, John W. "Planning-Programming-Budgeting (PPB)." *NEA Research Bulletin*, October 1969, pp. 94–95.

Douglas, Mary P. *Teacher-Librarian Handbook*, 2nd ed. Chicago: American Library Association, 1949.

Educational Facilities Laboratories. *Acoustical Environment of School Buildings*. Technical Report, no. 1. New York: Educ. Facilities Labs., n.d.

Educational Facilities Laboratories. *Contrast Renditions in School Lighting*. New York: Educ. Facilities Labs., 1970.

Educational Facilities Laboratories. *Design for ETV—Planning for Schools with Television*, rev. ed. New York: Educ. Facilities Labs., 1968.

Educational Facilities Laboratories. *The Early Learning Center*. New York: Educ. Facilities Labs., 1970.

Educational Facilities Laboratories. *Environmental Education/Facility Resources*. New York: Educ. Facilities Labs., 1970.

Educational Facilities Laboratories. *Found Spaces and Equipment for Children's Centers*. New York: Educ. Facilities Labs., 1972.

Educational Facilities Laboratories. *High School: The Process and the Place*. New York: Educ. Facilities Labs., 1972.

Educational Facilities Laboratories. *The Impact of Technology on the Library Building*. New York: Educ. Facilities Labs., 1967.

Educational Facilities Laboratories. *New Life for Old Schools*. New York: Educ. Facilities Labs., n.d.

Educational Facilities Laboratories. *Patterns for Designing Children's Centers*. New York: Educ. Facilities Labs., 1971.

Educational Facilities Laboratories. *Places and Things for Experimental Schools*. New York: Educ. Facilities Labs., 1972.

Educational Facilities Laboratories. *Planning Schools in Televised Design for ETV*. New York: Educ. Facilities Labs., 1960.

Educational Facilities Laboratories. *Schoolhouse*, newsletter. New York: Educ. Facilities Labs., May 1972.

Educational Facilities Laboratories. *The School Library: Facilities for Independent Study in the Secondary School*. New York: Educ. Facilities Labs., 1963.

Educational Facilities Laboratories. *School Renewal*. New York: Educ. Facilities Labs., 1972.

Educational Facilities Laboratories. *Schools for Early Childhood*. New York: Educ. Facilities Labs., 1970.

Educational Facilities Laboratories, Western Regional Center, Stanford, California. *Study Carrels—Designs for Independent Study Space*. New York: Educ. Facilities Labs., 1963.

Ellsworth, Ralph E., and Wagner, Hobart D. *The School Library: Facilities for Independent Study in the Secondary School*. New York: Educ. Facilities Labs., 1963.

Erickson, Carlton W. H. *Administering Instructional Media Programs*. New York: Macmillan, 1968.

Erickson, Carlton W. H., and David H. Curl. *Fundamentals of Teaching with Audiovisual Technology*. New York: Macmillan, 1972.

Fargo, Lucille F. *Preparation for School Library Work*. Columbia University Studies in Library Science, no. 3. New York: Columbia University Press, 1936.

Franklin, Ann. "From Alabama to Wyoming: School Library Certification Requirements." *School Library Journal*, December 1972, pp. 22–33.

Gaver, Mary V. *Emerging Media Centers, a 5 Year Report*. Chicago: Encyclopaedia Britannica, Inc., 1969.

Gaver, Mary V. *Services of Secondary School Media Centers: Evaluation and Development*. Chicago: American Library Association, 1971.

Gaver, Mary Virginia. "Services in Secondary Media Centers: A Second Appraisal." *School Libraries*, Fall, 1970, pp. 15–21.

Gerlach, Vernon S., and Ely, Donald P. *Teaching and Media: A Systematic Approach.* New Jersey: Prentice-Hall, 1971.

Glogau, Lillian, Krause, Edmund, and Wyler, Miriam. *Developing a Successful Elementary School Media Center.* West Nyack, N.Y.: Parker Publishing Company, 1972.

Grady, William F. "Certification of Audiovisual Personnel: A Nation-wide Status Report." *Audio-Visual Instruction,* March 1971, pp. 8–12.

Greenman, Edward D. "Development of Secondary School Libraries." *Library Journal,* April 1913, pp. 183–189.

Guidelines for School Library Media Programs in Kansas. Topeka: Kansas Association of School Librarians, Kansas State Department of Education, n.d.

Hall, Mary E. "The Development of the Modern School Library." *Library Journal,* September 1915, p. 672.

Hanna, Mary Ann. "Instructional Media Centers." *The Michigan Librarian,* Winter 1970, pp. 4–5.

Hartz, Frederic R., and Samuelson, Richard T. "Origin, Development and Present State of the Secondary School Library as a Materials Center." *Peabody Journal of Education,* July 1965, pp. 36–40.

Henne, Frances. "School Libraries." In *Library Surveys,* edited by Maurice F. Tauber and Irene R. Stephens. New York: Columbia University Press, 1967.

Henne, Frances, Ersted, Ruth, and Lohrer, Alice. *A Planning Guide for the High School Library Program.* Chicago: American Library Association, 1951.

Henry, Nelson B., ed. *The Library in General Education.* 42nd Yearbook of the National Society for the Study of Education, pt. 2. Chicago: University of Chicago, Department of Education, 1943.

Hensel, Evelyn, and Veilette, Peter D. *Purchasing Library Materials in Public and School Libraries.* Chicago: American Library Association, 1969.

Hicks, Warren B., and Tillin, Alma M. *Developing Multi-Media Libraries.* New York: Bowker, 1970.

Horton, Roger L., and Bishop, Kent W. "Keeping Up with the Budget Crunch." *Audiovisual Instruction,* December 1970, pp. 49–51.

Illuminating Engineering Research Institute. *IES School Lighting Handbook.* New York: Illuminating Engineering Research Inst., n.d.

Instructional Materials Committee. *The Instructional Materials Center.* Lansing, Michigan: The Michigan Department of Education, 1965.

Johnson, Elmer D. *A History of Libraries in the Western World.* New York: Scarecrow Press, 1965.

Kemp, Jerrold E. *Planning and Producing Audiovisual Materials,* 2nd ed. San Francisco: Chandler, 1968.

Knezevich, Stephen J. *Administrative Technology and the School Executive.* Washington, D.C.: American Association of School Administrators, 1969.

Lehan, Edward A. *Public Budgeting.* Hartford, Connecticut: University of Connecticut, Institute of Public Service, 1969.

Logassa, Hannah. *The High School Library: Its Function in Education.* New York: Harper and Bros., 1928.

Lohrer, Alice, ed. *The School Library Materials Center: Its Resources and their Utilization.* Champaign, Ill.: The Illini Union Bookstore, 1964.

Mahar, Mary Helen, ed., *The School Library as a Materials Center.* Washington, D.C.: Government Printing Office, 1963.

Minor, Ed, and Frye, Harvey R. *Techniques for Producing Visual Instructional Media.* New York: McGraw-Hill, 1970.

Montgomery County Public Schools. *Choices for Our Children–1971: A Budget Discussion Guide.* Rockville, Md.: Montgomery County Public Schools, 1971.

Morris, Barry. "Budgeting to Meet the New Standards." *School Activities and the Library* (1970): pp. 5–6.

Morton, Florrinell F. "Training for School Librarianship." *Library Trends,* January 1953, pp. 357–371.

National Education Association and American Library Association Joint Committee. *Elementary School Library Standards.* Chicago: A.L.A., 1925.

National Education Association, Committee on Library Organization and Equipment. *Standard Library Organization and Equipment for Secondary Schools.* Chicago: American Library Association, 1920.

National Study of Secondary School Education. *Evaluative Criteria.* Washington,

D.C.: Nat. Study of Sec. Sch. Ed., 1960.

New York Library Association, School Libraries Section. *The School Library's Teaching Program. A Section of Suggested Standards for School Libraries, A Preliminary Report.* New York: New York Library Assoc., 1957.

Nicholson, Margaret E. "The I.M.C." *School Libraries,* March 1964, pp. 39–43.

Nickel, Mildred L. "Standards and Certification." *Library Trends,* January 1953, pp. 345–356.

Ontario Department of Education, Division of School Planning and Building Research. *Suggestions for Library Materials Centres for Secondary Schools.* Ontario, Canada: Ontario Dept. of Educ., n.d.

Pula, Fred John. *Application and Operation of Audiovisual Equipment in Education.* New York: Wiley, 1968.

Rufsvold, Margaret. *Audio-Visual School Library Service.* Chicago: American Library Association, 1959.

Snider, Bob. "FTR from the NEA." *Audiovisual Instruction,* February 1971, p. 87.

Sullivan, Marjorie, ed. *Kansas Guidelines for the Supervision of School Library Media Programs.* Emporia: Kansas State Teachers College, Kansas School, Library Media Directors and Department of Librarianship, 1972.

Sullivan, Peggy. *Impact: The School Library and the Instructional Program.* Chicago: American Library Association, 1967.

Summers, William. "A Change in Budgetary Thinking." *American Libraries,* December 1971, pp. 1174–1180.

Swarthout, Charlene. *School Library as Part of the Instructional System.* Metuchen, N.J.: Scarecrow, 1966.

Take to the River, Michigan Association of School Libraries/Michigan Audio-Visual Association, rev. Sound Filmstrip. MASL/MAVA. Ann Arbor, Mich.:

Bureau of School Services, 1973.

Tracy, Margaret H. "The Great Certification Caper." *School Library Journal,* September 1972, pp. 31–35.

Tudor, Dean. *Planning-Programming-Budgeting Systems,* Exchange Bibliography, no. 121. Illinois: Council of Planning Librarians, 1970.

Vinson, Lu Ouida. "From the Secretary's Desk." *School Libraries* 21 (1972): 7–10.

Vought, Sabra W. "The Development of the School Library." *Library Journal,* February 15, 1923, pp. 161–164.

Weihs, Jean Riddle, Lewis, Shirley, and MacDonald, Janet. *Nonbook Materials, the Organization of Integrated Collections,* 1st ed. Ontario: Ontario Canadian Library Association, 1973.

Whitenack, Carolyn I. "Historical Development of the Elementary School Library." *Illinois Libraries,* June 1956, pp. 143–149.

Wildansky, Aaron B. "Budgeting as a Political Process." In Sills, David L., ed. *The International Encyclopedia of the Social Sciences,* vol. 2, pp. 192–199. New York: Crowell Collier and Macmillan, 1968.

Wiman, Raymond V. *Instructional Materials.* Worthington, Ohio: Charles A. Jones, 1972.

Wittich, Walter A., and Schuller, Charles F. *Instructional Technology: Its Nature and Use,* 5th ed. New York: Harper and Row, 1973.

Working with Volunteers, Leadership Pamphlet, no. 10. Washington, D.C.: Adult Education Association of the U.S.A., n.d.

Wofford, Azile. "School Library Evolution." *Phi Delta Kappan,* February 1940, pp. 285–288.

U.S. Office of Education. *Descriptive Case Studies of Nine Elementary School Media Centers in Three Inner Cities.* Washington, D.C.: U.S. Office of Education, 1969.

INDEX

227